KU-534-591

Television Fundamentals

John Watkinson

Focal Press
Butterworth-Heinemann
Linacre House, Jordan Hill, Oxford OX2 8DP
225 Wildwood Avenue, Woburn, MA 01801-2041
A division of Reed Educational and Professional Publishing Ltd

℞ A member of the Reed Elsevier plc group

OXFORD   BOSTON   JOHANNESBURG
MELBOURNE   NEW DELHI   SINGAPORE

First published 1996
Reprinted 1996, 1998

© John Watkinson 1996

All rights reserved. No part of this publication
may be reproduced in any material form (including
photocopying or storing in any medium by electronic
means and whether or not transiently or incidentally
to some other use of this publication) without the
written permission of the copyright holder except in
accordance with the provisions of the Copyright,
Designs and Patents Act 1988 or under the terms of a
licence issued by the Copyright Licensing Agency Ltd,
90 Tottenham Court Road, London, England W1P 9HE.
Applications for the copyright holder's written permission
to reproduce any part of this publication should be addressed
to the publishers

British Library Cataloguing in Publication Data
A catalogue record for this book is available from the British Library

Library of Congress Cataloguing in Publication Data
A catalogue record for this book is available from the Library of Congress

ISBN 0 2405 1411 4

Library
D.L.I.A.D.T.
Kill Ave.
Dun Laoghaire
Tel. 01-2144637

Composition by Genesis Typesetting, Rochester, Kent
Printed and bound in Great Britain by Biddles, Guildford and Kings Lynn

Contents

Preface

Literally 'to see at a distance', the word television today means moving pictures in colour with sound which have been brought to the viewer by terrestrial or satellite broadcast, cable or recording medium. The television industry exists to create and deliver those signals or recordings. The techniques and processes necessary to create, record, deliver and display television pictures form the major part of this book.

The subject of television is an enormous one, and it has been necessary to be reasonably selective in the choice of material presented here. The general criterion for inclusion is any process which attempts to convey the image unaltered. Consequently subjects such as encoding, decoding, recording and transmission are treated in depth, whereas production steps are omitted. Preference has been given to any subject which has far-reaching consequences, such as the working of the human eye and the portrayal of motion.

I have never written a conventional book, preferring instead to allow for potential readers with a wide range of backgrounds. Instead of stating facts, I prefer to unfold the fundamental reason behind them in a logical sequence and instead of pages of mathematics I prefer to use plain English. It is more important to understand the mechanisms at work in some process than it is to be able to quote an equation. Unable at one time to decide whether I was a scientist or an engineer, I no longer care and prefer to follow the theory of a subject with some practical applications and a guide to troubleshooting.

Although this is a fundamentals book it does not seek to simplify its subject matter. Oversimplification often leads to inaccuracy and gives the reader a false sense of knowledge. Consequently some of the concepts put forward here are quite advanced, but each is presented in the form of a logical sequence of small steps. Readers who are prepared to work through those steps will find themselves in a strong position.

John Watkinson
Burghfield Common

Acknowledgements

The author is indebted to the following for their assistance in the preparation of this book: David Lyon, Roderick Snell, Victor Steinberg, Mark Schubin, Charles Poynton, Graham Roe.

Chapter 1

Video concepts

In this chapter the concepts of image delivery are discussed, beginning with the scanning and synchronizing of monochrome cameras and displays. The concepts of contrast and resolution are discussed, along with an introduction to sampling theory and the two-dimensional spectra of analog video signals. Colour television is considered in Chapter 2. The term 'television' literally means to see at a distance and is generally taken to imply a broadcast. Where there is distance but no public broadcast, such as in security systems, the term 'closed circuit television' (CCTV) is used. In contrast, the term 'video' simply means 'I see'. Consequently we use devices such as *video* monitors and *video* recorders whether or not there is a transmission, but we would always use the term *television* transmitter.

1.1 Scanning

Monochrome, or 'black and white', television was developed some time before the addition of colour. The explanation of television principles is also simplified by considering monochrome systems first before complicating matters with colour.

It is difficult to convey two-dimensional images from one place to another directly, whereas electrical and radio signals are easily carried. The problem is to convert a two-dimensional image into a single voltage changing with time. The solution is to use the principle of scanning. Figure 1.1(a) shows that the camera produces a *video signal* whose voltage is a function of the image brightness at a single point on the sensor. This voltage is converted back to the brightness of the same point on the display. The points on the sensor and display must be scanned synchronously if the picture is to be re-created properly. If this is done rapidly enough it is largely invisible to the eye. Figure 1.1(b) shows that the scanning is controlled by a triangular or *sawtooth* waveform in each dimension which causes a constant-speed forward scan followed by a rapid return or *flyback*. As the horizontal scan is much more rapid than the vertical scan the image is broken up into lines which are not quite horizontal.

In the example of Figure 1.1(b), the horizontal scanning frequency or *line rate*, F_h, is an integer multiple of the vertical scanning frequency or *frame rate* and a *progressive scan* system results in which every frame is identical. Figure 1.1(c) shows an *interlaced scan* system in which there is an integer number of lines in *two* vertical scans or *fields*. The first field begins with a full line and ends on a half line and the second field begins with a half line and ends with a full line. The lines from the two fields interlace or mesh on the screen. Current terrestrial

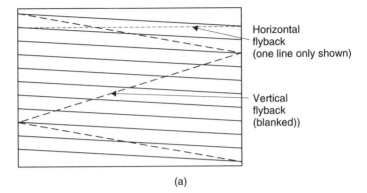

(a)

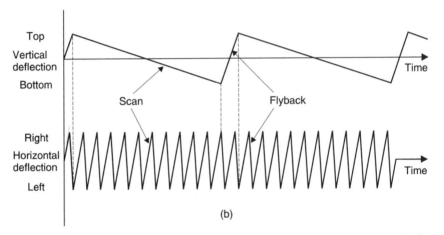

(b)

Figure 1.1 Scanning converts two-dimensional images into a signal which can be sent electrically. In (a) the scanning of camera and display must be identical. The scanning is controlled by horizontal and vertical sawtooth waveforms (b).

broadcast systems such as PAL and NTSC use interlace. The additional complication of interlace has both merits and drawbacks which will be discussed in Section 1.16.

1.2 Synchronizing

It is vital that the horizontal and vertical scanning at the camera is simultaneously replicated at the display. This is the job of the *synchronizing* or sync system which must send timing information to the display alongside the video signal. In very early television equipment this was achieved using two quite separate or *non-composite* signals. Figure 1.2(a) shows one of the first (US) television signal standards in which the video waveform had an amplitude of 1 volt pk–pk and the sync signal had an amplitude of 4 volts pk–pk. In practice, it was more convenient to combine both into a single electrical waveform then called *composite video* which carries the synchronizing information as well as the

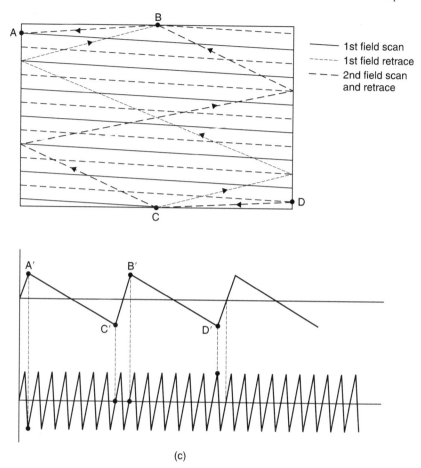

(c)

Figure 1.1 (*Continued*) Where two vertical scans are needed to complete a whole number of lines, the scan is interlaced as shown in (c). The frame is now split into two fields.

scanned brightness signal. The single signal is effectively shared by using some of the flyback period for synchronizing. The 4 volt sync signal was attenuated by a factor of ten and added to the video to produce a 1.4 volt pk–pk signal. This was the origin of the 10:4 video:sync relationship of US television practice. Later the amplitude was reduced to 1 volt pk–pk so that the signal had the same range as the original non-composite video. The 10:4 ratio was retained. As Figure 1.2(b) shows, this ratio results in some rather odd voltages and, to simplify matters, a new unit called the *IRE* unit (after the Institute of Radio Engineers) was devised. Originally this was defined as one per cent of the video voltage swing, independent of the actual amplitude in use, but it came in practice to mean one per cent of 0.714 volts. In European systems shown in Figure 1.2(c) the messy numbers were avoided by using a 7:3 ratio and the waveforms are always measured in millivolts. Whilst such a signal was originally called composite video, today it would be referred to as monochrome video or *Ys*, meaning luminance carrying syncs, although in practice the 's' is often omitted.

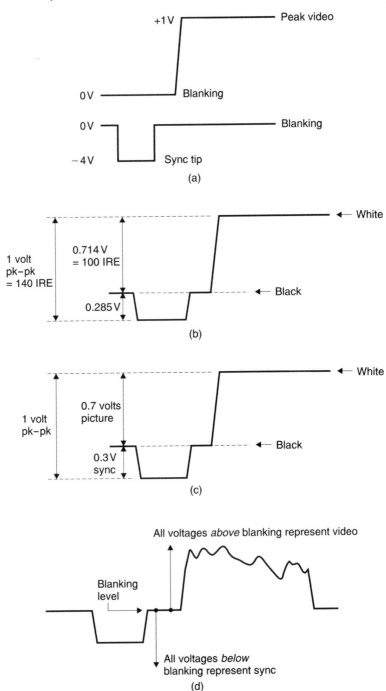

Figure 1.2 Early video used separate vision and sync signals shown in (a). The US one volt video waveform in (b) has 10:4 video/sync ratio. (c) European systems use 7:3 ratio to avoid odd voltages. (d) Sync separation relies on two voltage ranges in the signal.

Figure 1.2(d) shows how the two signals are separated. The voltage swing needed to go from black to peak white is less than the total swing available. In a standard analog video signal the maximum amplitude is 1 volt pk–pk. The upper part of the voltage range represents the variations in brightness of the image from black to white. Signals below that range are 'blacker than black' and cannot be seen on the display. These signals are used for synchronizing.

Figure 1.3(a) shows the line synchronizing system part-way through a field or frame. The part of the waveform which corresponds to the forward scan is called the *active line* and during the active line the voltage represents the brightness of the image. In between the active line periods are *horizontal blanking intervals* in which the signal voltage will be at or below black. Figure 1.3(b) shows that in some systems the active line voltage is superimposed on a *pedestal* or *black level set-up* voltage of 7.5 IRE. The purpose of this set-up is to ensure that the blanking interval signal is below black on simple displays so that it is guaranteed to be invisible on the screen. When set-up is used, black level and blanking level differ by the pedestal height. When set-up is not used, black level and blanking level are one and the same.

The blanking period immediately after the active line is known as the *front porch*, which is followed by the *leading edge of sync*. When the leading edge of sync passes through 50 per cent of its own amplitude, the horizontal retrace pulse is considered to have occurred. The flat part at the bottom of the horizontal sync pulse is known as *sync tip* and this is followed by the trailing edge of sync which returns the waveform to blanking level. The signal remains at blanking level during the *back porch* during which the display completes the horizontal flyback. The sync pulses have sloping edges because if they were square they would contain high frequencies which would go outside the allowable channel bandwidth on being broadcast.

The vertical synchronizing system is more complex because the vertical flyback period is much longer than the horizontal line period and horizontal synchronization must be maintained throughout it. The vertical synchronizing pulses are much longer than horizontal pulses so that they are readily distinguishable. Figure 1.4(a) shows a simple approach to vertical synchronizing. The signal remains predominantly at sync tip for several lines to indicate the vertical retrace, but returns to blanking level briefly immediately prior to the leading edges of the horizontal sync, which continues throughout. Figure 1.4(b) shows that the presence of interlace complicates matters, as in one vertical interval the vertical sync pulse coincides with a horizontal sync pulse whereas in the next the vertical sync pulse occurs half-way down a line. In practice the long vertical sync pulses were found to disturb the average signal voltage too much and so to reduce the effect extra *equalizing pulses* were put in, half-way between the horizontal sync pulses. The horizontal timebase system can ignore the equalizing pulses because it contains a flywheel circuit which only expects pulses roughly one line period apart. Figure 1.4(c) shows the final result of an interlaced system with equalizing pulses. The vertical blanking interval can be seen, with the vertical pulse itself towards the beginning.

1.3 Sync loss

Correct portrayal of a television image is only obtained when the synchronization system is working. Should the video signal be conveyed without the synchronizing

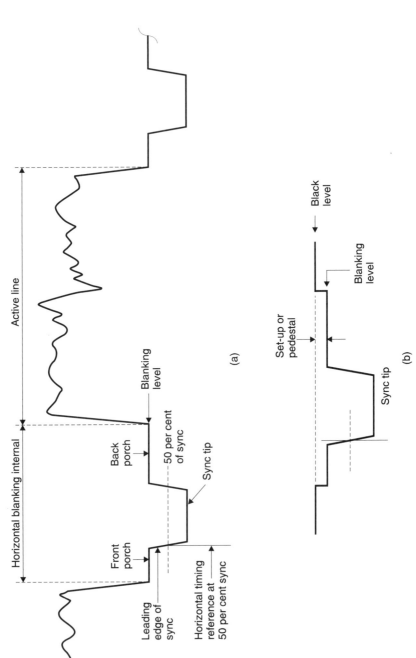

Figure 1.3 (a) Part of a video waveform with important features named. (b) Use of pedestal or set-up.

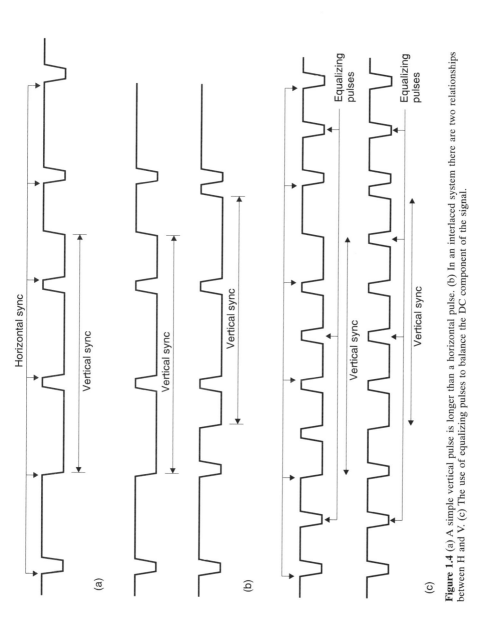

Figure 1.4 (a) A simple vertical pulse is longer than a horizontal pulse. (b) In an interlaced system there are two relationships between H and V. (c) The use of equalizing pulses to balance the DC component of the signal.

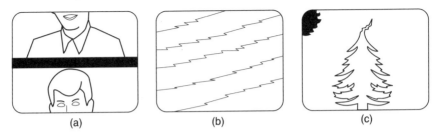

Figure 1.5 (a) Loss of vertical sync causes a frame roll. (b) Loss of horizontal sync causes diagonal picture breakup. (c) A marginal signal may cause tearing.

information, a condition called sync loss occurs, causing the picture to break up. Sometimes only one of the synchronizing signals is defective. If the vertical synchronizing is at fault, the vertical sweep of the CRT beam will begin at the wrong time and the picture will be 'wrapped around' the tube with the bottom at the top and vice versa. The vertical blanking period will be seen as a frame bar on the screen. This symptom, known as a frame roll, will be seen if a non-synchronous cut is made between two signal sources.

If horizontal sync is lost, the horizontal oscillator in the display will run at the wrong speed and vertical lines in the image will be displayed as diagonals. On a marginal signal, this fault may be evident only at the top of the screen and is known as tearing. The symptoms are illustrated in Figure 1.5.

1.4 Black-level clamping

As the synchronizing and picture content of the video waveform are separated purely by the voltage range in which they lie, it is clear that if any accidental drift or offset of the signal voltage takes place it will cause difficulty. Unwanted offsets may result from low frequency interference such as power line hum picked up by cabling. The video content of the signal also varies in amplitude with scene brightness, changing the average voltage of the signal. When such a signal passes down a channel not having a response down to DC, the baseline of the signal can wander. Such offsets can be overcome using a black-level clamp which is shown in Figure 1.6. The video signal passes through an operational

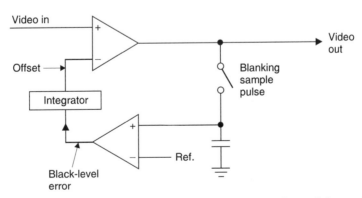

Figure 1.6 Black-level clamp samples video during blanking and adds offset until the sample is at black level.

amplifier which can add a correction voltage or DC offset to the waveform. At the output of the amplifier the video waveform is sampled by a switch which closes briefly during the back porch when the signal should be at blanking level. The sample is compared with a locally generated reference blanking level and any discrepancy is used to generate an error signal which drives the integrator producing the correction voltage. The correction voltage integrator will adjust itself until the error becomes zero.

1.5 Sync separation

It is essential to extract accurately the timing or synchronizing information from a sync or Ys signal in order to control some process such as the scanning of a display or the rotation of motors in a video recorder. Figure 1.7(a) shows a block diagram of a simple sync separator. The first stage will generally consist of a

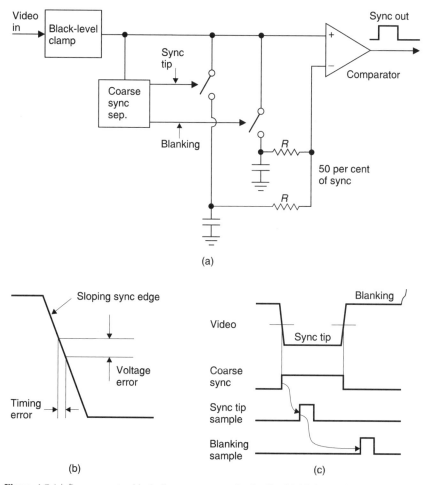

Figure 1.7 (a) Sync separator block diagram; see text for details. (b) Slicing at the wrong level introduces a timing error. (c) The timing of the sync separation process.

black-level clamp which stabilizes the DC conditions in the separator. Figure 1.7(b) shows that if this is not done the presence of a DC shift on a sync edge can cause a timing error.

The sync time is defined as the instant when the leading edge passes through the 50 per cent level. The incoming signal should ideally have a sync amplitude of either 0.3 volts pk–pk or 40 IRE, in which case it can be *sliced* or converted to a binary waveform by using a comparator with a reference of either 0.15 volts or 20 IRE. However, if the sync amplitude is for any reason incorrect, the slicing level will be wrong. Figure 1.7(a) shows that the solution is to measure both blanking and sync tip voltages and to derive the slicing level from them with a potential divider. In this way the slicing level will always be 50 per cent of the input amplitude. In order to measure the sync tip and blanking levels, a coarse sync separator is required, which is accurate enough to generate sampling pulses for the voltage measurement system. Figure 1.7(c) shows the timing of the sampling process.

Once a binary signal has been extracted from the analog input, the horizontal and vertical synchronizing information can be separated. All falling edges are potential horizontal sync leading edges, but some are due to equalizing pulses and these must be rejected. This is easily done because equalizing pulses occur part-way down the line. A flywheel oscillator or phase locked loop will lock to genuine horizontal sync pulses because they always occur exactly one line period apart. Edges at other spacings are eliminated. Vertical sync is detected with a timer whose period exceeds that of a normal horizontal sync pulse. If the sync waveform is still low when the timer expires, there must be a vertical pulse present. Once again a phase locked loop may be used which will continue to run if the input is noisy or disturbed. This may take the form of a counter which counts the number of lines in a frame before resetting.

The sync separator can determine which type of field is beginning because in one the vertical and horizontal pulses coincide whereas in the other the vertical pulse begins in the middle of a line.

1.6 The monochrome cathode ray tube

The CRT is a relative of the vacuum tube and is shown in Figure 1.8. Inside a glass envelope a vacuum is formed initially by pumping and completed by igniting a material called a *getter* which burns any remaining oxygen to form a harmless solid. The pressure differential across the tube face results in considerable force. For example, the atmosphere exerts a force of about a ton on the face of a 20 inch diagonal tube. As glass is weak in tension the tube is strengthened with a steel band which is stretched around the perimeter of the screen. As the tube face is slightly domed outwards, the pressure load is converted to a radial out-thrust to which the steel band provides a reaction.

The cathode is coated with a barium compound and contains an insulated heating element which raises its temperature. This heating causes the coating to emit electrons. The electrons have negative charge and so are attracted towards an anode which is supplied with a positive voltage. Between the cathode and the anode is a wire mesh grid. If this grid is held at a suitable negative voltage with respect to the cathode it will repel electrons from the cathode and they will be prevented from reaching the anode. If the grid voltage is reduced the effect diminishes and some electrons can pass. The voltage on the grid controls the

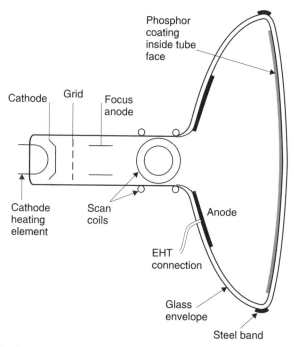

Figure 1.8 A simple CRT contains an electron gun and deflection mechanism for scanning. The cathode-to-grid voltage determines the beam current and hence brightness.

current. The anode contains a hole through which the electrons emerge in a beam. They are further accelerated by more electrodes at successively higher voltages, the last of these being the EHT (extra high tension) electrode which runs at 15–25 kilovolts. The electron beam strikes the inside of the tube face which is coated with material known as a phosphor. The impact of energetic electrons causes electrons in the phosphor to be driven to higher, unstable valence levels, and when they drop back, photons of a specific wavelength are released. By mixing a number of phosphor materials white light can be obtained. The intensity of the light is effectively controlled by the intensity of the electron beam which is in turn controlled by the grid voltage. As it is the relative voltage between the cathode and the grid which determines the beam current, some tubes are driven by holding the grid at a constant voltage and varying the voltage on the cathode. The electron impact may also generate low level X-rays and the face of the tube will be made from lead glass to absorb most of them.

The relationship between the tube drive voltage and the phosphor brightness is not linear, but an exponential function where the power is known as *gamma*. The power is the same for all CRTs as it is a function of the physics of the electron gun and it has a value of around 2.8. Since all CRTs exhibit gamma, all video signals are pre-distorted by an inverse gamma, so that the overall transfer function between light entering the camera and light emitted by the CRT is more linear. Figure 1.9 shows the principle. It will be seen in Section 1.9 that CRT gamma is not a nuisance, but is actually used to enhance the noise performance of a system.

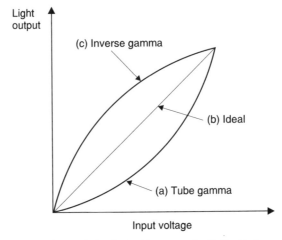

Figure 1.9 The non-linear characteristic of tube (a) contrasted with the ideal response (b). Non-linearity may be opposed by gamma correction with a response (c).

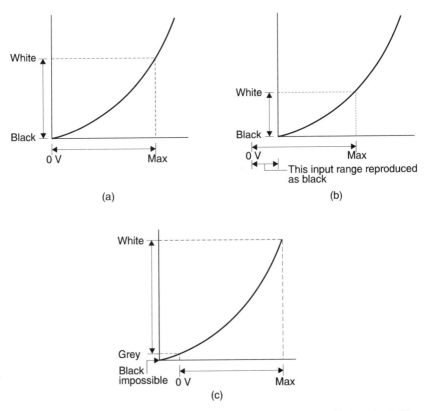

Figure 1.10 (a) Correctly set brightness control cuts off the electron beam at blanking level. (b) Control set too low causes black crushing. (c) Control set too high causes grey pedestal on picture, spoiling contrast. Brightness control is a misnomer as it has only one correct setting.

Virtually all CRT-based displays are fitted with two controls marked *brightness* and *contrast*. Figure 1.10(a) shows how the brightness control works. When correctly set, the lowest drive voltage, i.e. blanking level, results in the electron beam being just cut off so that the CRT displays black. If the brightness is set too low, as in Figure 1.10(b), the CRT cuts off prematurely and all inputs below a certain level are reproduced as black. The symptom is described as *black crushing*. If the control is set too high, as in Figure 1.10(c), video blanking results in a substantial light output such that all displayed images are superimposed on a grey level.

It should be clear that there is only one correct setting for a brightness control and so its name is somewhat misleading. In fact it is a tube bias control. In order to set a brightness control correctly the grey stepped scale of a test card is used. The brightness control is advanced until the black part of the scale appears obviously grey, and then it is turned down until the black part of the scale is just displayed as truly black, but not so far that the darkest grey step next to it becomes black as well. Once set in this way the CRT is correctly biased and further adjustment will only be needed if component values drift. Special test signals exist to assist with monitor alignment. One of these is known as PLUGE (Picture Line-Up GEnerator) pronounced 'plooj'. The PLUGE signal contains a black area in which there are two 'black' bars which sit typically ±20 mV above and below black level. If the 'brightness' control is adjusted downwards from an initial excessively bright setting, it will be found that the two bars become indistinguishable from the black background, due to black crushing, at slightly different times. The correct setting is achieved when one bar has vanished but the other is still visible.

The action of the contrast control is shown in Figure 1.11. This has the effect of increasing the amplitude of white signals whilst leaving black level unchanged. Thus in order to increase the brightness of a correctly biased display, the contrast control should be advanced. If the contrast is excessive the electron beam becomes larger in diameter and the resolution of the display is reduced. In critical monitoring, a light meter is used in conjunction with a peak white input signal to allow a standard brightness to be achieved. The PLUGE signal contains a peak white area to assist with this.

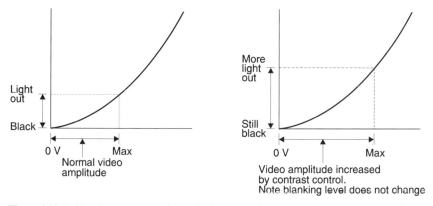

Figure 1.11 Action of contrast control. Paradoxically, the picture is made brighter by increasing contrast.

In practice the contrast of a CRT is also affected quite badly by ambient lighting. With black input voltage cutting off the beam, the brightness of a CRT cannot fall below the brightness of reflected ambient light. Thus ambient light reduces contrast. For best results CRTs should be viewed in subdued lighting where the best combination of contrast and resolution will be obtained. As all CRT tubes are reflective to some extent, it is important to ensure that no bright objects are positioned where they could be seen reflected in the screen.

The CRT phosphor continues to emit light in an exponentially decaying curve for some time after the electron beam has passed. This is known as *persistence*. The persistence time has to be short compared with that of oscilloscope CRTs because excessive values cause smearing on moving images.

The electron beam is an electric current and this can be deflected electro-statically by voltages applied to plates at the neck of the tube, or magnetically by coils outside the tube. Electrostatic deflection is fine for the small tubes used in oscilloscopes, but the large deflection angles needed in TV tubes can only be obtained with magnetic deflection.

The horizontal deflection coils are generally driven by a transformer. During the flyback period the flux in the transformer changes rapidly and this can be used to generate the EHT supply by providing an additional winding on the transformer which feeds a high voltage rectifier.

There is some evidence to suggest that the X-rays or magnetic fields from CRTs may present a health hazard after prolonged exposure.

The rate at which the electron beam can retrace is limited by the inductance of the scan coils which limit the rate at which the deflection current can change. The active line has to be made considerably shorter than the line period so that sufficient retrace time is available. Normally the horizontal and vertical retrace is invisible, but certain monitors have the facility to shift the scan phase with respect to incoming syncs by part of a line and part of a field. The result is that the blanking periods become visible for inspection on the screen in the form of a cross, hence the term *pulse cross monitor*.

1.7 The monochrome TV camera

There are two types of television camera, the older type based on an electron tube and the newer type based on charge coupled devices (CCDs).

The tube camera is basically a small CRT as described above, except that the tube face is not coated with a light-producing phosphor. Instead it is coated with a material which emits electrons when excited by light. The lens system focuses an image onto the tube face. As the tube contains a vacuum and the light-sensitive material is non-conductive the result is that a replica of the image is created in the distribution of electronic charge.

The face of the tube is scanned by an electron beam which forms the only conductive path by which electronic charge can leave. The variations in charge result in variations in tube current as the image is scanned and these are amplified to produce a video signal.

The shape and size of the image are determined entirely by the dimensions of the raster scan. Image distortions caused by the lens can be compensated by distorting the scan in the same way. Thus if the lens results in an image having pincushion distortion, the scan will also be given a degree of pincushion distortion so that the video signal represents a rectangular image.

The tubes used in cameras suffer from a number of shortcomings. They need a warm-up period, have a finite life and require periodic replacement. Their signal-to-noise ratio is marginal, and powerful lighting is required. Possibly the worst characteristic of tubes is that they suffer from smear on moving objects because the charge built up in an image cannot be discharged by a single pass of the electron beam.

The CCD camera breaks up the image area into a large number of discrete picture elements or pixels which are arranged in rows or columns. Each pixel is a small photosensor which builds up charge when exposed to light. When a frame pulse is generated, the charge in every pixel in a line is transferred to the various stages of an analog shift register based on analog switches and capacitors. The scanning process is replicated by shifting and the video signal appears at the end of the register.

The CCD element is small, light and has an indefinite life. It requires little power and does not need to warm up. The motion smear of tube cameras is eliminated as each pixel is completely reset every scan. As the CCD camera samples the image in one instant before scanning it electronically it is possible to fit a shutter so that the exposure time is less than the field period. This can be used in the same way as the exposure control on a still camera. By shortening the exposure, sharper pictures of moving objects can be obtained, or the depth of field can be reduced in bright light. The CCD elements are low-noise devices and can be made very sensitive so that economies in studio lighting can be made. Outdoor working in poor lighting conditions is possible. For most broadcast purposes the CCD camera has made the tube camera obsolete.

One drawback of the CCD camera is that the scanning pattern is determined by the geometry of the CCD chip and it is not possible to correct for lens distortions by scan correction. This puts extra demands on the lens performance.

Both tube and CCD cameras are nearly linear and this produces signals of excessive amplitude if there is a great deal of brightness range in the scene. Attenuating the signal to accommodate the range causes loss of contrast in the wanted range. Instead the camera signal is made non-linear so that a certain range of brightness is responsible for most of the signal range, whereas at the ends of the range the signal is compressed. Film is made with this characteristic and television cameras attempt to simulate the process electronically.

1.8 Aspect ratios

When television was in its infancy the production of cathode ray tubes (CRTs) was quite difficult because of the huge stress set up by the internal vacuum. Early tubes were circular as this shape resists pressure well. Early lenses had restricted coverage, and as the difficulty of obtaining coverage rises with distance from the optical axis, lens design is also eased by a circular picture. A square picture gives the largest area within a circle. Whatever the designers of television systems might have wanted for a picture aspect ratio, they had to compromise by choosing a rectangular shape which was close to the ideal square and this led to the 4:3 aspect ratio. Early film formats were also close to square for coverage reasons.

Now that lens and CRT design has advanced, these restrictions are no longer so severe. Newer types of display do not suffer the mechanical constraints of CRTs. As a result it is possible to have a wider picture without serious loss of quality and the aspect ratio of television will change to 16:9.

Figure 1.12 shows how a given picture is mapped onto an analog TV waveform. Neglecting the blanking interval which is needed for tube flyback, the distance across the picture is proportional to the time elapsed along the active line. The camera will break the picture into a standard number of lines, and again neglecting the vertical blanking interval, the distance down the picture will be proportional to the time through the frame in a non-interlaced system. If the format has a fixed number of lines per frame, the aspect ratio of the video format reflects in the ratio of the horizontal and vertical scan speeds. Neglecting blanking, the ratio of horizontal to vertical scan speed in an ideal 625 line system having a square picture would be 625 to 1. In a 4:3 system it would be more like 830 to 1. In a 16:9 system it would be about 1100 to 1. A viewpoint of this kind is useful because it is size independent. The picture can be any size as both axes then scale by the same amount.

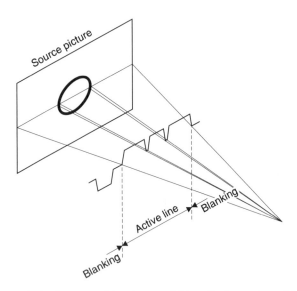

Figure 1.12 In all video standards, the source picture is mapped into a fixed percentage of the total line duration so that distance across the screen has a fixed proportional relationship to time along the line.

Clearly if the display is to be compatible with the resultant video format, it must have the same aspect ratio so that the vertical and horizontal mapping retains the correct relationship. If this is done, objects portrayed on the display have the same shape as they had in the original picture. If it is not done correctly there will be distortion. Most test cards contain a circular component to test for this distortion as it is easy to see non-circularity. If a circular object in front of a camera appears circular on the display, their scanning is compatible because both have the same aspect ratio. This test, however, does NOT mean that both camera and display are meeting any standard. For example both camera and display could be maladjusted to underscan by 10 per cent horizontally, yet the circularity test would still succeed. Thus the aspect ratio compatibility test should be made by checking the display with an electronically generated precision circle

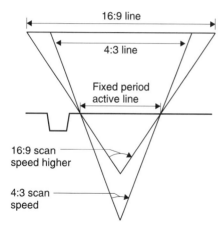

Figure 1.13 Using a higher scan speed, a longer source line can be mapped onto a standard active line. Note that for a given resolution, more bandwidth will be required because more cycles of detail will be scanned in a given time.

prior to assessing the camera output. Any discrepancy would then be removed by adjusting the camera.

Figure 1.13 shows how a 16:9 picture is mapped onto a video signal. If the frame rate and the number of lines in the frame are kept the same, the wider picture is obtained by simply increasing the horizontal scan speed at the camera. This allows the longer line to be scanned within the existing active line period. A 16:9 CRT will display the resulting signal with correct circularity.

Any television camera can instantly be adapted to work in this way by fitting an anamorphic lens with a ratio of 1.333...:1, which maps a 16:9 picture onto a 4:3 sensor. Clearly the viewfinder will need modification to reduce its vertical scan to 0.75 of its former deflection.

Some tube cameras can be converted to 16:9 by changing the scan amplitudes. Figure 1.14 shows that as the tube is circular, the change is made by reducing the vertical scan a good deal and increasing the horizontal scan by a little. Clearly with a CCD camera this is impossible as the scanning is locked into the pixel structure. In CCD cameras a wider sensor will be needed if an anamorphic lens is to be avoided.

Redefinition of the scanning speed ratio at the camera has produced a different video standard which is now incompatible with 4:3 displays even though a waveform monitor confirms that it meets all the timing specifications. By stretching the horizontal scan the video has been rendered anamorphic. Figure 1.15(a) shows the result of displaying 16:9 video on a 4:3 monitor. The

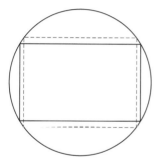

Figure 1.14 With a tube camera, the aspect ratio of the picture can be changed at will by controlling the deflection amplitudes. This is impossible with CCD.

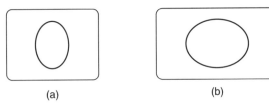

(a)   (b)

Figure 1.15 Displaying 16:9 video on a 4:3 monitor (a) results in a horizontal compression. The reverse case shown in (b) causes a horizontal stretch.

incompatible mapping causes circularity failure. Circular objects appear as vertical ellipses. Figure 1.15(b) shows the result of displaying 4:3 video on a 16:9 monitor. Circular objects appear as horizontal ellipses.

A form of standards converter is needed which will allow interchange between the two formats. There are two basic applications of such converters, as can be seen in Figure 1.16. If 16:9 cameras and production equipment are used, an aspect ratio converter is needed to view material on 4:3 monitors and to obtain a traditional broadcast output. Alternatively, conventional cameras can be used with a large safe area at top and bottom of the picture. 4:3 equipment is used for production and the aspect ratio converter is then used to obtain a 16:9 picture output.

The criterion for conversion must be that circularity has to be maintained otherwise the pictures will appear distorted. Thus an aspect ratio converter must change the aspect ratio of the picture frame, without changing the aspect ratio of portrayed objects.

If circularity is maintained, something else has to go. Figure 1.17(a) shows the result of passing 16:9 into a converter for 4:3 display. If the screen must be filled, the converter must perform a horizontal transform of 1.333...:1 to maintain

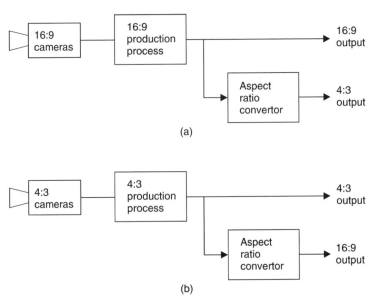

Figure 1.16 Two different approaches to dual-aspect ratio production which will be necessary during the change-over period.

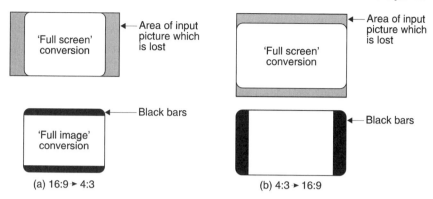

Figure 1.17 The extreme cases of 16:9 and 4:3 interchange are at the 'full image' and 'full screen' points.

circularity. The result of doing this alone is that the edges of the input picture are lost as they will be pushed outside the active line length. This may be acceptable if a pan/scan control is available. Alternatively, if no part of the image can be lost, the converter must perform a vertical transform of 0.75:1. This will result in the vertical blanking area of the 16:9 input entering the 4:3 screen area and the result will be black bars above and below the picture.

Figure 1.17(b) shows the reverse conversion process where 4:3 is being converted to 16:9. Again if 'full screen' mode is required, the converter must perform a vertical transform of 1.333. . .:1 to maintain circularity. This pushes the top and bottom of the input picture into 16:9 blanking. If the 4:3 material was shot with 16:9 safe areas this is no problem. However, if the input was intended for 4:3 it may have wanted detail near the top or bottom of the picture and a tilt (vertical pan) control may be provided to select the area which appears in the output. If no part of the image can be lost, i.e. 'full image' mode is required, a horizontal transform of 0.75:1 is needed, and this must result in the horizontally blanked areas of the 4:3 input entering the 16:9 screen area.

The above steps represent the two extremes of full screen or no image loss. In practice there is a scale between those extremes in which the black bars can be made smaller in one axis by an image loss in the other axis. In practice, then, an aspect ratio converter needs to perform vertical and horizontal transforms which may be magnification, translation or both. In order to maintain circularity, the ratio between the horizontal and vertical magnifications can only have three values, 1.333. . .:1 for 16:9 to 4:3 conversion, 1:1 for bypass and 0.75:1 for 4:3 to 16:9 conversion. Thus having selected the mode, a single magnification control would vary the conversion between 'full screen' and 'full image' modes. When not in full image mode, pan and tilt controls allow the user to select the part of the input image which appears in the output.

1.9 The eye

All television signals ultimately excite some response in the eye and the viewer can only describe the result subjectively. Familiarity with the operation and limitations of the eye is essential to an understanding of television principles.

The simple representation of Figure 1.18 shows that the eyeball is nearly spherical and is swivelled by muscles. The space between the cornea and the lens is filled with transparent fluid known as *aqueous humour*. The remainder of the eyeball is filled with a transparent jelly known as *vitreous humour*. Light enters the cornea, and the amount of light admitted is controlled by the pupil in the iris. Light entering is involuntarily focused on the retina by the lens in a process called *visual accommodation*. The lens is the only part of the eye which is not nourished by the bloodstream and its centre is technically dead. In a young person the lens is flexible and muscles distort it to perform the focusing action. In old age the lens loses some flexibility and causes *presbyopia* or limited accommodation. In some people the length of the eyeball is incorrect resulting in *myopia* (short sightedness) or *hypermetropia* (long sightedness). The cornea should have the same curvature in all meridia, and if this is not the case, *astigmatism* results.

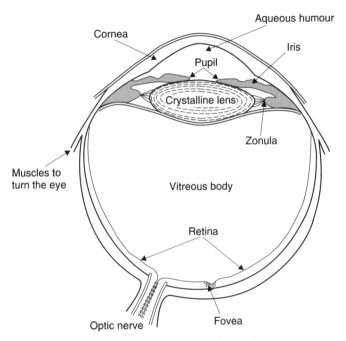

Figure 1.18 A simple representation of an eyeball; see text for details.

The retina is responsible for light sensing and contains a number of layers. The surface of the retina is covered with arteries, veins and nerve fibres and light has to penetrate these in order to reach the sensitive layer. This contains two types of discrete receptors known as *rods* and *cones* from their shape. The distribution and characteristics of these two receptors are quite different. Rods dominate the periphery of the retina whereas cones dominate a central area known as the *fovea* outside which their density drops off. Vision using the rods is monochromatic and has poor resolution but remains effective at very low light levels, whereas the cones provide high resolution and colour vision but require more light. Figure

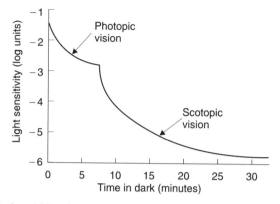

Figure 1.19 Retinal sensitivity changes after sudden darkness. The initial curve is due to adaptation of cones. At very low light levels cones are blind and monochrome rod vision takes over.

1.19 shows how the sensitivity of the retina slowly increases in response to entering darkness. The first part of the curve is the adaptation of cone or *photopic* vision. This is followed by the greater adaptation of the rods in *scotopic* vision. At such low light levels the fovea is essentially blind and small objects which can be seen in the peripheral rod vision disappear when stared at.

The cones in the fovea are densely packed and directly connected to the nervous system, allowing the highest resolution. Resolution then falls off away from the fovea. As a result the eye must move to scan large areas of detail. The image perceived is not just a function of the retinal response, but is also affected by processing of the nerve signals. The overall acuity of the eye can be displayed as a graph of the response plotted against the degree of detail being viewed. Detail is generally measured in lines per millimetre or cycles per picture height, but this takes no account of the distance from the eye. A better unit for eye resolution is one based upon the subtended angle of detail as this will be independent of distance. Units of cycles per degree are then appropriate. Figure 1.20 shows the response of the eye to static detail. Note that the response to very

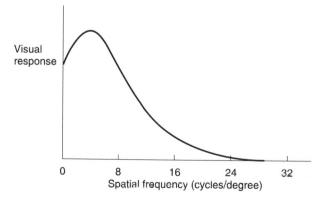

Figure 1.20 Response of the eye to different degrees of detail.

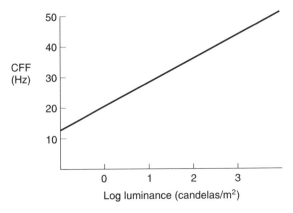

Figure 1.21 Critical flicker frequency varies with brightness. Rates used in television and film are marginal for bright displays.

low frequencies is also attenuated. An extension of this characteristic allows the vision system to ignore the fixed pattern of shadow on the retina due to the nerves and arteries.

The retina does not respond instantly to light, but requires between 0.15 and 0.3 seconds before the brain perceives an image. Scotopic vision experiences a greater delay than photopic vision as more processes are required. Images are retained for about 0.1 second – the phenomenon of *persistence of vision*. Flashing lights are perceived to flicker until the *critical flicker frequency* is reached, when the light appears continuous for higher frequencies. Figure 1.21 shows how the CFF changes with brightness. Note that the field rate of European television at 50 fields per second is marginal with bright images.

The response of the eye is effectively two dimensional as it is affected by spatial frequencies and temporal frequencies. Figure 1.22 shows the two-dimensional or

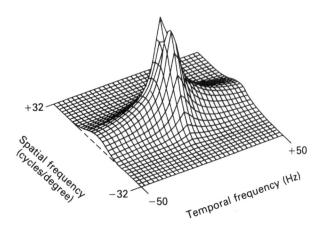

Figure 1.22 The response of the eye shown with respect to temporal and spatial frequencies. Note that even slow relative movement causes a serious loss of resolution. The eye tracks moving objects to prevent this loss.

spatio-temporal response of the eye. If the eye were static, a detailed object moving past it would give rise to temporal frequencies, as Figure 1.23(a) shows. The temporal frequency is given by the detail in the object, in lines per millimetre, multiplied by the speed. Clearly a highly detailed object can reach high temporal frequencies even at slow speeds, and Figure 1.22 shows that the eye cannot respond to high temporal frequencies; a fixed eye cannot resolve detail in moving objects. The solution is that in practice the eye moves to follow objects of interest. Figure 1.23(b) shows that when the eye is following an object the image becomes stationary on the retina and the temporal frequencies are brought to zero. The greatest resolution is then possible. Clearly whilst one object is being followed other objects moving differently will be blurred. This ability of the eye to follow motion has a great bearing on the way that discrete frames are perceived as a

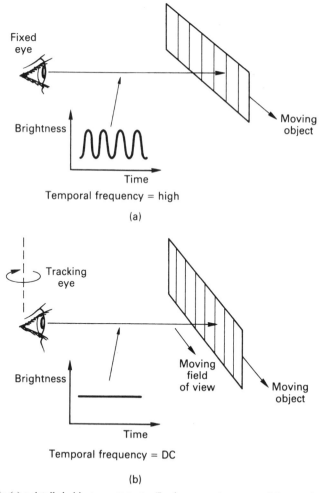

Figure 1.23 In (a) a detailed object moves past a fixed eye, causing temporal frequencies beyond the response of the eye. This is the cause of motion blur. In (b) the eye tracks the motion and the temporal frequency becomes zero. Motion blur cannot then occur.

continuously moving picture and affects the design of motion compensated equipment. This will be discussed further in Section 1.18.

The contrast sensitivity of the eye is defined as the smallest brightness difference which is visible. In fact the contrast sensitivity is not constant, but increases proportionally to brightness. Thus whatever the brightness of an object, if that brightness changes by about one per cent it will be equally detectable.

The true brightness of a television picture can be affected by electrical noise on the video signal. As contrast sensitivity is proportional to brightness, noise is more visible in dark picture areas than in bright areas. For economic reasons, video signals have to be made non-linear to render noise less visible. An inverse gamma function takes place at the camera so that the video signal is non-linear for most of its journey. Figure 1.24 shows a reverse gamma function. As a true power function requires infinite gain near black, a linear segment is substituted. It will be seen that contrast variations near black result in larger signal amplitude than variations near white. The result is that noise picked up by the video signal has less effect on dark areas than bright areas. After the gamma of the CRT has acted, noise near black is compressed with respect to noise near white. Thus a video transmission system using gamma correction at source has a better perceived noise level than if the gamma correction is performed near the display.

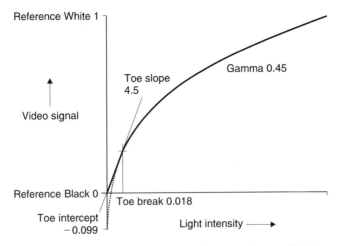

Figure 1.24 CCIR Rec.709 reverse gamma function used at camera has a straight line approximation at the lower part of the curve to avoid boosting camera noise. Note that the output amplitude is greater for modulation near black.

With an appropriate inverse gamma curve at the camera, the gamma characteristic of the CRT is put to good use as a signal linearizer. It is a happy but pure coincidence that the gamma function of a CRT follows roughly the same curve as human contrast sensitivity. It is widely thought that gamma is used in television simply because of the characteristics of the CRT but this is not the case. In fact it is used for noise reduction. Without gamma, vision signals would need around 30 dB better signal-to-noise ratio for the same perceived quality and digital video samples would need five or six extra bits.

In practice the system is not rendered perfectly linear by gamma correction and a slight overall exponential effect is usually retained in order further to reduce the effect of noise in darker parts of the picture. A gamma correction factor of 0.45 may be used to achieve this effect. As all standard video signals are inverse gamma processed, it follows that if a non-CRT display is to be used, some gamma conversion will be required at the display.

Electrical noise has no DC component and so cannot shift the average video voltage. However on extremely noisy signals, the non-linear effect of gamma is to exaggerate the white-going noise spikes more than the black-going ones. The result is that the black level appears to rise and the picture loses contrast.

1.10 Bandwidth and definition

As the conventional analog television picture is made up of lines, the line structure determines the *definition* or the fineness of detail which can be portrayed in the vertical axis. The limit is reached in theory when alternate lines show black and white. In a 625 line picture there are roughly 600 unblanked lines. If 300 of these are white and 300 are black then there will be 300 complete cycles of detail in one picture height. One unit of resolution, which is a unit of spatial frequency, is c/ph or cycles per picture height. In practical displays the contrast will have fallen to virtually nothing at this ideal limit and the resolution actually achieved is around 70 per cent of the ideal, or about 210 c/ph. The degree to which the ideal is met is known as the *Kell factor* of the display.

Definition in one axis is wasted unless it is matched in the other and so the horizontal axis should be able to offer the same performance. As the aspect ratio of conventional television is 4:3 then it should be possible to display 400 cycles in one picture width, reduced to about 300 cycles by the Kell factor. As part of the line period is lost due to flyback, 300 cycles per picture width becomes about 360 cycles per line period.

In 625 line television, the frame rate is 25 Hz and so the line rate F_h will be:

$$F_h = 625 \times 25 = 15\,625\,\text{Hz}$$

If 360 cycles of video waveform must be carried in each line period, then the bandwidth required will be given by:

$$15\,625 \times 360 = 5.625\,\text{MHz}$$

In the 525 line system, there are roughly 500 unblanked lines allowing 250 c/ph theoretical definition, or 175 lines allowing for the Kell factor. Allowing for the aspect ratio, equal horizontal definition requires about 230 cycles per picture width. Allowing for horizontal blanking this requires about 280 cycles per line period.

In 525 line video, $F_h = 525 \times 30 = 15\,750\,\text{Hz}$. Thus the bandwidth required is:

$$15\,750 \times 280 = 4.4\,\text{MHz}$$

If it is proposed to build a high definition television system, one might start by doubling the number of lines and hence double the definition. Thus in a 1250 line format about 420 c/ph might be obtained. To achieve equal horizontal definition, bearing in mind the aspect ratio is now 16:9, then nearly 750 cycles per picture width will be needed. Allowing for horizontal blanking, then around 890 cycles per line period will be needed. The line frequency is now given by:

$$F_h = 1250 \times 25 = 31\,250\,\text{Hz}$$

and the bandwidth required is given by:

$$31\,250 \times 890 = 28\,\text{MHz}$$

Note the dramatic increase in bandwidth. In general the bandwidth rises as the square of the resolution because there are more lines and more cycles needed in each line. It should be clear that, except for research purposes, high definition television will never be broadcast as a conventional analog signal because the bandwidth required is simply uneconomic. If and when high definition broadcasting becomes common, it will be compelled to use digital compression techniques to make it economic.

1.11 Sampling theory

Sampling is no more than the process of representing a continuous process by periodic measurements yet it is a technique which is used extensively in both analog and digital television. Sampling theory was not fully understood when the first television standards were being designed, and as a result many of their parameters were determined empirically and the principle of operation was difficult to explain. Now that sampling theory is well established, it is possible to explain the characteristics of television systems with relative ease. It is also easy to show that real television systems frequently violate sampling theory and the resultant artifacts can be explained.

Television systems sample along the time axis at frame rate, and sample down the vertical axis at the line spacing. Digital systems sample along the line as well. The sampling process originates with a pulse train which is shown in Figure 1.25 to be of constant amplitude and period. The input waveform amplitude-modulates the pulse train just as the carrier is modulated in an AM radio transmitter. In the same way that AM radio produces sidebands or images above and below the carrier, sampling also produces sidebands although the carrier is now a pulse train and has an infinite series of harmonics as shown in Figure 1.26(a). The sidebands repeat above and below each harmonic of the sampling rate as shown in Figure 1.26(b).

The sampled signal can be returned to the continuous-time domain simply by passing it into a low-pass filter. This filter has a frequency response which prevents the images from passing, and only the baseband signal emerges, completely unchanged. If considered in the frequency domain, this filter is called an anti-image or reconstruction filter. If an input is supplied having an excessive bandwidth for the sampling rate in use, the sidebands will overlap (Figure 1.26(c)) and the result is aliasing, where certain output frequencies are not the same as their input frequencies but instead become difference frequencies (Figure 1.26(d)). It will be seen that aliasing does not occur when the input frequency is equal to or less

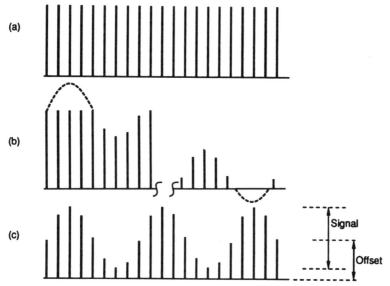

Figure 1.25 The sampling process requires a constant-amplitude pulse train as shown in (a). This is amplitude modulated by the waveform to be sampled. If the input waveform has excessive amplitude or incorrect level, the pulse train clips as shown in (b). For a bipolar waveform, the greatest signal level is possible when an offset of half the pulse amplitude is used to centre the waveform as shown in (c).

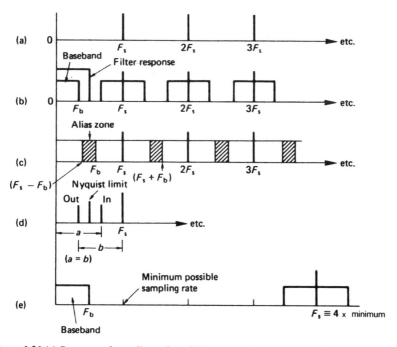

Figure 1.26 (a) Spectrum of sampling pulses. (b) Spectrum of samples. (c) Aliasing due to sideband overlap. (d) Beat-frequency production. (e) 4× oversampling.

than half the sampling rate, and this derives the most fundamental rule of sampling, which is that the sampling rate must be at least twice the highest input frequency. Whilst aliasing has been described above in the frequency domain, it can be described equally well in the time domain. In Figure 1.27(a) the sampling rate is obviously adequate to describe the waveform, but in Figure 1.27(b) it is inadequate and aliasing has occurred.

There is often no control over the spectrum of input signals and ideally it is necessary to have a low-pass filter at the input to prevent aliasing. This anti-aliasing filter prevents frequencies of more than half the sampling rate from reaching the sampling stage. In television cameras effective filters are impracticable and television signals may contain aliasing, particularly on the time axis. Temporal aliasing is commonly observed in films of rapidly revolving subjects. Stagecoach wheels are a classic example as the spoke-passing frequency can be quite high. When it reaches the frame rate of the camera the lower sideband reaches zero and the wheel appears to stop.

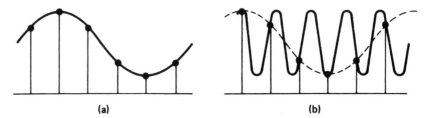

(a)   (b)

Figure 1.27 In (a), the sampling is adequate to reconstruct the original signal. In (b) the sampling rate is inadequate, and reconstruction produces the wrong waveform (dotted). Aliasing has taken place.

If ideal low-pass anti-aliasing and anti-image filters are assumed, having a vertical cut-off slope at half the sampling rate, an ideal spectrum is obtained as shown in Figure 1.28(a). The impulse response of a phase linear ideal low-pass filter is a $\sin x/x$ waveform in the time domain, and this is shown in Figure 1.28(b). Such a waveform passes through zero volts periodically. If the cut-off frequency of the filter is one-half of the sampling rate, the impulse passes through zero *at the sites of all other samples*. It can be seen from Figure 1.28(c) that at the output of such a filter, the voltage at the centre of a sample is due to that sample alone, since the value of *all* other samples is zero at that instant. In other words the continuous time output waveform must join up the tops of the input samples. In between the sample instants, the output of the filter is the sum of the contributions from many impulses, and the waveform smoothly joins the tops of the samples. It is a consequence of the band-limiting of the original anti-aliasing filter that the filtered analog waveform could only travel between the sample points in one way. As the reconstruction filter has the same frequency response, the reconstructed output waveform must be identical to the original band-limited waveform prior to sampling.

The ideal filter with a vertical 'brick-wall' cut-off slope is difficult to implement. As the slope tends to vertical, the delay caused by the filter goes to

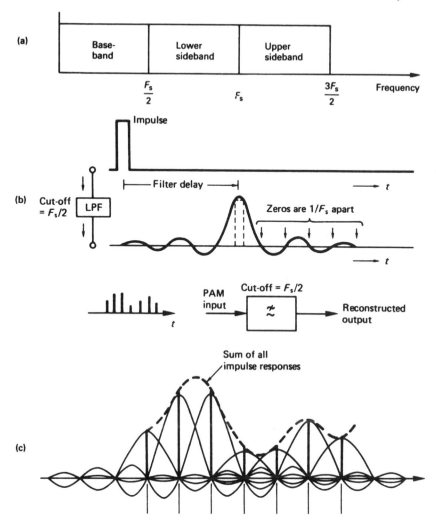

Figure 1.28 If ideal 'brick wall' filters are assumed, the efficient spectrum of (a) results. An ideal low-pass filter has an impulse response shown in (b). The impulse passes through zero at intervals equal to the sampling period. When convolved with a pulse train at the sampling rate, as shown in (c), the voltage at each sample instant is due to that sample alone as the impulses from all other samples pass through zero there.

infinity. In practice, a filter with a finite slope has to be accepted as shown in Figure 1.29.

1.12 Aperture effect

The reconstruction process of Figure 1.28 only operates exactly as shown if the impulses are of negligible duration. In many processes this is not the case, and many real devices have impulses which are of substantial size in comparison with the sample spacing. Sampling pulses of negligible width result in a uniform

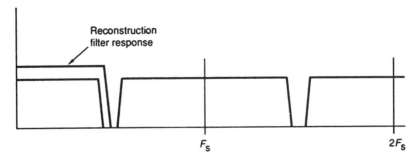

Figure 1.29 As filters with finite slope are needed in practical systems, the sampling rate is raised slightly beyond twice the highest frequency in the baseband.

spectrum, allowing a frequency response which is flat within the baseband. However if the impulses are of finite width, the ideal spectrum is not achieved. The frequency response will be given by the Fourier transform of the impulse.

The aperture effect will show up in many aspects of television in both the sampled and continuous domains. The image sensor has a finite aperture function. In tube cameras and in CRTs, the beam will have a finite radius with a Gaussian distribution of energy across its diameter. This results in a Gaussian spatial frequency response. Tube cameras often contain an *aperture corrector* which is a filter designed to boost the higher spatial frequencies which are attenuated by the Gaussian response. The horizontal filter is simple enough, but the vertical filter will require line delays in order to produce points above and below the line to be corrected. Aperture correctors also amplify aliasing products and an overcorrected signal may contain more vertical aliasing than resolution.

Some digital-to-analog converters keep the signal constant for a substantial part of or even the whole sample period. In CCD cameras, the sensor is split into elements which may almost touch in some cases. The element integrates light falling on its surface. In both cases the aperture will be rectangular. The case where the pulses have been extended in width to become equal to the sample period is known as a zero-order hold system and has a 100 per cent aperture ratio.

Rectangular apertures have a $\sin x/x$ spectrum which is shown in Figure 1.30. With a 100 per cent aperture ratio, the frequency response falls to a null at the sampling rate, and as a result is about 4 dB down at the edge of the baseband.

The temporal aperture effect varies according to the equipment used. Tube cameras have a long integration time and thus a wide temporal aperture. Whilst this reduces temporal aliasing, it causes smear on moving objects. CCD cameras do not suffer from lag and as a result their temporal response is better. Some CCD cameras deliberately have a short temporal aperture as the time axis is resampled by a mechanically driven revolving shutter. The intention is to reduce smear, hence the popularity of such devices for sporting events, but there will be more aliasing on certain subjects.

The eye has a temporal aperture effect which is known as persistence of vision, and the phosphors of CRTs continue to emit light after the electron beam has passed. These produce further temporal aperture effects in series with those in the camera.

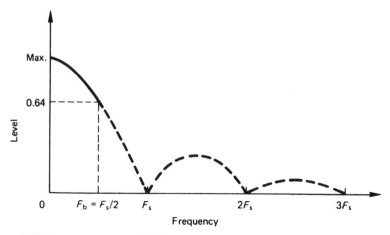

Figure 1.30 Frequency response with 100 per cent aperture nulls at multiples of sampling rate. Area of interest is up to half sampling rate.

In analog television systems, the vertical axis is sampled by the line structure whereas the horizontal axis is continuous. This causes a disparity between the resolution which is possible in the two axes. The imperfect sampling on the vertical axis permits less resolution than on the continuous horizontal axis. The ratio of the two resolutions is known as the Kell factor. In fact the Kell factor is describing an aperture effect and so it is a superfluous unit.

1.13 MTF, contrast and sharpness

The modulation transfer function (MTF) is a way of describing the ability of an imaging system to carry detail. It is the spatial equivalent of frequency response in electronics. Prior to describing the MTF it is necessary to define some terms used in assessing image quality.

Spatial frequency is measured in cycles per millimetre (mm^{-1}). The Contrast Index (CI) is shown in Figure 1.31(a). The luminance variation across an image has peaks and troughs and the relative size of these is used to calculate the Contrast Index as shown. A test image can be made having the same Contrast Index over a range of spatial frequencies as shown in Figure 1.32(b). If a non-ideal optical system is used to examine the test image, the output will have a Contrast Index which falls with rising spatial frequency.

The ratio of the output CI to the input CI is the MTF as shown in Figure 1.31(c). In the special case where the input CI is unity the output CI is identical to the output MTF. It is common to measure resolution by quoting the frequency at which the MTF has fallen to one-half. This is known as the 50 per cent MTF frequency. The limiting resolution is defined as the point where the MTF has fallen to 10 per cent.

Whilst MTF resolution testing is objective, human vision is subjective and gives an impression we call sharpness. However, the assessment of sharpness is affected by contrast. Increasing the contrast of an image will result in an increased sensation of sharpness even though the MTF is unchanged. When CRTs having black areas between the phosphors were introduced, it was found

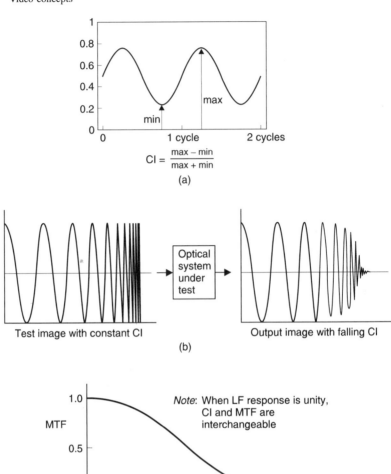

$$CI = \frac{max - min}{max + min}$$

(a)

(b)

Note: When LF response is unity, CI and MTF are interchangeable

(c)

Figure 1.31 (a) The definition of contrast index (CI). (b) Frequency sweep test image having constant CI. (c) MTF is the ratio of output and input CIs.

that the improved contrast resulted in subjectively improved sharpness even though the MTF was unchanged. Similar results are obtained with CRTs having non-reflective coatings.

Figure 1.32 shows a test image consisting of alternating black and white bars. When scanned by a point, the result is a square wave which contains odd harmonics in addition to the fundamental. However, in practice the scanner will suffer from an aperture effect and its aperture function will not be a delta function but will be Gaussian or rectangular. In the waveform domain the impulse response will be convolved with the input waveform to produce the output waveform which will not be square, but will be rounded off to some extent.

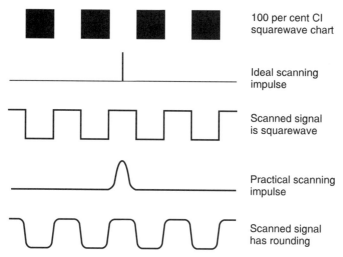

Figure 1.32 An ideal black/white grating should produce a squarewave when scanned, but the aperture effect of the scanner prevents this. The waveform produced will be the convolution of the square wave and the aperture function.

As convolution is difficult, the frequency domain can be used instead. The spectrum of the output can be obtained by multiplying the input spectrum by the frequency response. The MTF is essentially an optical frequency response and is a function of depth of contrast with respect to spatial frequency. The MTF is given by the Fourier transform of the aperture function. As the Fourier transform of a Gaussian impulse is also Gaussian, a cathode ray tube with spot having a Gaussian intensity distribution will also have a Gaussian frequency response.

A CCD camera has discrete square sensors and a rectangular aperture function. Its frequency response will be the Fourier transform of a rectangle, which is a $\sin x/x$ function.

1.14 Oversampling

Oversampling means using a sampling rate which is greater (generally substantially greater) than the Nyquist rate. Neither sampling theory nor quantizing theory *require* oversampling to be used to obtain a given signal quality, but Nyquist rate conversion places extremely high demands on component accuracy when a converter is implemented. Oversampling allows a given signal quality to be reached without requiring very close tolerance, and therefore expensive, components.

Figure 1.33 shows how vertical oversampling can be used to increase the resolution of a TV system. A 1250 line camera is used as the input device, but the 1250 line signal is fed to a form of standards converter which reduces the number of lines to 625. The standards converter must incorporate a vertical low-pass spatial filter to prevent aliasing when the vertical sampling rate is effectively halved. As this will be a digital filter, it can have arbitrarily accurate performance, including a flat passband and steep cut-off slope. The combination of the vertical aperture effect of the 1250 line camera and the vertical LPF in the

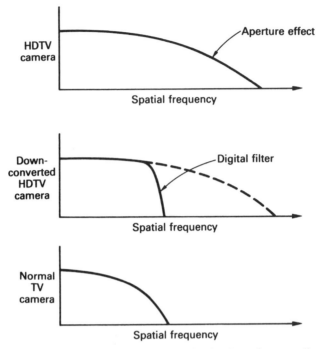

Figure 1.33 Using an HDTV camera with downconversion is a form of oversampling and gives better results than a normal camera because the aperture effect is overcome.

standards converter gives a better spatial frequency response than could be achieved with a 625 line camera. The improvement in subjective quality is quite noticeable in practice.

In the case of display technology, oversampling can also be used, this time to render the raster invisible and to improve the vertical aperture of the display. Once more a standards converter is required, but this now, for example, doubles the number of input lines using interpolation. Again the filter can have arbitrary accuracy. The vertical aperture of the 1250 line display does not affect the passband of the input signal because of the use of oversampling.

Oversampling can also be used in the time domain in order to reduce or eliminate display flicker. A different type of standards converter is necessary which doubles the input field rate by interpolation. The standards converter ought to use motion compensation otherwise moving objects will not be correctly positioned in intermediate fields and will suffer from judder. Motion compensation is considered in Section 1.22.

1.15 2D spectrum of luminance

Analog video samples in the time domain and vertically down the screen so a two-dimensional vertical/temporal sampling spectrum will result. In the absence of interlace there is a rectangular matrix of sampling sites vertically and temporally where the sample spacing reflects the vertical and temporal sampling rates. The sampling spectrum will be obtained according to Section 1.11 and consists of the baseband spectrum repeated as sidebands above and below harmonics of the two-dimensional sampling frequencies. The corresponding spectrum is shown in Figure 1.34. The baseband spectrum is in the centre of the diagram, and the repeating sampling sideband spectrum extends vertically and horizontally. The vertical aspects of the star-shaped spectrum result from vertical spatial frequencies in the image. The horizontal aspect is due to image movement. Note that the star shape is rather hypothetical; the actual shape depends heavily on the source material. On a still picture the horizontal dimensions collapse to a line structure. In order to return a non-interlaced video signal to a continuous moving picture, a two-dimensional low-pass filter having a rectangular response is required.

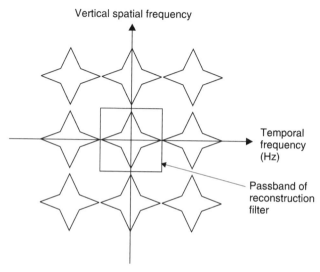

Figure 1.34 The vertical/temporal spectrum of a non-interlaced video signal.

The use of interlace has a profound effect on the vertical/temporal spectrum. Figure 1.35 shows that the lowest sampling frequency on the time axis is the frame rate, and the lowest sampling frequency on the vertical axis is the number of lines in a field. The arrangement is called a quincunx pattern because of the similarity to the five of dice. In order to return to a continuous signal, a quincuncial spectrum requires a triangular low-pass filter. The triangular passband has exactly half the area of the rectangular passband of Figure 1.34 illustrating that half the information rate is available.

1.16 The merits of interlace

Interlace is a primitive form of compression in which the system bandwidth is typically halved by sending only half the frame lines in the first field, with the remaining lines being sent in the second field. As a consequence of the triangular passband of an interlaced signal, if the best vertical frequency response is to be obtained, no motion is allowed. It should be clear from Figure 1.35 that a high vertical spatial frequency resulting from a sharp horizontal edge in the picture is only repeated at frame rate, resulting in an artifact known as *interlace twitter*. Conversely, to obtain the best temporal response, the vertical resolution must be impaired. Thus interlaced systems have poor resolution on moving images; in other words their *dynamic resolution* is poor. The artifacts of interlaced systems are compression artifacts.

It is often claimed that interlace allows the video bandwidth to be halved because only half the picture lines are sent per vertical scan. This is not correct. In a tube camera the intensity distribution of the beam is so wide that the image surface is effectively discharged every field. Thus the aperture effect of the camera combined with that of a CRT ensures that the effective resolution obtained in practice is around half that which is theoretically possible. The

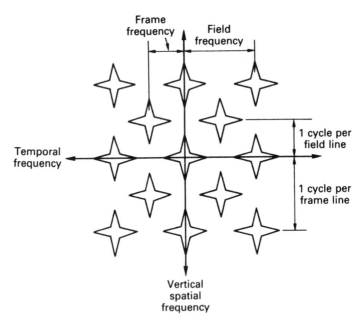

Figure 1.35 The vertical/temporal spectrum of monochrome video due to interlace.

vertical resolution is given by the number of lines in a field, not by the number of lines in the frame. Virtually the same resolution would be obtained with a progressive scan system using the same vertical line spacing. The only difference is that the vertical raster frequency is halved. Thus the real reason for the adoption of interlace emerges: it made the raster less visible in early tube camera/CRT television systems.

Now that techniques such as digital compression and spatial oversampling are available, the format used for display need not be the same as the transmission format. Thus it is difficult to justify the use of interlace in a transmission format. In fact interlace causes difficulties which are absent in progressive systems. Progressive systems are separable. Vertical filtering need not affect the time axis and vice versa. Interlaced systems are not separable, and two-dimensional filtering is mandatory. A vertical process requires motion compensation in an interlaced system whereas in a progressive system it does not. Interlace, however, makes motion estimation more difficult. When compression is used, compression systems should not be cascaded. As digital compression techniques based on transforms are now available, it makes no sense to use an interlaced, i.e. compressed, video signal as an input. Better results will be obtained if a progressive scan signal is used.

Computer-generated images and film are not interlaced, but consist of discrete frames spaced on a time axis. As digital technology is bringing computers and television closer the use of interlaced transmission is an embarrassing source of incompatibility. The future will bring image delivery systems based on computer technology and oversampling cameras and displays which can operate at resolutions much closer to the theoretical limits. With the technology of the day, interlace had a purpose whereas it now impedes progress.

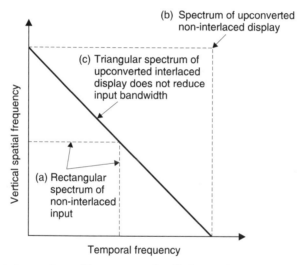

Figure 1.36 Interlace can be used in an oversampling display to reduce the line frequency of that display; see text for details.

If interlace has a place in modern systems, it is in display technology. Figure 1.36 shows a progressive scan transmission system with a rectangular passband (Figure 1.36(a)). For display purposes, the signal could be upconverted or oversampled by a factor of two in both dimensions to reduce flicker and render the raster invisible. Upconverting to a progressive scan format would require the display line rate to be quadrupled as Figure 1.36(b) shows. The use of interlace in the display upconverter shown in Figure 1.36(c) allows the full input passband through but only requires the display line rate to be doubled. The benefits of oversampling are achieved without the display becoming very expensive.

1.17 Telecine

Telecine is a significant source of video signals as film continues to be an important medium. Film cameras and projectors both work by means of synchronized shutters and intermittently driven sprockets. When the shutter is closed, the film is mechanically advanced by one frame by driving the intermittent sprocket. When the film has come to rest at the next frame, the shutter opens again. This process is repeated at the frame rate of film, the most common of which is 24 Hz. In order to reduce flicker, the projector works in a slightly different way to the camera. For each film frame, the shutter opens two or three times, instead of once, multiplying the flicker frequency accordingly.

In telecine traditionally some liberties are taken because there was until recently no alternative. In 50 Hz telecine the film is driven at 25 fps, not 24, so that each frame results in two fields. In 60 Hz telecine the film runs at 24 fps, but odd frames result in two fields, even frames result in three fields – a process known as 3:2 pulldown. On average there are two and a half fields per film frame giving a field rate of 60 Hz. The field repetition of telecine causes motion judder, which is explained in Section 1.19.

Essentially a telecine machine is a form of film projector which outputs a video signal instead of an image on a screen. Early telecine machines were no more than a conventional projector which shone light into a modified TV camera, but these soon gave way to more sophisticated devices. As television pictures are scanned vertically down the screen, it is possible to scan film using the linear motion of the film itself. In these machines there is no intermittent motion and the film is driven by a friction roller. This causes less wear to the film, and if the sprocket holes are damaged, there is less vertical instability in the picture position.

The first constant speed telecines used the 'flying spot' scanning principle. A CRT produces a small spot of white light which is focused on the film. The spot is driven back and forth across the tube by a sawtooth waveform and consequently scans the film transversely. The film modulates the intensity of the light passing through and sensors on the other side of the film produce a video output signal. It is easy to see how a constantly moving film can produce a progressively scanned video signal, but less easy to see how interlace or 3:2 pulldown can be achieved. A further problem is that on the film the bottom of one frame is only separated from the top of next frame by a thin black bar. Scanning of the next frame would begin as soon as that of the previous frame had ended, leaving no time for the vertical interval required by the television display for vertical retrace.

In flying spot telecines, these problems were overcome by deflecting the spot along the axis of film motion in addition to the transverse scan. By deflecting the spot steadily against film motion for one frame and then jumping back for the next, the film frame would be scanned in less than real time, creating a vertical interval in the video output. By jumping the spot in the same direction as the film travel by one frame and making a further scan, two interlaced fields could be produced from one film frame.

The two-dimensional motion of the flying spot caused it to produce what is known as a 'patch' on the CRT. If the film is stopped, the shape of the patch can be changed to be the same as the shape of the frame in order to display a still picture in the video output. More complex patch generation allows a picture to be obtained with the film running at any linear speed. The patch slides along the CRT to follow a given frame, and then omits or repeats frames in order to produce a standard field rate in the video whatever the film frame rate. By controlling both the width and height of the patch independently, films of any frame size can be handled, and anamorphic formats can be linearized. Smaller parts of a film frame can be made to fill the TV screen by shrinking the patch, and the patch can be rotated for effect or to compensate for a film camera which was not level.

In order to obtain a 3:2 pulldown interlaced output, there must be five different patch positions on the CRT where one frame is scanned twice but the next is followed for three scans. This caused great difficulty in early flying spot telecines because any physical error in the relative positioning of the patches would cause the image on the TV screen to bounce vertically. The solution was to use digital field stores between the scanner and the video output. Each frame of the film could then be scanned into two fields, and the 3:2 pulldown effect is obtained by outputting from one of the field stores twice. Figure 1.37 shows the procedure which produces a correctly interlaced 60 Hz output.

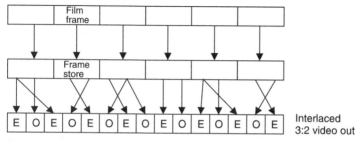

E = Even lines from framestore
O = Oddlines from framestore

Figure 1.37 When a field store is available, 3:2 pulldown is obtained by repeating fields from the store, so the film scanning process is regular.

Progress in field store technology made it possible to build a telecine in which the vertical motion of the patch was replaced by a process of electronic timebase correction. The line scanning mechanism is obtained by projecting the steadily moving film onto a sensor consisting of a single line of CCD elements. The entire film frame is scanned progressively in one frame period and this information is stored. By reading alternate lines from the store, an interlaced output is possible. 3:2 pulldown is obtained in the same way. By reading the store faster than it is written, the film frame area can be fitted into the active picture area, leaving time for blanking. The linear sensor cannot move, so a still frame cannot be obtained; however, output is possible over a range of speeds using the frame store as a buffer.

1.18 Introduction to motion portrayal

Section 1.9 showed that a fixed eye has poor resolution of moving objects. Many years ago this was used as an argument that people would never be able to fly because they would not be able to see properly at speeds needed for flight. As all birds know, the argument is false, because the eye can move to follow objects of interest. In real life we can see moving objects in some detail unless they move faster than the eye can follow. The brain follows motion by moving the eyeball in order to keep transitions in the image stationary on the retina as was shown in Figure 1.23. Exceptions are in the case of irregular motion which the eye cannot track, or rotational motion since the eyeball cannot rotate on the optical axis!

The process is not exclusive to the eyeball; the technique of panning to follow moving objects is used by still photographers and film/television camera operators alike because it renders moving objects stationary with respect to the camera sensor.

When the eye is tracking an object of interest it will be kept in the foveal area in the centre of the eye's field of view where the highest resolution is available. Anything in the field of view which is moving at a different velocity will suffer motion blur. This is not obvious because it occurs outside the foveal area where the resolution of the eye is lower. The effect is clearly visible on a panned still photograph, where motion blur of the background is often deliberately exaggerated by a long exposure in order to emphasize the subject.

Figure 1.38 shows what happens when the eye follows correctly a moving object displayed on a film or television system. Effectively the original scene and the retina are stationary with respect to one another, but the camera sensor and display are both moving through the field of view. As a result the temporal frequency at the eye due to the object being followed is brought to zero and no aliasing is perceived by the viewer due to the field/frame rate sampling. The effect of sampling is simply to make the stationary image intermittent and persistence of vision renders it continuous to the viewer. As a result field rates are chosen for the purpose of flicker

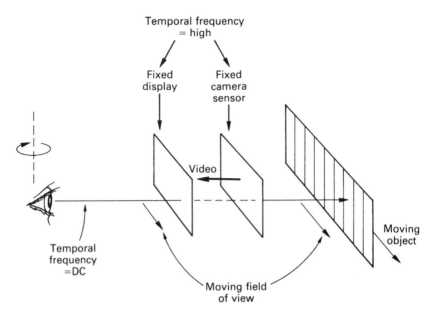

Figure 1.38 An object moves past a camera, and is tracked on a monitor by the eye. The high temporal frequencies cause aliasing in the TV signal, but these are not perceived by the tracking eye as this reduces the temporal frequency to zero. Compare with Fig. 1.23.

prevention rather than for accurate motion portrayal. 50 Hz is marginal, 60 Hz is better, but there is reason to suggest that higher rates would reveal an improvement, particularly on modern bright displays.

Whilst the result of eye tracking is highly desirable, we have not actually disproved sampling theory, because the effect only works if several assumptions are made, including the requirement for the motion to be smooth and for the eye to track accurately.

What is seen in this example is not quite the same as if the scene were being viewed through a piece of moving glass because of the movement of the image relative to the camera sensor and the display. Here, high temporal frequencies do exist, and the temporal aperture effect (lag) of both will reduce perceived resolution. When there is relative movement of the image and the sensor, the image will be smeared across the sensor by a distance which depends upon the velocity and the exposure time. In conventional television cameras, the exposure time is one field period. In film cameras the shutter is closed for approximately half the frame period in order to pull down the film and as a result the exposure is about the same as a TV camera.

A reduction in motion blur can be obtained by shortening the exposure. This is the reason that shutters are sometimes fitted to CCD cameras used at sporting events. The mechanically rotating shutter allows light onto the CCD sensor for only part of the field period thereby reducing the temporal aperture. The result is obvious from conventional photography in which one naturally uses a short exposure for moving subjects. The shuttered CCD camera effectively has an exposure control.

With the advent of sensitive film stock, certain film cameras are available in which the exposure can advantageously be made shorter than 50 per cent of the frame time. In film and CCD cameras, each field or frame is independently sensed whereas a tube camera displays considerable lag causing an instantaneous input to be evident in several fields. Motion portrayal is poor and there is no point in fitting a shutter to a tube camera as little improvement will result.

In practice the temporal aperture of cameras is a compromise. If the scene contains difficult subjects such as stagecoach wheels, fans or propellers, a long temporal aperture is beneficial in blurring the image to disguise the aliasing. If such subjects are absent, the shorter the temporal aperture the better the motion portrayal.

1.19 Motion in film and video systems

Although film and television are intended to convey moving images, they do so in very different ways, which are incompatible. Today it is common to convert material shot on film into television signals using a telecine machine. The incompatibility of motion portrayal between film and television leads to artifacts. For a long time these artifacts had to be accepted because dealing with them was simply too complex. With today's processing power this is no longer the case.

The motion handling characteristics of various imaging systems will now be contrasted. Figure 1.39(a) shows the simplest time axis, that of film, where entire frames are simultaneously exposed, or sampled, and the result is that the two-dimensional image is effectively at right angles to the time axis. Early cameras and projectors could not achieve a high enough frame rate to prevent flicker, and, to overcome this problem, each frame of a film is generally projected twice or

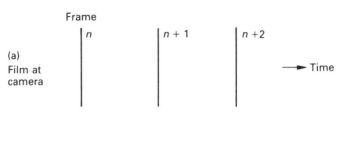

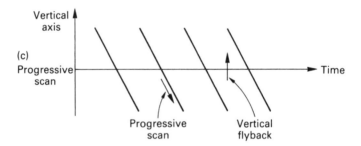

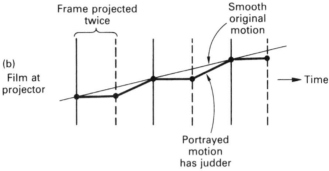

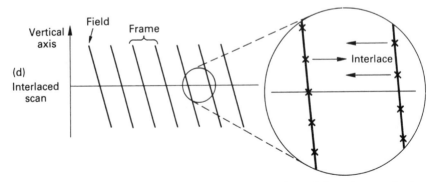

Figure 1.39 (a) The spatio-temporal characteristic of film. Note that each frame is repeated twice on projection. (b) The frame repeating results in motion judder as shown here. (c) The spatio-temporal characteristic of progressive scan TV. Note the characteristic tilt of the image planes. (d) The result of interlaced scan.

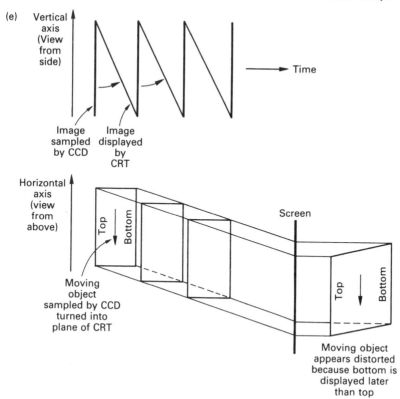

(e) Vertical axis (View from side)

Time

Image sampled by CCD

Image displayed by CRT

Horizontal axis (view from above)

Top Bottom

Screen

Top Bottom

Moving object sampled by CCD turned into plane of CRT

Moving object appears distorted because bottom is displayed later than top

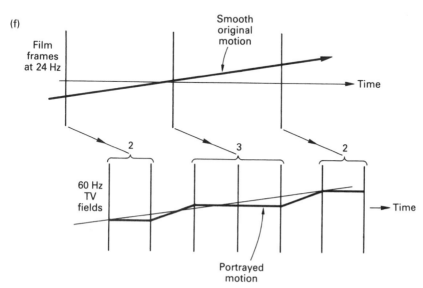

(f)

Film frames at 24 Hz

Smooth original motion

Time

2   3   2

60 Hz TV fields

Time

Portrayed motion

Figure 1.39 (*Continued*) (e) Displaying sampled CCD images on a scanned CRT results in distortion in the presence of motion. (f) Telecine machines must use 3:2 pulldown to produce 60 Hz field rate video.

three times using a shutter which is geared up with respect to the film pulldown. In addition to reducing flicker, the film consumption is reduced. Unfortunately there is a penalty to be paid for this gain. The result with a moving object is that the motion is not properly portrayed and there is judder. Figure 1.39(b) shows the origin of the judder. It should be appreciated that the judder is not actually present on the film, but results from the projection method. Information from one place on the time axis appears in two places. It is therefore wrong to call the artifact film judder; it should be called projector judder.

Tube cameras do not sample the image all at once, but scan it from top to bottom. Scanning may be progressive or interlaced. Figure 1.39(c) shows the time axis of progressive scan television cameras and CRT displays. The vertical scan takes a substantial part of the frame period and so the image is tilted with respect to the time axis. As both camera and display have the same tilt, the tilt has no effect on motion portrayal.

Figure 1.39(d) shows the time axis of interlaced scan cameras and displays. The vertical scan is twice as fast and so the tilt is now over a field period. Again as camera and CRT display have the same tilt, the tilt does not affect motion portrayal.

Interlace in video is the rough equivalent of double frame projection in film. Sending fields instead of frames requires half as much bandwidth for the same flicker frequency. Again there is a penalty which is that fields will only superimpose correctly when there is no motion. In the presence of motion with a tracking eye the moving object is portrayed with the line spacing of a field, not a frame.

In CCD cameras, when the parallel transfer to the shift registers takes place, the image is sampled instantaneously, like film, and thus the fields are at right angles to the time axis. If displayed on a scanning CRT, the time axis is distorted such that things are displayed later than they should be towards the bottom of the screen. Transversely moving objects have speed-dependent sloping verticals, as shown in Figure 1.39(e). The same effect is evident if film is displayed on a CRT via telecine. The film frames are sampled, but the CRT is scanned. Thus CCD cameras to a certain extent and telecines to a much greater extent are not compatible with scanning (CRT) displays.

The motion portrayal (or lack of it) of telecine is shown in Figure 1.39(f). The judder is not on the film, but is due to a flawed process. The problem is worse in 60 Hz telecine because of the effects of 3:2 pulldown.

1.20 Video slow motion

The provision of picture playback at reduced speed has been a useful tool for many years and a great deal of effort has been expended to obtain high quality. Slow motion may be used for artistic effect, or to study a phenomenon more easily. The earliest approach was to use high speed film cameras, but this was expensive and required advanced knowledge that slow motion reproduction was required. The development of the helical scan video recorder led to machines with automatically deflecting heads which could follow tracks on tape at non-standard speed. In order to maintain the standard output signal structure, the drum speed remained locked to reference video, but to constrain the deflection amplitude, the head would periodically need to jump, repeating one or more fields. Thus the output field rate was correct, but the repeating of fields did not

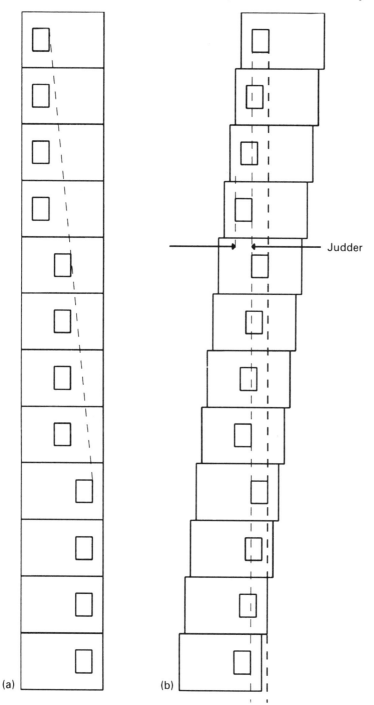

Figure 1.40 Conventional slow motion using field repeating with stationary eye shown in (a). With tracking eye (b) the source of judder is seen.

give an accurate portrayal of motion. Figure 1.40 shows that a moving object would remain in the same place on the screen during field repeats, but jump to a new position as a new field was played. The eye follows a selected moving object on the screen, attempting to render it stationary on the retina. Figure 1.40 also shows that the field repeating process of a conventional VTR causes the location of a moving object to wander with respect to the trajectory of the eye, and this is visible as judder. Effectively a VTR in slow motion is behaving like a telecine, repeating images to obtain the correct field rate. Once more this is a standards conversion problem.

1.21 Motion in standards conversion

Standards converters need to convert the number of lines in the image, perhaps the colour modulation scheme, and the field rate. Out of these, the field rate change is the most difficult, not least because the field rates involved are so low compared with the temporal frequencies which are created when objects move. Thus temporal aliasing in the input signal is the norm rather than the exception. It was seen above that the eye would not see this aliasing in a normal television system because it would follow motion. However, a conventional standards converter is not transparent to motion portrayal, and the effect is judder and loss of resolution.

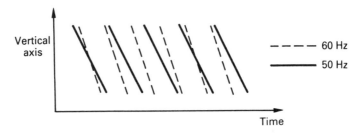

Figure 1.41 The different temporal distribution of input and output fields in a 50/60 Hz converter.

Figure 1.41 shows what happens on the time axis in a conversion between 60 Hz and 50 Hz (in either direction). Fields in the two standards appear in different planes cutting through the spatio-temporal volume, and the job of the standards converter is to interpolate between input planes in one standard in order to estimate what an intermediate plane in the other standard would look like. With still images, this is easy, because planes can be slid up and down the time axis with no ill effect. Sixty fields a second can be turned into 50 fields a second simply by dumping one field in six. However, if the programme material contains motion, this approach fails. Figure 1.42 shows that field dumping results in a 10 Hz jerkiness in the movement and so it cannot be used in practice.

The 10 Hz is a beat or difference frequency between the two field rates and practical converters attempt to filter it out by incorporating low-pass filtering in the time axis. The frequency response of the filter must extend no further than permitted by sampling theory. In other words the temporal frequency response must not exceed one-half of the lowest sampling rate, i.e. 25 Hz. Filtering to this

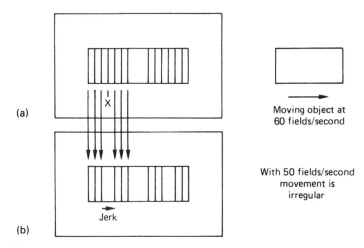

Figure 1.42 In (a) a rectangular object is moving smoothly to the right, and seven superimposed fields are shown in the frame in a 60 Hz system. If an attempt is made to convert to 50 Hz by omitting fields, as in (b), there will be jerky movement where the image moves a greater distance due to the omission. This is subjectively highly disturbing.

low frequency can only be achieved by having a temporal impulse response which spreads over at least four fields along the time axis, hence the conventional four-field standards converter.

Four-field converters interpolate through time, using pixel data from four input fields in order to compute the likely values of pixels in an intermediate output field. This gets rid of 10 Hz effects, but does not handle motion transparently.

Figure 1.43(a) shows that if an object is moving, it will be in a different place in successive fields. Interpolating between several fields results in multiple images of the object. The position of the dominant image will not move smoothly, an effect which is perceived as judder. If, however, the camera is panning the moving object, it will be in much the same place in successive fields and Figure 1.43(b) shows that it will be the background which judders.

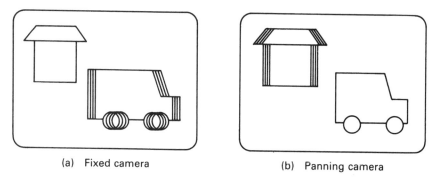

Figure 1.43 (a) Conventional four-field converter with moving object suffers multiple images. (b) If the moving object is panned, the judder moves to the background.

The four-field aperture of a conventional standards converter has the effect of turning cuts into dissolves and often the impulse response is made adaptive so that if a cut is sensed the output is prevented from averaging images across the cut.

1.22 Motion compensation

The basic principle of motion compensation is quite simple, even if the actual implementation is not. Motion compensation can be applied in principle to any process in which the input consists of images sampled along the time axis where the output is required with a different time axis. Standards conversion is an obvious application where a moving object appears in different places in successive source images and motion compensation computes where the object should be in an intermediate target image and then shifts the object to that position. Motion compensation is also important in compression systems where

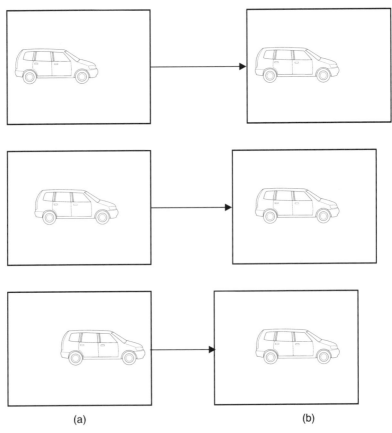

(a)   (b)

Figure 1.44 In the presence of motion, objects are in different places in successive fields as shown in (a). Motion compensation cancels the motion so that different versions of a moving object superimpose, (b).

it is intended to use redundancy or similarity between successive images. Where moving objects are involved, the redundancy between images can only be exploited if the relative motion is cancelled before a comparison is made.

There are various ways of considering motion compensation, depending upon whether we use the object or the frame as a reference. Figure 1.44 takes the moving object as a reference. Figure 1.44(a) shows the source images, and Figure 1.44(b) shows that motion compensation can be considered to shift successive source images so that an object of interest is in the same place in each field after shifting. Interpolation can then be performed between source images without any multiple imaging or judder whatsoever. This simple explanation is only suitable for illustrating the processing of a single motion such as a pan, but it does show the potential of the concept.

An alternative way of looking at motion compensation is to consider what happens with respect to the frame. When a two-dimensional image is moved along the time axis the result is a three-dimensional tube which we can call the spatio-temporal volume. A conventional standards converter interpolates only along the time axis which is parallel to the sides of the spatio-temporal volume. In contrast, a motion-compensated standards converter can swivel its inter-polation axis so that it is no longer parallel to the time axis. Figure 1.45(a) shows the input fields in which three objects are moving in a different way. In Figure 1.45(b) it will be seen that the interpolation axis is aligned with the trajectory or optic flow of each moving object in turn.

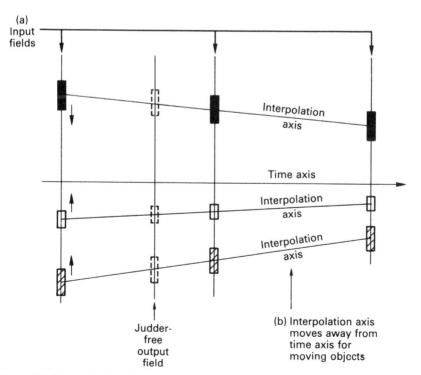

Figure 1.45 (a) Input fields with moving objects. (b) Moving the interpolation axes to make them parallel to the trajectory of each object.

This has a dramatic effect. Each object is now stationary with respect to its own interpolation axis, and so on that axis it no longer generates temporal frequencies due to motion and temporal aliasing cannot occur. Interpolation along the correct axes will then result in a sequence of output fields in which motion is properly portrayed. It should also be clear that locating the axes where temporal frequencies vanish is advantageous in compression.

Effectively, in motion-compensated devices, the tracking technique of the human eye has been replicated in hardware. The motion estimation system is essentially 'watching television' and tracks moving objects to render them stationary with respect to the interpolation axis. There is, however, a major difference. The human viewer chooses one object to track and everything else loses resolution. The unfortunate motion estimator cannot know what the viewer will want to track and so it has to track every moving object in parallel. This requires a good deal of computation, and a few years ago the cost would have been prohibitive; today that is no longer the case.

1.23 The Dallas effect

Judder on 60 Hz telecine has been the norm for a long time and has been accepted as the best that could be achieved. Similarly, judder in conventional standards converters has had to be accepted. There is, however, a worst case effect which is obtained when 60 Hz telecine material is standards converted to 50 Hz video. The 3:2 pulldown judder inherent in the 60 Hz video is compounded by the judder resulting from 60/50 conversion and the result is indescribable. If an adaptive or motion-compensated standards converter is used, the motion compensation system is confused by the 3:2 pulldown where there are two identical fields, then a change followed by three identical fields.

The solution to standards converting 60 Hz telecine video is to use an intelligent system which can detect the 3:2 sequence even in the presence of video edits. The third version of the frame is discarded, and the remaining pairs of fields are de-interlaced to re-create the original film frames at 48 Hz. The 525 line frames are then interpolated to 625 lines, and output to a specially adapted video recorder which can accept a 48 Hz signal. This produces a standard tape which, when played at 50 Hz, gives the same result as if a 50 Hz telecine had been used.

Chapter 2

Colour television

In this chapter the principles of colour vision and colorimetry will be used to introduce colour television component signals. Composite video will also be introduced as a method of conveying the three components of a colour television picture in a single waveform, generally for the purpose of broadcasting.

2.1 A short history of colour television

The United States almost adopted a field sequential colour system which would have been incompatible with the existing 525 line monochrome system. The US monochrome standard dated from the first National Television System Committee (NTSC-1) in 1940 and 1941. The manufacturers and broadcasters re-formed the NTSC as NTSC-2 in 1950, but it made slow progress until the FCC, acting as a catalyst, ruled that a sequential system would be adopted unless a better system was proposed. However, the compatible subcarrier-based NTSC-2 coding system won the day and transmissions began in 1954.

NTSC was found to suffer from colour instabilities due to multipath reception and transmitter imperfections and receivers needed a hue control to alleviate the effects. Development of the PAL system was led by Dr Bruch in Germany who decided that PAL would have to overcome the NTSC instability and eliminate the hue control. PAL was also designed to be different to NTSC in order to keep out non-European manufacturers from the TV set market. This ploy failed when the Japanese designed PAL decoders which circumvented the PAL patents by treating the signal like NTSC but decoding only every other line. France meanwhile went its own way with SECAM, a system which also overcame the problems of NTSC but in a different way.

The three systems were adopted by the rest of the world primarily on a political basis rather than on technical grounds, except for South America, where PAL-M (basically PAL encoding used with NTSC line and field rate) and PAL-N (625/50 PAL having NTSC channel spacing) were local compromises.

In the mid-1980s Direct Satellite Broadcasting (DSB) was starting to become viable and a new coding scheme known as MAC (Multiplexed Analog Components) was developed. Although technically superior to earlier systems, MAC failed to achieve widespread use primarily for political reasons.

By the early 1990s it was becoming clear that the aspect ratio of television pictures would change from 4:3 to 16:9. European terrestrial broadcasters, concerned at competition from new widescreen delivery systems, developed a

16:9 version of PAL known as PALplus. As part of the PALplus project, an improved coding scheme was developed for use in the studio environment. Extended Studio PAL, also known as COM^3 is designed to offer higher horizontal resolution for widescreen working.

2.2 Colour vision

Colour vision is made possible by the cones on the retina which occur in three different types, responding to different colours. Figure 2.1 shows that human vision is restricted to a range of light wavelengths from 400 nanometres to 700 nanometres. Shorter wavelengths are called ultraviolet and longer wavelengths are called infrared. Note that the response is not uniform, but peaks in the area of green. The response to blue is very poor and makes a nonsense of the traditional use of blue lights on emergency vehicles.

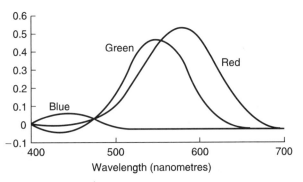

Figure 2.1 All human vision takes place over this range of wavelengths. The response is not uniform, but has a central peak. The three types of cone approximate to the three responses shown to give colour vision.

Figure 2.1 shows an approximate response for each of the three types of cone. If light of a single wavelength is observed, the relative responses of the three sensors allow us to discern what we call the colour of the light. Note that at both ends of the visible spectrum there are areas in which only one receptor responds; all colours in those areas look the same. There is a great deal of variation in receptor response from one individual to the next and the curves used in television are the average of a great many tests. In a surprising number of people the single receptor zones are extended and discrimination between, for example, red and orange is difficult.

The full resolution of human vision is restricted to brightness variations. Our ability to resolve colour details is only about a quarter of that.

2.3 Colorimetry

The triple receptor characteristic of the eye is extremely fortunate as it means that we can generate a range of colours by adding together light sources having just three different wavelengths in various proportions. This process is known as *additive colour matching* and should be clearly distinguished from the subtractive colour matching which occurs with paints and inks. Subtractive matching begins with white light and selectively removes parts of the spectrum by filtering. Additive matching uses coloured light sources which are combined.

An effective colour television system can be made in which only three pure or single wavelength colours or *primaries* can be generated. The primaries need to be similar in wavelength to the peaks of the three receptor responses, but need not be identical. Figure 2.2 shows a rudimentary colour television system. Note that the colour camera is in fact three cameras in one, where each is fitted with a different coloured filter. Three signals, *R*, *G* and *B*, must be transmitted to the display which produces three images which have to be superimposed to obtain a colour picture.

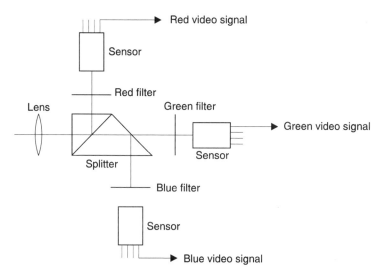

Figure 2.2 Simple colour television system. Camera image is split by three filters. Red, green and blue video signals are sent to three primary coloured displays whose images are combined.

In practice the primaries must be selected from available phosphor compounds. Once the primaries have been selected, the proportions needed to reproduce a given colour can be found using a colorimeter. Figure 2.3 shows a colorimeter which consists of two adjacent white screens. One screen is illuminated by three light sources, one of each of the selected primary colours. Initially, the second screen is illuminated with white light and the three sources are adjusted until the first screen displays the same white. The sources are then calibrated. Light of a single wavelength is then projected on the second screen. The primaries are once more adjusted until both screens appear to have the same colour. The proportions of the primaries are noted. This process is repeated for the whole visible spectrum, resulting in *colour mixture curves* shown in Figure 2.4. In some cases it will not be possible to find a match because an impossible negative contribution is needed. In this case we can simulate a negative contribution by shining some primary colour on the test screen until a match is obtained. If the primaries were ideal, monochromatic or single wavelength

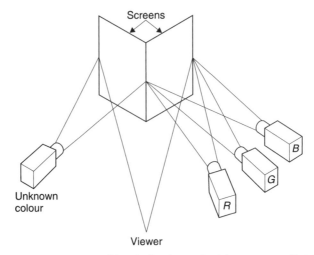

Figure 2.3 Simple colorimeter. Intensities of primaries on the right screen are adjusted to match the test colour on the left screen.

sources, it would be possible to find three wavelengths at which two of the primaries were completely absent. However, practical phosphors are not monochromatic, but produce a distribution of wavelengths around the nominal value, and in order to make them spectrally pure other wavelengths have to be subtracted.

The colour mixing curves dictate what the response of the three sensors in the colour camera must be. The primaries are determined in this way because it is easier to make camera filters to suit available CRT phosphors rather than the other way round.

As there are three signals in a colour television system, they can only be simultaneously depicted in three dimensions. Figure 2.5 shows the *RGB* colour space, which is basically a cube with black at the origin and white at the diagonally opposite corner. Figure 2.6 shows the colour mixture curves plotted in

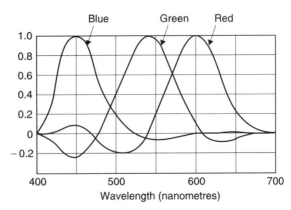

Figure 2.4 Colour mixture curves show how to mix primaries to obtain any spectral colour.

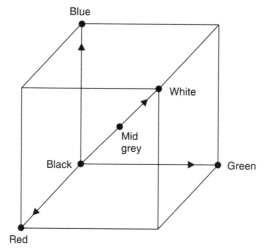

Figure 2.5 *RGB* colour space is three-dimensional and not easy to draw.

RGB space. For each visible wavelength a vector exists whose direction is determined by the proportions of the three primaries. If the brightness is allowed to vary this will affect all three primaries and thus the length of the vector in the same proportion.

Depicting and visualizing the *RGB* colour space are not easy and it is also difficult to take objective measurements from it. The solution is to modify the diagram to allow it to be rendered in two dimensions on flat paper. This is done by eliminating luminance (brightness) changes and depicting only the colour at constant brightness. Figure 2.7(a) shows how a constant luminance unit plane

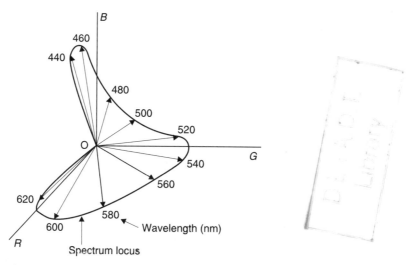

Figure 2.6 Colour mixture curves plotted in *RGB* space result in a vector whose locus moves with wavelength in three dimensions.

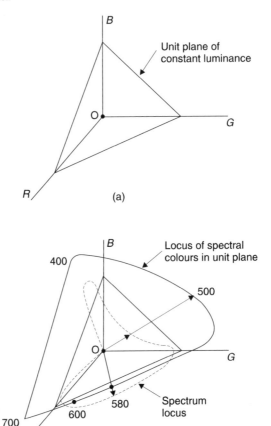

Figure 2.7 (a) A constant luminance plane intersects *RGB* space, allowing colours to be studied in two dimensions only. (b) The intersection of the unit plane by vectors joining the origin and the spectrum locus produces the locus of spectral colours which requires negative values of *R*, *G* and *B* to describe it.

intersects the *RGB* space at unity on each axis. At any point on the plane the three components add up to one. A two-dimensional plot results when vectors representing all colours intersect the plane. Vectors may be extended if necessary to allow intersection. Figure 2.7(b) shows that the 500 nm vector has to be produced (extended) to meet the unit plane, whereas the 580 nm vector naturally intersects. Any colour can now uniquely be specified in two dimensions.

The points where the unit plane intersects the axes of *RGB* space form a triangle on the plot. The horseshoe shaped locus of pure spectral colours goes outside this triangle because, as was seen above, the colour mixture curves require negative contributions for certain colours.

Having the spectral locus outside the triangle is a nuisance, and a larger triangle can be created by postulating new coordinates called *X*, *Y* and *Z* representing hypothetical primaries that cannot exist. This representation is shown in Figure 2.7(c).

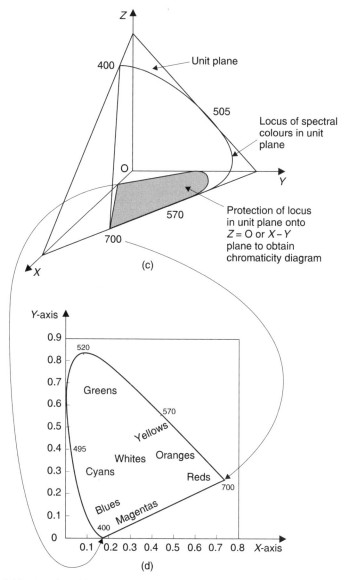

Figure 2.7 (*Continued*) In (c) a new coordinate system, *X*, *Y*, *Z*, is used so that only positive values are required. The spectrum locus now fits entirely in the triangular space where the unit plane intersects these axes. To obtain the CIE chromaticity diagram (d), the locus is projected onto the *X–Y* plane.

The Commission Internationale d'Eclairage (CIE) standard *chromaticity diagram* shown in Figure 2.7(d) is obtained in this way by projecting the unity luminance plane onto the *X–Y* plane. This projection has the effect of bringing the red and blue primarics closer together. Note that the curved part of the locus is due to spectral or single wavelength colours. The straight base is due to non-spectral colours obtained by additively mixing red and blue.

As negative light is impossible, only colours within the triangle joining the primaries can be reproduced and so practical television systems cannot reproduce all possible colours. Clearly efforts should be made to obtain primaries which embrace as large an area as possible. Figures 2.8 and 2.9 show how the colour range or gamut of television compares with paint and printing inks and illustrates that the comparison is favourable. Most everyday scenes fall within the colour gamut of television. Exceptions include saturated turquoise, spectrally pure iridescent colours formed by interference in ducks' feathers or reflections in Compact Discs. For special purposes displays have been made having four primaries to give a wider colour range, but these are uncommon.

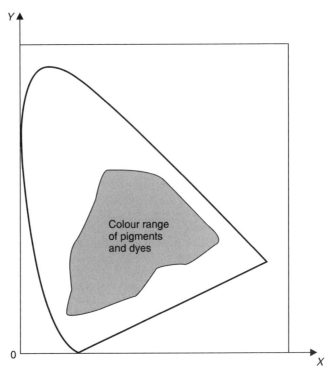

Figure 2.8 The colour range of television compares well with printing and photography.

Figure 2.9 shows the primaries initially selected for NTSC. However, manufacturers looking for brighter displays substituted more efficient phosphors having a smaller colour range. This was later standardized as the SMPTE C phosphors which were also adopted for PAL.

Whites appear in the centre of the chromaticity diagram corresponding to roughly equal amounts of primary colour. Two terms are used to describe colours: *hue* and *saturation*. Colours having the same hue lie on a straight line between the white point and the perimeter of the primary triangle. The saturation of the colour increases with distance from the white point. As an example, pink is a desaturated red.

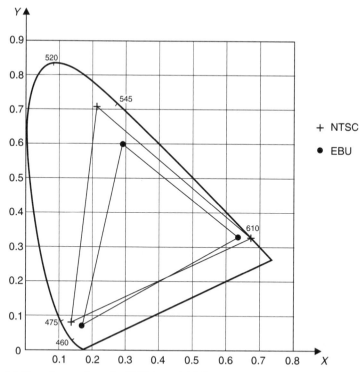

Figure 2.9 The primary colours for NTSC were initially as shown. These were later changed to more efficient phosphors which were also adopted for PAL. See text.

The apparent colour of an object is also a function of the illumination. The 'true colour' will only be revealed under ideal white light, which in practice is uncommon. An ideal white object reflects all wavelengths equally and simply takes on the colour of the ambient illumination. Figure 2.10 shows the location of three 'white' sources or *illuminants* on the chromaticity diagram. Illuminant A corresponds to a tungsten filament lamp, illuminant B corresponds to midday sunlight and illuminant C corresponds to typical daylight, which is bluer because it consists of a mixture of sunlight and light scattered by the atmosphere. In everyday life we accommodate automatically to the change in apparent colour of objects as the sun's position or the amount of cloud changes and as we enter artificially lit buildings, but colour cameras accurately reproduce these colour changes. Attempting to edit a television programme from recordings made at different times of day or indoors and outdoors would result in obvious and irritating colour changes unless some steps are taken to keep the white balance reasonably constant.

2.4 The colour cathode ray tube

In order to display colour pictures, three simultaneous images must be generated, one for each primary colour. The colour CRT does this geometrically. Figure 2.11(a) shows that three electron beams pass down the tube from guns mounted

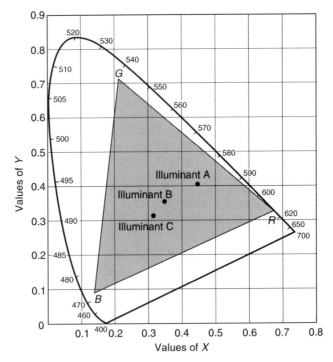

Figure 2.10 Position of three common illuminants on chromaticity diagram.

in a triangular or delta array. Immediately before the tube face is mounted a perforated metal plate known as a shadow mask. The three beams approach holes in the shadow mask at a slightly different angle and so fall upon three different areas of phosphor which each produce a different primary colour. The sets of three phosphors are known as triads. Figure 2.11(b) shows an alternative arrangement in which the three electron guns are mounted in a straight line and the shadow mask is slotted and the triads are rectangular. This is known as a PIL (precision-in-line) tube. The triads can easily be seen upon close inspection of an operating CRT.

During the manufacturing process the shadow mask is fitted and the tube is assembled except for the electron guns. The inside of the tube is coated with photoresist and a light source is positioned at the point where the scan coils would deflect an electron beam such that the resist is exposed in all locations where one colour of phosphor should be deposited. The process is repeated for each phosphor.

In early tubes the space between the phosphor dots was grey. Later tubes replaced this with black in order to reduce reflection of ambient light and thereby increase contrast and apparent sharpness.

When the tube is completed, the scan coils have to be installed in exactly the right place otherwise the correct beam geometry will not result and beams may fall on part of the wrong phosphor in the triads. Adjusting the scan coils to ensure correct triad registration is called the *purity* adjustment. The shadow mask is heated by electron impact in service, and is not readily cooled because it is in a vacuum. Should the shadow mask overheat, it may distort due to thermal expansion and damage the purity. This effect limits the brightness of shadow mask CRTs. Purity can also be damaged by stray magnetic fields which may magnetize the shadow mask. Most monitors incorporate coils which degauss the shadowmask when the unit is first switched on. Many loudspeakers produce stray magnetic fields sufficiently strong to affect nearby CRTs and it is advisable to use loudspeakers which have been designed to contain their fields.

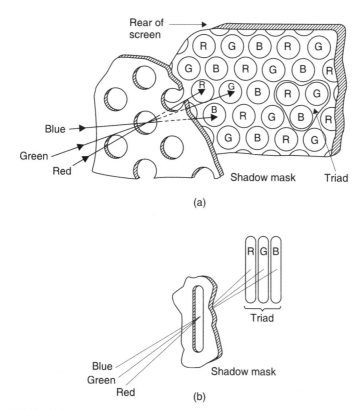

Figure 2.11 (a) Triads of phosphor dots are triangular and electron guns are arranged in a triangle. (b) Inline tube has strips of phosphor side by side.

The three electron beams must also be arranged to scan over exactly the same area of the tube so that the three images correctly superimpose. Static shifts of the beams can be obtained by the *static convergence* controls which register the three beams in the tube centre. All three beams are deflected by the same horizontal and vertical scan coils, and the geometry is such that there will be registration errors between the beams which increase with the deflection. These errors are cancelled by providing subsidiary individual scan coils for two of the beams with correction waveforms. This is known as *dynamic convergence*. In order to adjust the convergence, a test pattern which produces a white cross-hatch is used. If the convergence is incorrect, separate coloured lines can be seen instead of one white line. The inline tube has the advantage that the dynamic convergence waveforms are simpler to generate.

2.5 Colour difference signals

There are many different ways in which television signals can be carried; these will be considered here. A monochrome camera produces a single luminance signal Y or Ys whereas a colour camera produces three signals, or *components*, R, G and B, which are essentially monochrome video signals representing an image in each primary colour. In some systems sync is present on a separate signal (*RGBS*). Rarely is it present on all three components – most commonly it is only present on the green component, leading to the term *RGsB*. The use of the green component for sync has led to suggestions that the components should be called *GBR*. As the original and longstanding term *RGB* or *RGsB* correctly reflects the sequence of the colours in the spectrum it remains to be seen whether *GBR* will achieve common usage. Like luminance, *RGsB* signals may use 0.7 or 0.714 volt signals, with or without set-up.

RGB and Y signals are incompatible, yet when colour television was introduced it was a practical necessity that it should be possible to display colour signals on a monochrome display and vice versa.

Creating or *transcoding* a luminance signal from R, Gs and B is relatively easy. Figure 2.1 showed the spectral response of the eye, which has a peak in the green region. Green objects will produce a larger stimulus than red objects of the same brightness, with blue objects producing the least stimulus. A luminance signal can be obtained by adding R, G and B together, not in equal amounts, but in a sum which is *weighted* by the relative response of the eye. Thus:

$$Y = 0.299R + 0.587G + 0.114B$$

Syncs may be regenerated, but will be identical to those on the Gs input and when added to Y result in Ys as required.

If Ys is derived in this way, a monochrome display will show nearly the same result as if a monochrome camera had been used in the first place. The results are not identical because of the non-linearities introduced by gamma correction.

As colour pictures require three signals, it should be possible to send Ys and two other signals which a colour display could arithmetically convert back to R, G and B. There are two important factors which restrict the form which the other two signals may take. One is to achieve reverse compatibility. If the source is a monochrome camera, it can only produce Ys and the other two signals will be completely absent. A colour display should be able to operate on the Ys signal only and show a monochrome picture. The other is the requirement to conserve bandwidth for economic reasons.

These requirements are met by sending two *colour difference signals* along with Ys. There are three possible colour difference signals, $R - Y$, $B - Y$ and $G - Y$. As the green signal makes the greatest contribution to Y, then the amplitude of $G - Y$ would be the smallest and would be most susceptible to noise. Thus $R - Y$ and $B - Y$ are used in practice as Figure 2.12 shows.

R and B are readily obtained by adding Y to the two colour difference signals. G is obtained by rearranging the expression for Y above such that:

$$G = \frac{Y - 0.3R - 0.11B}{0.59}$$

If a colour CRT is being driven, it is possible to apply inverted luminance to the cathodes and the $R - Y$ and $B - Y$ signals directly to two of the grids so that the tube performs some of the matrixing. It is then only necessary to obtain $G - Y$ for the third grid, using the expression:

$$G - Y = -0.51(R - Y) - 0.186(B - Y)$$

If a monochrome source having only a Ys output is supplied to a colour display, $R - Y$ and $B - Y$ will be zero. It is reasonably obvious that if there are no colour difference signals the colour signals cannot be different from one another and $R = G = B$. As a result the colour display can only produce a neutral picture.

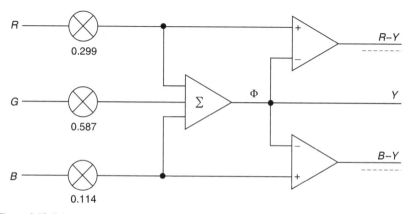

Figure 2.12 Colour components are converted to colour difference signals by the transcoding shown here.

The use of colour difference signals is essential for compatibility in both directions between colour and monochrome, but it has a further advantage which follows from the way in which the eye works. In order to produce the highest resolution in the fovea, the eye will use signals from all types of cone, regardless of colour. In order to determine colour the stimuli from three cones must be compared. There is evidence that the nervous system uses some form of colour difference processing to make this possible. As a result the acuity of the human eye is only available in monochrome. Differences in colour cannot be resolved so well. A further factor is that the lens in the human eye is not achromatic and this means that the ends of the spectrum are not well focused. This is particularly noticeable on blue.

If the eye cannot resolve colour very well there is no point is expending valuable bandwidth sending high resolution colour signals. Colour difference working allows the luminance to be sent separately at full bandwidth. This determines the subjective sharpness of the picture. The colour difference signals can be sent with considerably reduced bandwidth, as little as one-quarter that of luminance, and the human eye is unable to tell.

In practice, analog component signals are never received perfectly, but suffer from slight differences in relative gain. In the case of *RGB* a gain error in one signal will cause a colour cast on the received picture. A gain error in Y causes no colour cast and gain errors in $R - Y$ or $B - Y$ cause much smaller perceived colour casts. Thus colour difference working is also more robust than *RGB* working.

The overwhelming advantages obtained by using colour difference signals mean that in broadcast and production facilities *RGB* is seldom used. The outputs from the *RGB* sensors in the camera are converted directly to $Y, R - Y$ and $B - Y$ in the camera control unit and output in that form. Standards exist for both analog and digital colour difference signals to ensure compatibility between equipment from various manufacturers. The M-II and Betacam formats record analog colour difference signals, and there are a number of colour difference digital formats.

Whilst signals such as Y, R, G and B are *unipolar* or positive only, it should be stressed that colour difference signals are *bipolar* and may meaningfully take on levels below zero volts.

The wide use of colour difference signals has led to the development of test signals and equipment to display them. The most important of the test signals is the ubiquitous *colour bars*. Colour bars are used to set the gains and timing of signal components and to check that matrix operations are performed using the correct weighting factors. Further details will be found in Chapter 4. The origin of the colour bar test signal is shown in Figure 2.13. In *100 per cent amplitude bars*, peak amplitude binary *RGB* signals are produced, having one, two and four

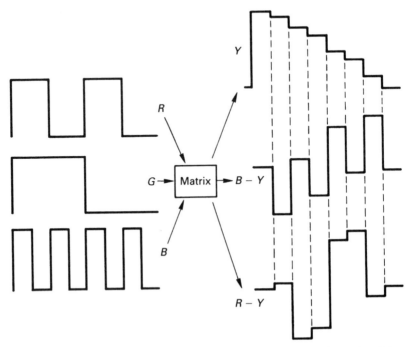

Figure 2.13 Origin of colour difference signals representing colour bars. Adding R, G and B according to the weighting factors produces an irregular luminance staircase.

cycles per screen width. When these are added together in a weighted sum, an eight-level luminance staircase results because of the unequal weighting. The matrix also produces two colour difference signals, $R - Y$ and $B - Y$ as shown. Sometimes *75 per cent amplitude bars* are generated by suitably reducing the *RGB* signal amplitude. Note that in both cases the colours are fully saturated; it is only the brightness which is reduced to 75 per cent. Sometimes the white bar of a 75 per cent bar signal is raised to 100 per cent to make calibration easier. Such a signal is sometimes erroneously called a 100 per cent bar signal.

Figure 2.14(a) shows an SMPTE/EBU standard colour difference signal set in which the signals are called *Ys*, P_b and P_r. 0.3 volt syncs are on luminance only and all three video signals have a 0.7 volt pk–pk swing with 100 per cent bars. In order to obtain these voltage swings, the following gain corrections are made to the components:

$$P_r = 0.71327(R - Y)$$

and

$$P_b = 0.56433(B - Y)$$

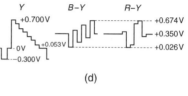

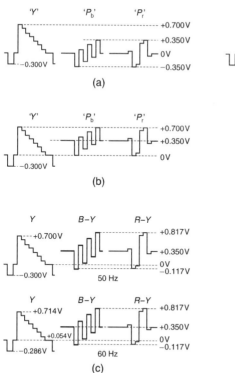

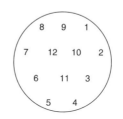

Pin no.	Signal
1	Y in
2	Y in ground
3	P_r in
4	P_r in ground
5	P_b in
6	P_b in ground

(e)

Figure 2.14 (a) 100 per cent colour bars represented by SMPTE/EBU standard colour difference signals. (b) Level comparison is easier in waveform monitors if the $B-Y$ and $R-Y$ signals are offset upwards. (c) Early Betacam equipment operated with the levels shown here. (d) M-II equipment signal levels. Interchange between these standards requires no more than gain changes. (e) Betacam equipment uses a twelve-pin connector.

Within waveform monitors, the colour difference signals may be offset by 350 mV as in Figure 2.14(b) to match the luminance range for display purposes.

Whilst the Betacam SP format is compatible with these signal levels, the older Betacam equipment operated with colour difference signals in which the amplitude had been increased by $\frac{4}{3}$ as shown in Figure 2.14(c). In addition the Y signal used a 10:4 video:sync relationship in 60 Hz products.

The analog M-II format uses SMPTE/EBU standard signals in 50 Hz products, but uses the levels shown in Figure 2.14(d) in 60 Hz products. The colour difference signals are scaled to the peak luminance amplitude minus set-up.

Transcoding between any of these analog standards is only a matter of applying gain changes. In many cases the range of adjustments is sufficient; in some cases resistors may need to be changed on circuit boards. Some equipment can operate with more than one standard and the levels can be changed by moving links or jumpers.

Ys,P_r,P_b signals are distributed as 75 ohm impedance waveforms and generally three parallel BNC connectors are used. For compactness, Betacam equipment uses a twelve-pin connector as shown in Figure 2.14(e).

2.6 Quadrature modulation

Section 2.5 showed how the colour bar test signal results in standard colour difference signals. Figure 2.15 shows that both signals can be displayed at once on a component vectorscope. The screen of a component vectorscope represents a constant-luminance chromaticity diagram with white in the centre and

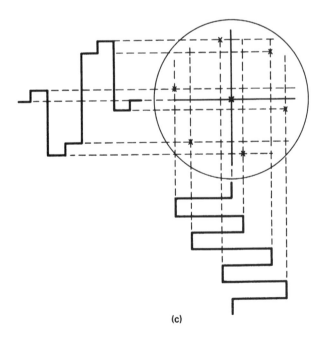

(c)

Figure 2.15 Colour difference signals can be shown two-dimensionally on a vectorscope.

saturation increasing outwards with radius. The $B - Y$ signal causes horizontal deflection, and $R - Y$ causes vertical deflection. It will be seen that this results in a display having six peripheral dots and two central dots. The central dots result from the white and black bars which are not colours and in which the colour difference signals are both zero.

Figure 2.16 shows how a particular dot or colour can be reached on a two-dimensional display. In component signals, the dot is reached by travelling a given distance horizontally, followed by a given distance vertically. This is the way a map reference works; mathematicians call the components Cartesian coordinates. It is just as easy to reach the same dot by travelling a suitable distance at the right heading or angle. Mathematicians call these components polar coordinates. Instead of two signals, we can convey distance and angle in the amplitude and phase of a waveform. That is precisely how PAL and NTSC chroma work. The radius of the dot is the chroma amplitude which is proportional to the saturation, and the angle is the phase. The phase angle of the vector literally points to the appropriate hue in the chromaticity diagram.

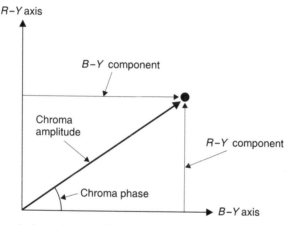

Figure 2.16 The equivalence of polar (radius and angle) and XY coordinates in locating a specific colour.

Simultaneous modulation of amplitude and phase is performed by a quadrature modulator. Figure 2.17 shows how this works. A pair of amplitude modulators (analog multipliers) are supplied with the same carriers except that one has been phase shifted by 90 degrees. The outputs of the two modulators are linearly added and the resultant signal will be found to be amplitude and phase modulated. The phase is a function of the relative proportions and polarities of the two inputs. The original subcarrier is suppressed in the output of the modulator. The picture frequencies in the baseband result in sidebands above and below the centre frequency after modulation. As a result it is incorrect to refer to the quadrature modulator output as subcarrier; the correct term is chroma. As the chroma signal carries the information from both colour difference signals, it is possible to carry a colour picture by sending two signals: luminance and chroma, abbreviated Y/C. This is also shown in Figure 2.17. Y/C is used in S-VHS VCRs (see Chapter 5) in which the chroma signal is kept separate from the luminance through the whole record and playback process in order to avoid cross-effects. It is difficult to define a *Y/C* standard. As there are two signals involved, strictly speaking it is a component standard.

As will be seen in Figure 2.17 and in the next section, a composite system linearly adds chroma to luminance for broadcasting. At the receiver the two signals must undergo *Y/C* separation before the chroma can be demodulated back to a pair of colour difference signals.

This can be done using a pair of synchronous demodulators also driven in quadrature. These need reference carriers which are identical in phase to the original pair of carriers. As there is no subcarrier in the chroma signal it is necessary to send a reference subcarrier separately. This is the purpose of the burst which is sent during horizontal blanking. A heavily damped phase locked loop synchronizes to the burst and continues to run for the rest of the line to provide a reference for the decoder.

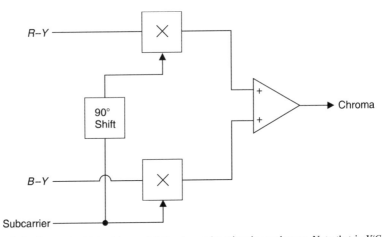

Figure 2.17 Chroma is obtained by modulating two subcarriers in quadrature. Note that in *Y/C* working the resultant chroma is kept separate from the luminance whereas in composite video the two are added.

One way of considering how quadrature modulation works is that when one of the carrier inputs reaches its peak, the other is passing through zero. At that time the signal voltage can only be a function of, say, the *B − Y* input. Ninety degrees later the relationships exchange and the signal voltage can then only be a function of the *R − Y* input. Demodulation is a question of sampling the signal every 90 degrees. Odd samples reflect the state of one component; even samples reflect the state of the other. The demodulators have the effect of inverting alternate samples. A simple low-pass filter removes the harmonics of the subcarrier frequency to recreate the input waveform.

2.7 Basic composite video

Composite video was originally designed as a monochrome compatible system for broadcasting in which subcarrier-based colour-difference information was added to an existing line standard in such a way that existing sets could still display a monochrome picture. A further requirement was that the addition of colour should not increase the bandwidth of the TV channel. In that respect composite video has to be viewed as an early form of compression.

Whilst the details vary, all composite signals have in common the need to include a subcarrier-based *chroma* signal within the luminance band in such a way that it will be effectively invisible on an unmodified monochrome TV set. This is achieved in much the same way in all three systems. Figure 2.18 shows that if a chroma signal is linearly added to a luminance signal it has the effect of making it alternately too bright and too dark. If it is arranged that the chroma is inverted on the next picture line the effect is that areas which are too bright on one line are adjacent to areas which are too dark on the next. The eye will see the average brightness of the line pairs which is almost the original luminance. In the absence of gamma correction the cancellation would be perfect; in the presence of gamma it is imperfect but generally adequate.

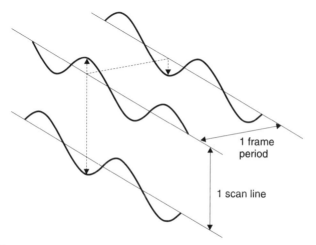

Figure 2.18 In composite video the subcarrier frequency is arranged so that inversions occur between adjacent lines and pictures to help reduce the visibility of the chroma.

Efforts are also made to ensure that the phase of the chroma also reverses from frame to frame so that the same point on the screen alternates in brightness on the time axis about the value determined by the luminance signal. Clearly the exact frequency of the subcarrier has to be carefully chosen with respect to line and frame rates. NTSC and PAL use quadrature modulation as in Section 2.6 so that two components can be sent simultaneously whereas SECAM frequency modulates the subcarrier and sends the components on alternate lines. The effect of composite modulation is to produce an extremely complex signal spectrum, especially in PAL. It is only by considering this spectrum in detail that it becomes clear how the components can effectively be separated.

2.8 NTSC encoding

Figure 2.19 shows an NTSC encoder which works strictly according to the original specification. The *RGsB* to colour difference matrix operates as

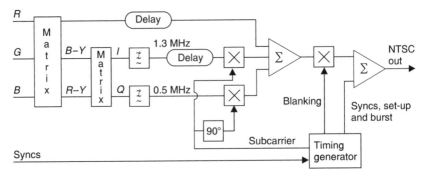

Figure 2.19 A simple NTSC encoder; see text for details.

described in Section 2.5 to produce a Ys signal. Where used, a pedestal level of 7.5 IRE will be added to black level.

The quadrature modulation process also operates as described above except that a psycho-visual coding scheme was used where the greatest perceived colour resolution is obtained with the minimum overall chroma bandwidth. This was achieved by matrixing the $R - Y$ and $B - Y$ colour difference signals to produce new signals I and Q on different axes as shown in Figure 2.20. The following scale factors were used to obtain the I and Q signals:

$$I = -0.27(B - Y) + 0.74(R - Y)$$
$$Q = 0.41(B - Y) + 0.48(R - Y)$$

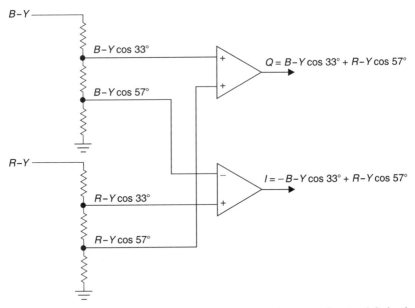

Figure 2.20 The colour difference signals are matrixed as shown here to produce I and Q signals to drive the modulators.

The I axis is at 123 degrees to $B - Y$ and the Q axis is at 33 degrees to $B - Y$. The I signal was low-pass filtered to 1.3 MHz whereas the Q signal was filtered to only 0.5 MHz. This was possible because the latter lies upon an axis on which the eye is least sensitive to detail. The wider bandwidth filter causes less delay than the narrow band filter, and a compensating delay was needed to time-align the filtered signals. The filtered I signal drove a modulator which was fed with subcarrier shifted by 123 degrees to cancel the phase rotation caused by the matrix operation, hence the term I which stands for In-phase. The filtered Q signal drove a modulator which was fed by subcarrier shifted by:

$$123 - 90 = 33 \text{ degrees}$$

hence the term Q for Quadrature. A compensating delay was needed for time alignment of the luminance with the chroma. The sync generator produced burst gates which allowed inverted subcarrier at the correct amplitude to be added to the quadrature modulator output during the blanking period following horizontal sync. Alternatively the burst could have been produced by subtracting a burst envelope waveform from the $B - Y$ signal.

Adding Y, C and syncs together produced the NTSC signal which was band-limited to 4.2 MHz for broadcast.

It will be recalled that Chapter 1 defined composite video as a signal in which the syncs were combined with the vision signal. Unfortunately the term composite video is also used to describe a video signal having luminance, syncs and subcarrier in order to distinguish it from $RGsB$ or Ys, P_r, P_b signals which are described as component video. As a result composite video may mean a signal having mixed syncs or a signal with subcarrier-based chroma. It is generally obvious from the context which is the case.

Whilst the NTSC encoder described above met the ideal NTSC specification, ideal decoding also required the demodulators to be fed with I and Q references and to have reconstruction filters of two different bandwidths followed by a matrix to return to $R - Y$ and $B - Y$. However, many television set manufacturers ignored the extra bandwidth and demodulated on the $R - Y$ and $B - Y$ axes. Similarly numerous encoder manufacturers discarded the additional complexity of the second matrix and the different bandwidths and encoded on the colour difference axes. The restricted Q bandwidth was later found to be unnecessary

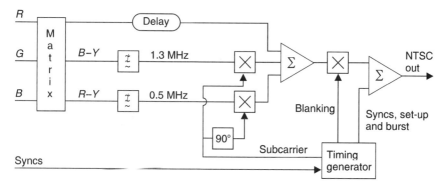

Figure 2.21 An equal bandwidth NTSC encoder.

and the requirement was dropped, resulting in the equal bandwidth coder of Figure 2.21 which needs no colour difference delay. In 525 line Y/C systems the C signal is obtained exactly as described above, but it is not added to Ys.

2.9 PAL encoding

The PAL (Phase Alternating Line) system was designed to overcome the susceptibility to hue errors inherent in NTSC and to eliminate the hue control from receivers. Figure 2.22 shows that the $RGsB$ input is matrixed as before to produce Ys, $B - Y$ and $R - Y$ and the latter two are gain weighted and result in signals called U and V where:

$$U = 0.49(B - Y)$$
$$V = 0.88(R - Y)$$

The chroma modulation system uses quadrature as in NTSC, but on alternate lines the phase of the carrier feeding the V modulator is inverted by a vertical axis switch (V-switch). The demodulator in the decoder has to re-invert the V signal and in order to synchronize the receiver inversion the PAL burst is arranged to swing by ±45 degrees with respect to $-U$ in synchronism with the encoder inversion.

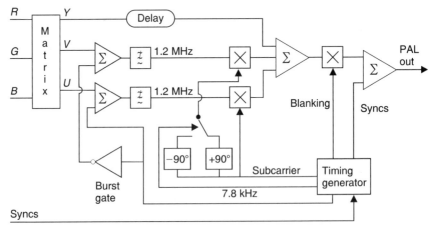

Figure 2.22 A simple PAL encoder; see text for details.

Figure 2.23 shows how the inclusion of V-switch allows phase errors to be rejected. If a phase error should occur, rotating the received phase, for example, clockwise, then on one line the U signal will be too small on demodulation whereas the V signal will be too large. However, on the next line the same phase error causes U to be too large and V to be too small. Thus by averaging the colour difference signals over two lines the effect of the phase error is prevented from affecting the hue. There is a small second order loss of saturation instead, but this is considerably less obvious. In simple receivers (PAL-S), the averaging is left to the viewer and severe phase errors result in brightness differences between lines which cause picture patterning known as Hanover bars or blinds.

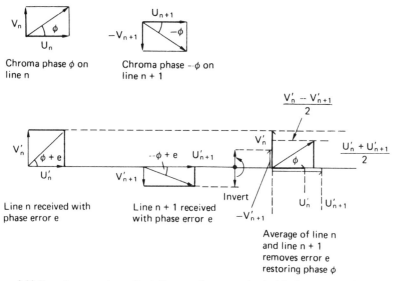

Chroma phase ϕ on line n

Chroma phase $-\phi$ on line n + 1

Line n received with phase error e

Line n + 1 received with phase error e

Invert

Average of line n and line n + 1 removes error e restoring phase ϕ

Figure 2.23 Top, chroma as transmitted. Bottom, chroma received with phase error. V is reversed on second line and the two lines are averaged, eliminating phase error, and giving a small saturation error.

In PAL-D receivers a one-line delay is used to allow electronic averaging of the colour difference signals. This results in a loss of vertical colour resolution, but this is unimportant as the horizontal colour resolution has already been seriously reduced by the encoding filters to take advantage of the reduced colour resolution of the eye.

Returning to Figure 2.22, the PAL encoder has equal bandwidth filters for U and V. V-switch is obtained by either inverting the quadrature subcarrier on

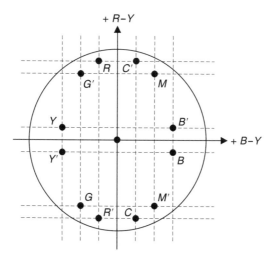

Figure 2.24 In PAL, V-switch has the effect of producing an extra six dots on the vectorscope colour-bar display.

alternate lines or by inverting the baseband V signal. The swinging burst is obtained by adding an inverted burst envelope to the baseband U signal and a non-inverted burst envelope of equal amplitude to the baseband V-signal. This results in a burst of 135 degrees or −135 degrees according to the state of V-switch. The luminance signal is passed through a compensating delay before the addition of the chroma and syncs. PAL does not use set-up. For broadcast purposes the composite signal is band-limited to 5.75 MHz. Once more the C signal in 625 line Y/C is identical to PAL chroma.

PAL appears quite different on the vectorscope although the interpretation techniques needed are exactly the same. The swinging burst results in two burst vectors and V-switch results in two vectors mirrored around the U axis for each colour. Figure 2.24 shows the result for colour bars.

2.10 SECAM encoding

SECAM was also designed to overcome the hue instability of NTSC. Whilst PAL retained the quadrature modulation system and modified it with V-switch, the French approach was to abandon quadrature modulation altogether and to send the colour difference signals on alternate lines instead of simultaneously. The receiver requires a one-line delay in order to time-align the sequential signals; hence the name SEquentiel Couleur Avec Memoire or SECAM. Line averaging is then used to obtain the colour difference signals on every line. The colour subcarrier is frequency modulated and then subject to pre-emphasis.

$RGsB$ inputs are matrixed to Ys as for PAL, but the colour difference signals D_r and D_b are obtained by the following scaling:

$$D_r = -1.9020(R - Y)$$
$$D_b = 1.505(B - Y)$$

D_r is inverted so that it causes deviation opposite to D_b. On typical programme material this results in a slightly cleaner spectrum. Prior to frequency modulation D_r and D_b are pre-emphasized according to the following:

$$A1(f) = \frac{1 + j(f/f1)}{1 + j(f/f1)}$$

As the colour difference signals are sent sequentially, it is necessary to synchronize the receiver so that they are not accidentally transposed. This is done by using different centre frequencies for D_b ($282F_h$) and D_r ($272F_h$). Instead of a burst for phase reference, an undeviated subcarrier of the appropriate frequency is sent at the run-in to active video to act as a reference. The centre frequencies of the two subcarriers are quite close together, and so in some versions of SECAM the vertical interval carries identification signals to help maintain colour synchronism. These consist of bursts of subcarrier which are frequency swept along the line. The pre-emphasis causes the subcarrier amplitude to vary and the resultant envelope shape has led to them being called 'bottles'. In order to reduce chroma visibility on monochrome receivers, the chroma is inverted on alternate lines. As the subcarrier is frequency modulated, this cannot be done by selecting a suitable frequency as is done in PAL and NTSC, but instead requires a switchable inverter following the frequency modulator.

Figure 2.25 shows a SECAM encoder. The identification (bottle) signal envelopes are added if required to the D_r and D_b signals from the matrix. A DC offset is added to D_b. The D_r and D_b signals are selected alternately at half line rate, and low-pass filtered to 1.2 MHz prior to pre-emphasis. The baseband signals drive a frequency modulator. The DC offset in D_b results in a higher centre frequency. Following the frequency modulator the chroma signal is selectively inverted. As SECAM has a two-line sequence, two frames have to elapse before the same picture line carries the same component.

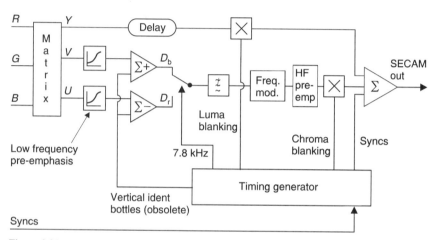

Figure 2.25 A simple SECAM encoder; see text for details.

SECAM works well for transmission as the frequency modulated chroma is immune to differential gain and phase errors. This characteristic also makes it resistant to timebase errors in analog VTRs. In fact the timebase accuracy required in SECAM is no greater than in monochrome. However, it is not possible to carry out any manipulation of the SECAM signal. Even a simple fade is impossible as it has no effect on the frequency of the chroma. The result is that the luminance fades and the chroma becomes noisier until it cuts out. In practice many countries which use SECAM produce in PAL and transcode for transmission. It is hardly surprising that France has been at the forefront of component video development as this was a matter of necessity.

2.11 Spectrum of PAL and NTSC

The composite video systems must incorporate the chroma signals into the same channel bandwidth as the existing monochrome signal. This is done using spectral interleaving in which frequencies which are unused in the luminance spectrum are occupied by the chroma and vice versa. A detailed knowledge of the spectra of both is important to an understanding of composite video decoding and editing. As television signals describe two-dimensional images changing with time they contain three-dimensional information and the resulting spectra are also three dimensional. However, careful use of sampling theory can predict exactly what takes place. Sampling theory was considered in Chapter 1 in which the spectrum of monochrome interlaced video was deduced in Figure 1.35. The structure of the vertical/temporal spectrum of the two colour difference signals is the same as the that of luminance because both have the same field and line rates.

As the colour and luminance signals have gaps in their spectra at integer multiples of line rate vertically and integer multiples of field rate temporally, it follows that the two spectra can be made to interleave and share the same spectrum if an appropriate subcarrier frequency is selected which causes the chroma spectrum to shift by an odd multiple of half of the spectral period in both dimensions.

2.12 Detailed spectrum of NTSC

The subcarrier frequency of NTSC is an odd multiple of half line rate; 227.5 times to be precise. Figure 2.26 shows that this frequency means that on successive lines the chroma will appear phase inverted. There is thus a two-line sequence of subcarrier, responsible for a vertical frequency of half line frequency.

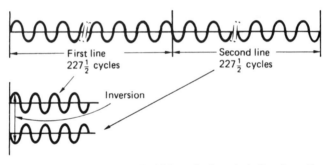

Figure 2.26 The two-line sequence of NTSC which results from the half-cycle-per-line subcarrier offset.

As there is an odd number lines in the frame, the existence of line pairs means that the chroma at a given point on the screen will also appear to invert from frame to frame. There are thus two types of frame in NTSC: one in which the subcarrier commences normally and one in which it is inverted. Two frames or four fields must elapse before the same relationship between line pairs and frame sync repeats. This is responsible for a temporal frequency component of half the frame rate. These two frequency components can be seen in the vertical/temporal spectrum of Figure 2.27. The chroma interleaves with the luminance spectrum in two dimensions as required.

The effect of the chroma added to luminance is to make the luminance alternately too dark or too bright. The phase inversion causes this effect to cancel over pairs of lines and over pairs of frames, minimizing visibility on monochrome receivers. The half frame rate component is responsible for the familiar four-field colour framing sequence. When editing NTSC recordings, this four-field sequence must not be broken.

The spectrum of Figure 2.27 does not show the whole story, because the luminance and chroma do not have the same horizontal frequency. Figure 2.28 shows a vertical/horizontal spectrum in which it will be seen that the chroma is

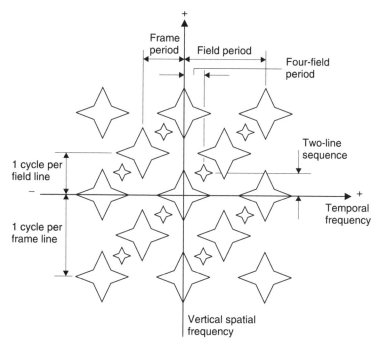

Figure 2.27 The vertical/temporal spectrum of NTSC.

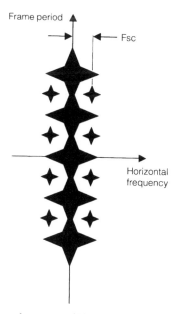

Figure 2.28 The vertical/temporal spectrum of NTSC. Note the one-quarter field rate component responsible for the four-field sequence.

displaced on the horizontal frequency axis by the subcarrier frequency. If Figure 2.27 is considered whilst viewing Figure 2.28 it will be possible to imagine the chroma components being displaced above and below the plane of the diagram.

An alternative approach to understanding composite video is to consider the spectrum of the actual video waveform in the area where the chroma and luminance overlap in Figure 2.28. The video signal as displayed on a spectrum analyser has a one-dimensional spectrum. This results from the temporal sampling spectrum being itself sampled by a vertical sampling process at the line rate. The situation is inevitably complicated by interlace. Considering luminance only, the fundamental temporal sampling rate is 60 Hz. The temporal sampling spectrum thus contains multiples of 30 Hz as shown in Figure 2.29(a). In an interlaced system there is an odd number of lines in the frame and so the line frequency is not a multiple of field rate.

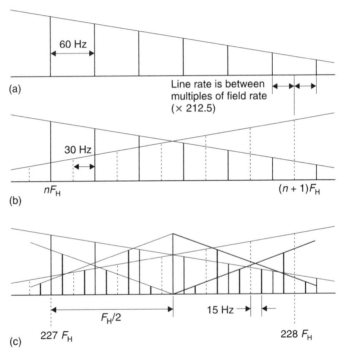

Figure 2.29 The one-dimensional spectrum of NTSC.

The effect of interlace is that the line rate is positioned half-way between multiples of field rate as shown in Figure 2.29(b). The sidebands at 60 Hz spacing mesh with the 60 Hz spacing of the baseband to produce a signal which has spectral entries repeating at 30 Hz which is, of course, the frame rate. There is a coarse spectrum repeating at line rate, and a fine spectrum repeating at frame rate. The colour difference components in NTSC have the same spectral structure as they are sampled in the same way. The subcarrier frequency must be such that the resulting chroma spectrum meshes with luminance on both the coarse and the fine scale. This means that the subcarrier frequency must be as far as possible from multiples of line rate and field rate. A frequency half-way between multiples of line rate also falls half-way between the 30 Hz spaced fine spectral entries. The use of 227.5 times line rate also meets this requirement. It will be seen from Figure 2.29(c) that this allows the luminance and chrominance spectra to mesh on both the coarse and fine scales. The fundamental spacing in the spectrum is now 15 Hz, which is further evidence of the four-field sequence of NTSC.

2.13 Detailed spectrum of PAL

The periodicity of the vertical temporal spectrum of the U signal is identical to that of luminance. However, in PAL the hue instability of NTSC is overcome by the inversion of V on alternate lines. This makes the V spectrum different to that of the U signal. V-switch causes a two-line sequence which is responsible for a vertical frequency component of half line rate. As the two-line sequence does not divide into 625 lines, two frames elapse before the same relationship between V-switch and the line number repeats. This is responsible for a half frame rate temporal frequency component. Figure 2.30 shows the resultant vertical/temporal

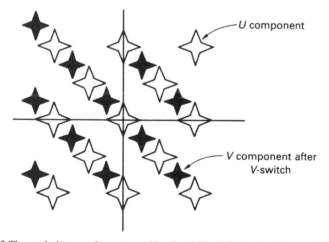

Figure 2.30 The vertical/temporal spectrum of baseband U and V signals prior to modulation.

spectrum of PAL baseband colour difference signals after V-switch. The two-frame sequence of V-switch moves the V spectrum horizontally between the U spectral entries, and the two-line sequence moves the V spectrum vertically in the same way. The effect of both is that the V component has shifted diagonally so that its spectral entries lie half-way between the U component entries.

Spectral interleaving with a half-cycle offset of subcarrier frequency as in NTSC will not work, as Figure 2.31 shows that this only interleaves the U component properly. As V-switch has halved the spectral repeat rate of chroma, the solution is to shift the chroma not half-way between the luminance spectral

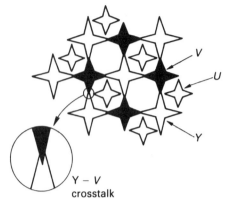

Figure 2.31 Using the subcarrier offset of NTSC causes crosstalk in PAL.

entries, but one-quarter and three-quarters of the way. In order to obtain this spectrum it is necessary to adopt a subcarrier frequency with a quarter-cycle per line offset. Multiplying the line rate by $283\frac{3}{4}$ allows the luminance and chrominance spectra to mesh as in Figure 2.32.

The quarter-cycle offset produces line quartets instead of line pairs, and this is necessary to obtain the vertical frequency component of one-quarter of line rate which is necessary for spectral interleaving. Furthermore, four frames or eight fields have to elapse before the same relationship of subcarrier to frame timing repeats. This results in a temporal frequency component of one-quarter of frame rate which is also visible in the figure. This component is also necessary for spectral interleaving, but restricts the way in which PAL recordings can be edited. Note that there is an area of the spectrum which appears not to contain signal energy in PAL. This is known as the Fukinuki hole.

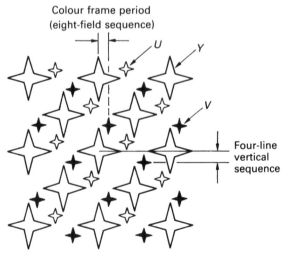

Figure 2.32 Interleaving of Y, U and V in PAL.

The three-quarter-cycle offset of subcarrier also means that the line pair cancellation of NTSC is absent, and another means has to be found to achieve visibility reduction. This is done by adding a frequency of half-frame-rate to the subcarrier frequency, such that an inversion in subcarrier is caused from one field to the next. Since in an interlaced system lines one field apart are adjacent on the screen, effective cancellation is achieved. The penalty of this approach is that subcarrier phase creeps forward with respect to H-sync at one cycle per frame. The eight-field sequence contains 2500 unique lines all having the subcarrier in a slightly different position. Observing burst on an H-triggered oscilloscope shows a stable envelope with a blurred interior.

The one-dimensional spectrum of the PAL signal in the area of the subcarrier will now be considered. Beginning with the luminance signal, as for NTSC the effect of interlace is that there is a coarse spectrum based on multiples of line rate and a fine spectrum repeating at multiples of 50 Hz as shown in Figure 2.33(b).

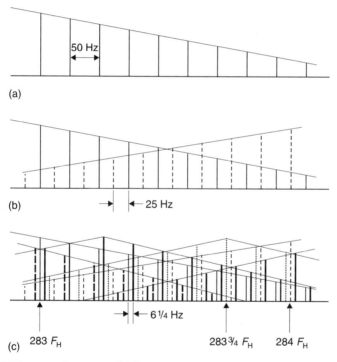

Figure 2.33 The temporal spectrum of PAL.

In PAL, the presence of V-switch alters the spectrum in comparison with NTSC. The U-signal is unaffected and has the same spectrum as luminance. However, V-switch effectively modulates a half-line-rate square wave with the V signal. The result is that the V spectrum is displaced by half line rate such that the line rate multiples of V fall between the line rate multiples of U as shown in Figure 2.33(c). The half line rate offset of NTSC clearly cannot be used as this would cause the V-component spectrum to have identical frequencies to luminance. Instead a three-quarter line rate offset must be used.

Figure 2.33(c) shows that on a coarse scale the U component resides at three-quarters of the way between luminance line rate multiples and the V component resides one-quarter of the way. Meshing is also achieved on the fine spectral scale. The fundamental spectral spacing here is $6\frac{1}{4}$ Hz, which is responsible for the eight-field sequence. Note that the addition of 25 Hz to the subcarrier frequency does not affect the meshing of the coarse or fine spectra. The 25 Hz component neither causes nor affects the eight-field sequence.

2.14 Broadcasting television signals

So far only baseband television signals have been discussed. In order to broadcast such signals, they need to modulate a suitable carrier. In terrestrial television systems, amplitude modulation (AM) is used. Figure 2.34 shows that in AM, the voltage of the video signal is used to control a multiplier which

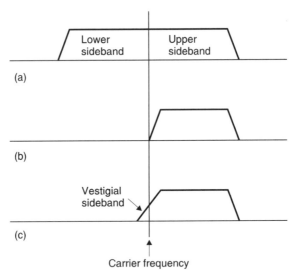

Figure 2.34 In conventional AM, upper and lower sidebands are produced as in (a). In single sideband (SSB) the carrier is suppressed (b) requiring a complex receiver. For television broadcast, a compromise (c) is used in which there is a vestigial lower sideband (VSB).

determines the amplitude of the carrier. In practice there are some complications. Firstly, conventional AM produces symmetrical sidebands above and below the carrier frequency, effectively doubling the spectrum width required. Conventional AM is also known as double sideband (DSB). In communications, a technique known as single sideband (SSB) exists, in which only one sideband is transmitted. This occupies half the spectrum space, but requires a complex receiver which has to regenerate the carrier frequency. This approach was considered too expensive for TV receivers and so a compromise was reached in which the carrier and the upper sideband is transmitted intact, but most of the lower sideband is suppressed to leave what is called a vestigial sideband. In vestigial sideband working (VSB or AM-VSB) the receiver is no more complex than in the double sideband system, but a useful spectrum saving is obtained.

Figure 2.35 shows that in addition to the vision carrier, a sound carrier is also present. This could be amplitude modulated, but frequency modulation gave better sound quality allowing lower noise. Thus all conventional TV receivers are actually double receivers allowing simultaneous sound and picture reception.

It is a characteristic of AM that the presence of the carrier blots out interference. Thus less interference will be experienced when the modulator produces full carrier amplitude. However, in video signals, noise is more visible when it affects dark picture areas. The optimum solution is to invert the baseband video signal before it drives the modulator. In this way the carrier amplitude is

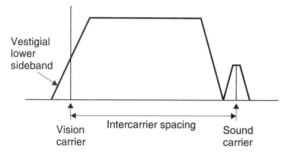

Figure 2.35 Typical transmitted TV channel showing VSB video and sound carrier.

maximum during the sync pulses and minimum at peak white. Black level or blanking corresponds to a significant carrier level which helps reduce noise in dark picture areas.

2.15 Colour framing and ScH phase

Composite video was originally designed purely for transmission and all three systems work well in that role. However, the low temporal frequencies resulting from the deliberate measures to render the chroma invisible caused some difficulties when editing composite video recordings was attempted. Monochrome editing requires only that the line and frame synchronizing is unbroken at the edit, but the presence of chroma adds the requirement that the low frequency components continue undisturbed across the edit. VTRs require a colour framing signal in the control track to specify the field in which the lowest frequency begins a cycle.

Timebase correctors attempt to make the off-tape chroma sequence the same as in the reference. The timebase corrector will rephase the low frequency components of non-colour framed edit by moving the picture vertically or horizontally as required and in some cases these picture shifts will be visible.

In composite vision mixers the most critical aspect of the signal is that the subcarrier phase of all inputs should be the same. Timebase correctors are designed to align subcarrier phase with reference so that signals from tapes can be mixed with other sources. If the ScH (subcarrier to horizontal) phase on the tape is not the same as that of the reference the picture is once more shifted horizontally by the TBC. A further problem is that certain ScH phases make it impossible unambiguously to identify the field in which the lowest frequency begins a cycle and consistent colour framing is not then possible. As a result definitions of acceptable ScH phase have been produced which specify the time relationship between a zero crossing of subcarrier and the 50 per cent point of sync on a specified line. In order to meet the specification subcarrier has to be generated with a mathematical relationship to sync.

2.16 Composite decoding

Composite decoding takes place in two stages which are usually sequential. One is to separate the chrominance signal from the luminance; the other is to demodulate the chrominance into the original colour difference signals. In NTSC and PAL it is not necessary to perform these processes in a particular order. The quadrature demodulation process requires multiplication by a subcarrier and is indistinguishable from a modulation process. Thus the act of *demodulating* composite video without prior *Y/C* separation has the effect of *modulating* the luminance to new frequencies which can then be filtered from the colour difference signals.

Figure 2.36(a) shows an ideal *Y/C* separator whereas Figure 2.36(b) shows what happens in practice. Ideal separation is impossible and there is always some

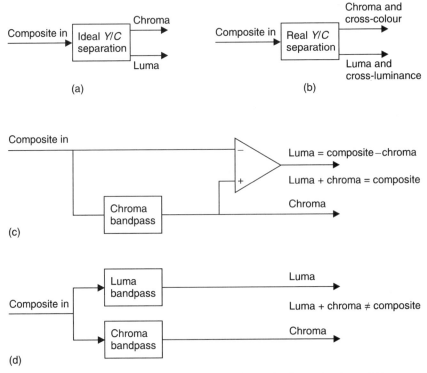

Figure 2.36 An ideal *Y/C* separator in (a) achieves perfect results. In practice there will be cross-products shown in (b). It is possible to use imperfect decoding if it is complementary, so on a subsequent encoding the cross-products re-merge. Complementary decoders (c) subtract one signal from the composite input so that by definition the input is the sum of the outputs. A high performance decoder (d) need not be complementary.

crosstalk. The luminance signal contains some residual chroma which is called cross-luminance and the chroma signal contains some cross-colour. If the decoded components are subsequently re-encoded to composite, it is possible to return the cross-colour and cross-luminance to their original places in the composite spectrum provided that the subcarrier used in the second encoder has the same relationship to syncs as the subcarrier in the original signal. If this relationship is not maintained, artifacts will result. This is the reason why component video recorders still have colour framing systems: it allows them to record composite inputs using simple decoders and correctly to re-encode the original composite signal on replay. This effect is only obtained if the filtering is complementary. A complementary *Y/C* filter is defined as one whose outputs when linearly added will recreate the original input waveform exactly. This is easily achieved in practice by constructing a filter as shown in Figure 2.36(c) which selects chroma from the input. This chroma signal is simply subtracted from the composite input to produce luminance, in which case the outputs are complementary by definition.

In practice simple decoders need to be complementary so that re-encoding can be used, whereas high quality decoders will achieve sufficient separation to make complementary operation unnecessary. In fact the requirement for complementary signals is a restriction in advanced decoder design and is undesirable as well as unnecessary. A non-complementary filter is shown in Figure 2.36(d). Each output is obtained by a separate filtering process.

It was shown in the section above that in ideal PAL and NTSC signals the chroma resides in a different space to the luminance and so it is theoretically possible to make a filter which efficiently separates them. In NTSC the *I* and *Q* signals share the same spectrum and can only be separated in the quadrature demodulation process. In PAL, the *U* and *V* signals also reside in different spaces to one another and so it is also possible to separate *U* and *V* spectrally prior to demodulation.

This theory does not tell us how to design such a filter or how complicated it will be. In practice real picture material can result in non-ideal spectra where the components may overlap. In this case ideal separation is impossible. However, there is a possibility that suitable pre-filtering may be used before or during composite encoding to ensure that no such crosstalk is allowed in the composite spectrum. In this case effective separation would be possible with all types of picture material.

At the moment such pre-filters are uncommon, and as a result colour artifacts are generated by certain luminance patterns. Herringbone suits and zebras at the right distance from the camera can both produce luminance frequencies which extend into and are indistinguishable from chroma frequencies. Without pre-filtering, the decoder produces false colours.

2.17 Simple *Y/C* separation

Early decoders were rather crude and simply contained a notch filter centred around subcarrier frequency which removed chroma from the composite signal as well as removing high frequency luminance. The resulting picture was quite soft. When displays were small and of moderate performance this was acceptable, except when highly saturated colours or sharp detail were present when cross-effects would be evident. A bandpass filter centred on subcarrier was used to produce the chroma signal. In the presence of luminance detail this contained a great deal of cross-luminance. Such performance is totally unacceptable for production purposes. In NTSC and PAL more sophisticated filters can be used based on the predictable phase changes of chroma from one line or field to the next. These cannot be used for SECAM because the chroma is frequency modulated and the phase becomes arbitrary. SECAM Y/C separation must use a notch filter. Cross-colour is less of a problem in SECAM because the colour information is carried in the frequency of the chroma. An improvement in cross-luminance performance can be obtained if the notch filter in the luminance channel is programmable in depth and width so that its frequency response can vary according to the chroma content.

2.18 Comb filter Y/C separation

In composite signals the spectrum is repetitive. The luminance energy exists at multiples of line rate with the chroma between. Comb filters are attractive for such signals because of their periodic frequency response. Figure 2.37(a) shows the ideal frequency response of a comb filter for NTSC and Figure 2.37(b) shows

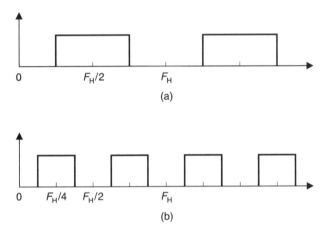

Figure 2.37 The ideal line comb filter responses for (a) NTSC and (b) PAL.

the ideal response for PAL in which the 'teeth' are spaced half as far apart. The ideal square teeth shown cannot be achieved in practice because the number of points in the filter has to be infinite. In practice little more than the fundamental frequency of the teeth will be obtained. Figure 2.38(a) shows a simple line comb for NTSC and its frequency response. The delays needed are of one line period. The configuration for PAL is shown in Figure 2.38(b), in which the delays need to be of two line periods.

Line-based comb filters work quite well in NTSC but less well in PAL. The reason can be seen in Figure 2.39 which shows the response of a comb filter superimposed on the vertical/temporal spectrum. Quite a lot of vertical luminance resolution is being lost, and becoming cross-colour. This is particularly noticeable in PAL. In the same way, high vertical frequencies in chroma become cross-luminance.

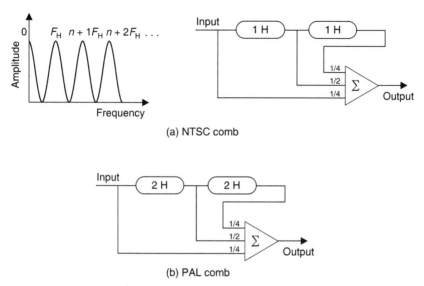

(a) NTSC comb

(b) PAL comb

Figure 2.38 Comb filters for NTSC and PAL.

Some of this resolution loss can be overcome by restricting the action of the comb filter to a bandpass region as shown in Figure 2.40(a). The result can be seen in Figure 2.40(b) which is a vertical/horizontal spectrum. At low horizontal frequencies the full vertical resolution is restored and the loss of vertical resolution only occurs at high horizontal frequencies. Although the full luminance bandwidth is available, this is restricted to picture detail having vertical edges. Man-made subjects such as buildings give good results, but more natural scenes containing diagonal edges are less successful.

2.19 Adaptive comb filters

Possibly the main drawback of the line-based comb filter is the cross-colour due to high vertical frequencies in the colour difference signals. Figure 2.39 showed

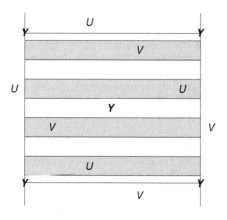

Figure 2.39 The vertical/temporal response of a PAL comb filter having two-line delays.

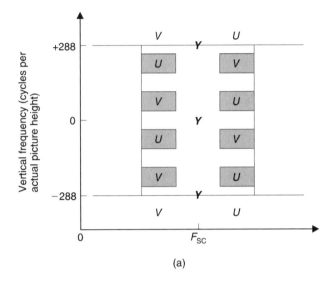

(a)

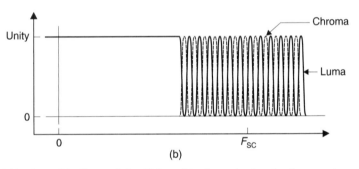

(b)

Figure 2.40 A better PAL line comb in which combing is restricted to the chroma region.

how these frequencies are accepted by the luminance passband. It is possible to visualize how this cross-colour occurs by considering how the comb filter handles chroma. The line comb effectively adds lines together. In NTSC the chroma inversion between lines and in PAL the inversion over two lines results in chroma cancellation. However, this is only true if the *chroma* phase is the same on the three lines being added. Whilst the *subcarrier* inverts as required, there is no subcarrier in chroma. If there are vertical colour changes in the image, there will be chroma phase changes from line to line and the chroma cancellation will break down. This is known as *comb mesh failure* and the result is that uncancelled chroma breaks through onto the luminance signal and causes dots at vertical transitions.

In practical line comb filters, it is necessary to revert to simple Y/C separation when comb mesh failure occurs. A low-pass filter is used to produce narrow-band luminance which is free of dots. Additional circuitry is required which compares chroma phase over the line delays to predict when failure will occur. A tuned circuit may also be provided in the comb luminance output which produces a signal if comb failure actually occurs. The output of either of these systems can select the narrow-band luminance signal instead of the comb output.

The switch between operating modes can be visible in an adaptive filter. It is particularly noticeable on moving objects where the difference between static and dynamic resolution becomes obvious. It is difficult to detect the conditions in which one or other mode should be selected because of the complex spectrum of real signals. Additionally there will always be signals which will not be handled well by any mode. Noisy signals may result in undesirable frequent mode switching.

2.20 Multidimensional filtering

Conventional line or field comb filters are not the ideal solution to Y/C separation, particularly in PAL as they only work in one dimension at a time. The reason this fails is the strong diagonal distribution of chroma in the vertical/ temporal domain. However, the shortcomings of these filters can largely be overcome by designing filters having two-dimensional responses which can follow the diagonal chroma structure.

Caution is necessary because of the vertical and temporal phase (and V-switch in PAL) changes in composite signals. If composite signals are to be combined in a multitap filter it may be necessary to invert or phase shift certain taps before adding in order to avoid corrupting the chroma. In the case of PAL it may be necessary to have two filters, one feeding the U demodulator and one feeding the V demodulator so that lines containing opposing states of V-switch can be added in one case and subtracted in the other. In a filter which is designed to reject chroma from luminance this is unnecessary as it is only required to remove the correct frequencies. It will be clear that if such techniques are used, the Y/C separation will not be complementary. However, if the performance is good enough this is not a concern.

Figure 2.41(a) shows a diagonal comb filter based on 312 line delays and the corresponding vertical/temporal response. 312 lines is one field period to the nearest line. A delay of 312 lines has the same state of V-switch on input and output so can meaningfully be combined to create chroma. Owing to interlace, summing three points at a spacing of 312 lines places the impulse response diagonally on three different picture lines vertically and in three different fields temporally, hence the diagonal response.

A second comb filter having a spatio-temporal response at right angles to that of Figure 2.41(a) is required, but the spacing of the comb 'teeth' must be halved because of the periodicity of U and V energy. A comb filter based on 313 line delays has a response in the vertical/temporal diagram with the opposite slant to that of the 312 line comb but the period is too great and the delay has to be doubled to 626 lines as shown in Figure 2.41(b). Combining the two filters as in Figure 2.41(c) has the effect of selecting diamond-shaped areas in the two-dimensional spectrum in which the U and V signals reside. Another way of looking at this result is to consider that the diagonal spectrum of video is due to interlace in the first place and it is intuitive that a filter having points on an interlaced scan is bound to have a diagonal response.

Using a three-tap comb filter it is only possible to obtain a sinusoidal frequency response. Increasing the number of taps allows more terms in the

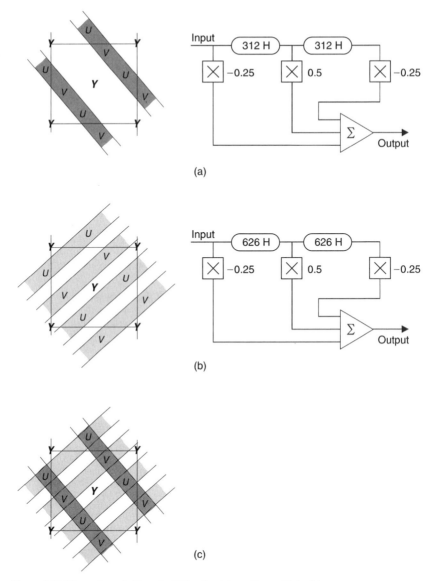

Figure 2.41 Diagonal comb filters in PAL using integer-line-multiple delays.

Fourier series to be admitted and the response can be improved to make the passband flatter and the cut-off steeper. However, this increase cannot be taken too far. Firstly, the cost of the filter rises dramatically with the number of points, particularly when increasing the impulse response window along the time axis requires additional fields of storage which also cause the filter delay to rise. Secondly a large number of points on the time axis can result in the response becoming too sharp, in which case ringing will occur due to the filter ripple. This is evident as multiple images of moving objects. Similarly an excessive number

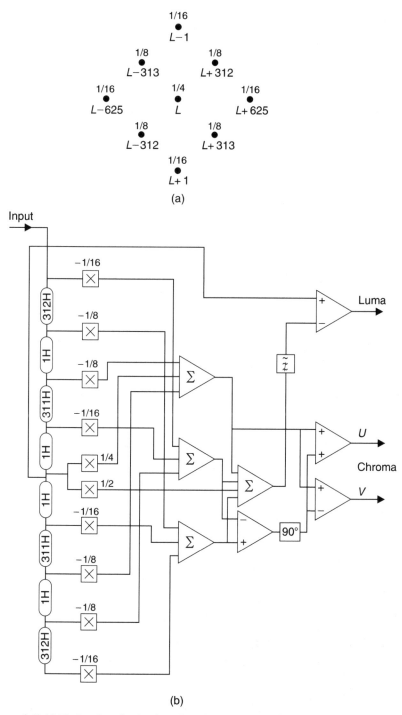

Figure 2.42 (a) The location of points in a nine-tap PAL filter. (b) Block diagram of nine-tap filter.

of vertical points can result in spatial ringing, particularly on horizontal edges between coloured areas.

The selection of the number of filter points is thus a compromise, but to keep matters in perspective the final result is considerably better than in any simpler approach. A particularly desirable result in spatio-temporal filters of this kind is that the need for adaptation is eliminated. Figure 2.42(a) shows the location of points in a nine-tap PAL filter and the structure of such a filter is shown in Figure 2.42(b). Note that this is not a complementary filter: the luminance signal is obtained by producing a two-dimensional chroma passband regardless of V-switch and subtracting it from luminance. The U and V outputs are obtained after a 90 degree phase shift to counteract the effects of subcarrier quadrature from line to line. Separate additions and subtractions are used to produce U and V signals allowing for the effect of V-switch.

2.21 Chroma demodulators

In SECAM the colour difference signals are sent on alternate lines on a frequency modulated subcarrier. Following Y/C separation the chroma will be decoded to baseband colour difference signals. Figure 2.43 shows that there are two

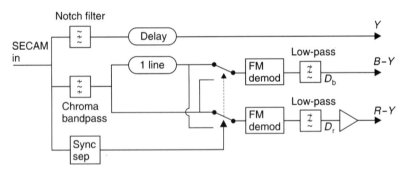

Figure 2.43 A simple SECAM demodulator.

frequency discriminators, one for each centre frequency. Input chroma is passed through a one-line delay. As the colour difference signals are sent alternately, when one type of signal is entering the delay, the other type will be emerging. The demodulator will lock to the two-line sequence by using the unmodulated subcarrier at the beginning of each line and will use the sequence to operate a two-pole changeover switch which ensures that the correct colour difference signal is always fed to the appropriate discriminator. Following the discriminators are two low-pass filters which remove any residual subcarrier in the baseband output. The D_r signal is re-inverted to oppose the inversion in the encoder. The luminance signal has been obtained by passing the composite input through a notch filter and a compensating delay which time-aligns luminance with the demodulated colour difference signals. If RGB is required, a further matrix can be used.

2.22 NTSC demodulation

Figure 2.44 shows an NTSC demodulator. The composite input is Y/C separated. A sync separator recognizes horizontal sync edges and produces a burst gate which allows input bursts into the burst locked oscillator which is used to locally regenerate subcarrier. The hue control changes the phase of the local oscillator with respect to burst. The oscillator output is provided with a quadrature phase shift for

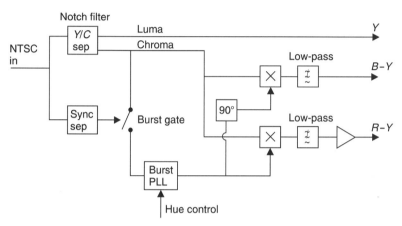

Figure 2.44 A simple NTSC demodulator.

one of the demodulators. Following the demodulators, low-pass filters of 1.3 MHz bandwidth are used to remove residual subcarrier frequencies from the baseband colour difference signals. Luminance passes through a compensating delay.

2.23 PAL demodulation

Simple PAL demodulation (PAL-S) can be obtained by a slight modification to Figure 2.44 which is shown in Figure 2.45. The burst locked oscillator is heavily

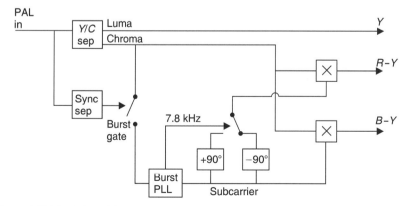

Figure 2.45 PAL-S demodulator requires the line averaging to be done in the eye of the viewer.

damped and runs at the average phase of burst. As a result, burst swing will cause a phase error at the oscillator which has a frequency of 7.8 kHz. This is the V-switch signal and it is used to invert the V-signal on alternate lines. This can be done either by switching the quadrature reference between ±90 degrees, or by switching in and out an inverter in the baseband V signal.

This simple demodulator relies upon the eye to average out phase errors and if these are serious, the result will be an artifact known as *Hanover blinds*. The proper PAL decode (PAL-D) requires the colour difference signals to be averaged over two lines. This requires a one-line delay which is best implemented before demodulation where the signal contains fewer octaves. The delay is slightly increased from one line to make it a whole number of cycles of subcarrier long. Figure 2.46 shows the configuration of the line averager. As the U signal is unswitched, after a delay of 284 cycles it will have the same phase. Adding the input of the delay to the output results in reinforcement of the U signal but

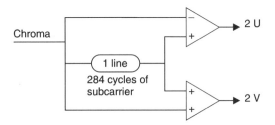

Figure 2.46 Averager used in PAL-D decoder uses 284 cycle delay.

cancellation of V. On the other hand V-switch means that after a delay of 284 cycles the V signal will be inverted. Adding the inverted input to the delay output reinforces the V signal but cancels U. These signals are both the average of two lines and so phase errors will have been cancelled. The separated U and V signals are fed to a pair of demodulators followed by low-pass filters to remove residual subcarrier. In early PAL-D TV sets the accurate 284 cycle delay was an expensive item. In the digital domain it is much easier to implement.

2.24 Introduction to the MAC system

Early television systems used signals which were directly compatible with the requirements of the display. This was out of economic necessity as it was essential to keep the complexity of the receiver to a minimum when electronic circuitry was expensive. MAC (Multiplexed Analog Components) was the first television standard to break with that tradition. MAC was designed for Direct Satellite Broadcasting (DSB), in which individual viewers have their own satellite receiver. In MAC the receiver has to be more complex than a traditional PAL or NTSC set.

Composite video such as PAL, NTSC and SECAM was constrained from the outset because it had to be backwards compatible with existing monochrome TV sets and with the existing terrestrial broadcast channel width. There was no alternative but to use frequency division multiplexing (FDM) in which the chroma signal was interleaved into relatively empty spaces in the luminance spectrum.

MAC had no such constraints as it was designed as a DBS system. Without the constraint of monochrome compatibility and with the benefit of lower cost electronic processing, MAC was implemented with time division multiplexing (TDM) instead of FDM.

2.25 Time division multiplexing

TDM relies on the concept of time compression shown in Figure 2.47. In time compression, the time required to transmit a TV line is somewhat less than the time it takes to scan or display it. If several signals are time compressed they can be transmitted in turn down the same channel.

In practice, time compression is achieved by temporarily entering the digital domain. Samples obtained by digitizing a TV line are stored in a memory. If the memory is read out with a clock rate which is higher than the original sampling rate, the duration of the line will be reduced in the same proportion as the bandwidth is increased.

MAC retains the line scanning parameters of 625/50 2:1 interlace so that it can be transcoded to PAL or SECAM without a standards converter. There is no 525/60 equivalent.

In MAC the video components are sampled in according to CCIR-601 (see Chapter 3). The luminance signal will be sampled at 13.5 MHz and the colour difference signals are sampled at 6.75 MHz. This has the effect of halving the bandwidth of the colour difference signals in the horizontal direction. Vertical low-pass filtering is used in the MAC encoder to reduce the vertical colour difference resolution by the same amount. Once this is done, the colour difference signals need not be sent on every line; they need only be sent every other line. In practice they are sent on alternate lines in a manner analogous to the approach of SECAM (see Section 2.10).

Luminance and colour difference signals are time compressed by being read out at a rate of 20.25 MHz. This results in a time compression factor of 3 for colour difference and a factor of 3/2 for luminance. Accordingly a line of luminance occupies two-thirds of its original duration, leaving one-third of the line for a colour difference signal.

Figure 2.47 shows how the three signal components are time multiplexed over a two-line period. The digital audio signals are carried by a burst of data which doubles as a video sync pulse.

In D-MAC, the audio burst contains 198 data bits and the time compression process has the effect of raising the bandwidth to around 8.5 MHz. For applications where less bandwidth was available, the D2-MAC system halves the number of audio channels and can operate in a bandwidth of 7 MHz with a slight reduction in resolution.

2.26 MAC transmission

For cable distribution MAC can be modulated using AM-VSB, but for satellite use this would give inadequate noise performance. Satellite transmission of MAC uses pre-emphasis and frequency modulation to spread the signal over a 27 MHz satellite channel. In order to make the transmitted spectrum more uniform the signal is superimposed on a triangle wave having a frequency of

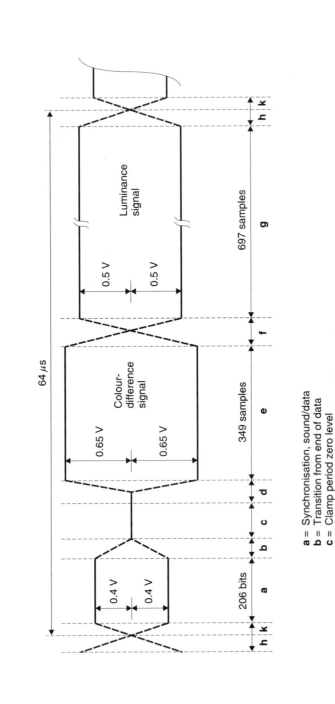

Figure 2.47 The MAC signal is created using time compression so that audio, luminance and colour difference signals fit sequentially into one line period.

a = Synchronisation, sound/data
b = Transition from end of data
c = Clamp period zero level
d = Weighted transition to colour-difference signal
e = Colour-difference component
f = Weighted transition between colour-difference signal and luminance signal
g = Luminance component
h = Weighted transition from luminance signal
k = Transition into data

25 Hz as Figure 2.48 shows. The black-level clamp in the receiver automatically removes this energy dispersal signal.

Figure 2.49 shows how a D-MAC decoder functions. The data burst on the incoming signal drives a phase locked loop which produces a 20.25 MHz signal. There are exactly 1296 cycles of this frequency in a standard 64 μs line. The decoder uses the 20.25 MHz clock to sample the analog part of the incoming line. The samples are stored in memory and this memory is then read out at 6.75 MHz for colour difference and 13.5 MHz for luminance. This has the effect of returning the components to their correct duration. As each colour difference signal is only available on every other line, it is necessary to use an interpolator to produce the missing lines. The vertical interpolator takes lines above and below the missing one and averages them. This process causes delay and to avoid the need for a corresponding luminance delay in every receiver, a delay is introduced at the encoder instead.

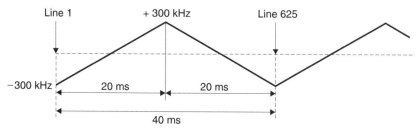

Figure 2.48 For transmission, the MAC signal has a 25 Hz triangle wave added to improve energy dispersion.

Although the video signals MAC transmits are analog, digital processes are required to produce and decode those signals. As a result MAC has to be described as a digitally assisted analog system and as such represents a half-way house between pure analog systems such as PAL and the pure digital approach of DVB (Digital Video Broadcasting).

2.27 PALplus

PALplus is a transmission system which is backward compatible with conventional PAL but which delivers 16:9 pictures on a suitable widescreen set. PALplus production starts with 625/50 component video which is scanned at 16:9 aspect ratio as shown in Section 1.8. Figure 2.50 shows that the 576 active lines of the video signal are passed into a vertical bandsplitting filter (see Chapter 5) which separates the top quarter of the spectrum from the bottom three-quarters. The low band signal has effectively been filtered to $\frac{3}{4}$ of its previous vertical bandwidth and so it can be expressed with $\frac{3}{4}$ as many lines. A vertical interpolator resamples the vertical dimension to take up only the centre 432 lines of the raster. This part of the picture is encoded with a standard PAL encoder.

On a standard 4:3 PAL receiver the 432 active lines create a 16:9 area in the centre of the screen in which the picture appears. The top and bottom of the screen appears black as shown in Figure 2.50.

The top quarter of the vertical spectrum (luminance only) is known as the helper signal, which will restore vertical resolution on suitable receivers. This signal is

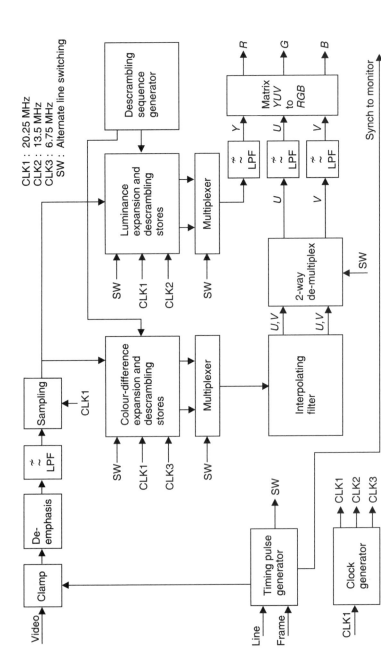

Figure 2.49 A D-MAC decoder contains time expansion circuitry to re-create simultaneous continuous outputs.

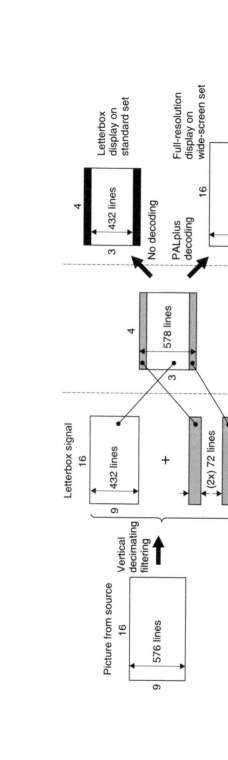

Figure 2.50 The PALplus system; see text for details.

similarly interpolated to take up 144 lines. These lines are divided into two areas of 72 lines each which fit above and below the centre 432 lines. In order to make these areas appear black on a standard PAL receiver, a number of steps are necessary. The helper signal is subject to a horizontal bandwidth limit and a non-linear compression at the encoder which limits its amplitude to ±150 mV. It then modulates a standard PAL subcarrier, but not with the normal quadrature technique. Instead AM-VSB (see Section 2.14) is used. This makes the signal DC-free and the usual subcarrier cancellation helps render it invisible.

A PALplus receiver demodulates the AM-VSB helper signal and reverses the compression. A vertical filter then recombines the helper signal with the vertical luminance spectrum residing in the centre 432 lines. The resultant signal is interpolated back to 576 active lines for full resolution display on a 16:9 screen.

An improved Y/C separation method has been developed for PALplus. In the absence of motion, advantage is taken of the inversion of chroma over a field period. Motion Adaptive Colourplus can switch between field cancelling and normal filtering according to the degree of motion in signals from video cameras. In the case of video from telecine, pairs of fields will have come from the same film frame and by definition relative motion cannot occur. In this case Fixed Colourplus decoding is used where the motion sensing is disabled.

A control system is required so that a 16:9 PALplus receiver can correctly display all possible PAL and PALplus signals. In the first part of line 23 the widescreen signalling code is found. This can be decoded to produce an aspect ratio flag which indicates the presence of a PALplus transmission, without which a PALplus receiver has to assume a standard 4:3 PAL transmission which it will display with black borders. A further flag denotes the presence of the vertical helper signal. Finally the camera/film flag determines the type of colour processing to be used.

2.28 Extended Studio PAL

As part of the PALplus project, the Extended Studio PAL (ESP) system was developed to provide a suitable production format for broadcasters currently

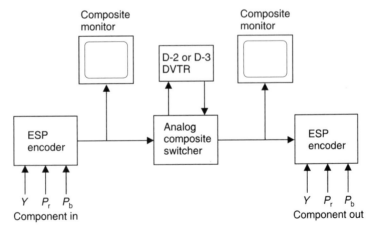

Figure 2.51 An Extended Studio PAL production system can use standard mixers and monitors.

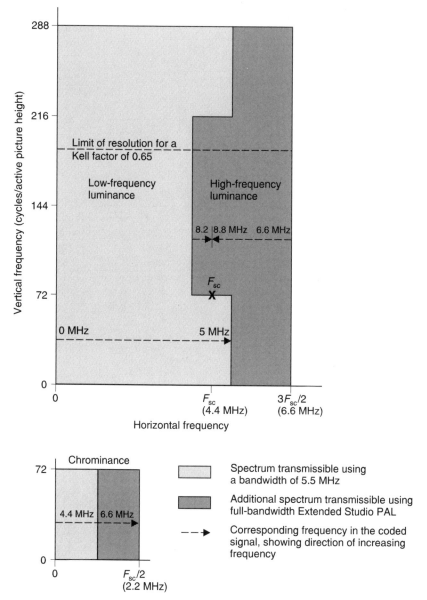

Figure 2.52 Extended Studio PAL pre-filtering. Note the dramatic increase in horizontal colour difference bandwidth.

using D-2 and D-3 composite digital VTRs. These VTRs sample at $4F_{sc}$ and have a signal bandwidth which is comfortably in excess of that required for regular composite video. Most analog vision mixers have sufficient bandwidth to equal the DVTR performance. ESP takes advantage of that extra bandwidth to produce a PAL-like signal which has better Y/C separation characteristics, more luminance bandwidth and considerably more colour difference bandwidth. This

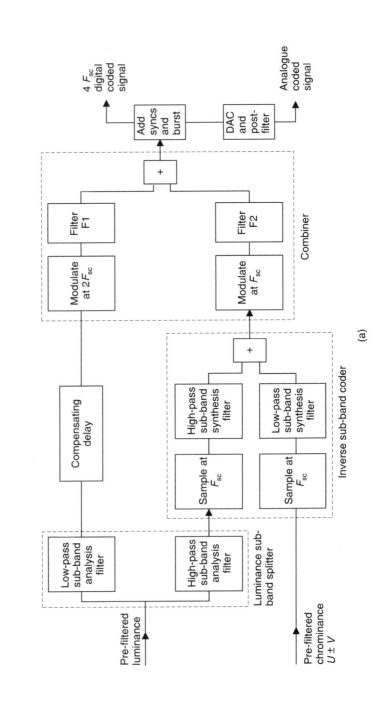

(a)

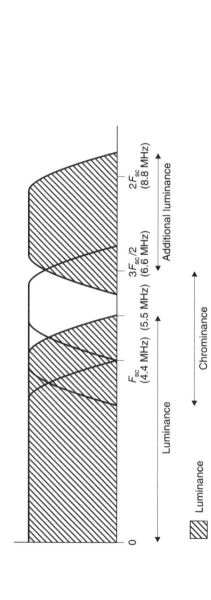

Figure 2.53 ESP encoding (a) relies upon band splitting and heterodyning to put the h.f. luma above the usual band. The resulting spectrum is shown in (b).

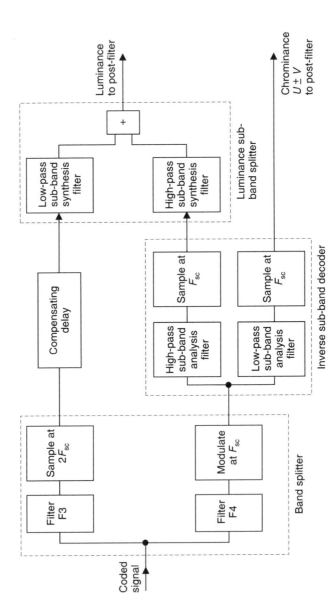

Figure 2.54 ESP decoder; see text for details.

is a particular advantage for 16:9 working. These attributes are only obtained when the signal is decoded by a full ESP decoder. However, the ESP signal can be fed to standard PAL monitors which will produce a picture which is good enough for production purposes.

Figure 2.51 shows an ESP production system using standard PAL DVTRs, mixer and monitors. The incoming component signal enters an ESP encoder but from then on standard PAL equipment is used. Following production, an ESP decoder produces the wide bandwidth components once more. The ESP signal is sufficiently compatible that it can be keyed with a standard PAL signal.

Figure 2.52 shows how the components are filtered prior to ESP encoding. The vertical low-pass filtering of the colour difference signals results in equal vertical and horizontal chroma resolution and permits an improved Y/C separation technique known as phase segregation to be used. Note that the chroma bandwidth is twice that available from standard PAL.

Figure 2.53(a) shows the ESP encoder. The luminance signal passes into a band splitter which divides the signal into frequencies above and below subcarrier frequency. The low band signal goes on to become the normal luminance signal. The high band signal having a bandwidth of one-half subcarrier frequency is heterodyned so that it fits above the baseband colour difference frequencies in a channel having a bandwidth equal to subcarrier frequency. This chroma/h.f. luma signal is then used to modulate a standard PAL subcarrier. It is filtered so that the h.f. luma only appears in the upper sideband. The resulting spectrum is shown in Figure 2.53(b) where it will be seen that the h.f. luminance has been shifted above the normal PAL band. With this approach, a conventional PAL decoder will reproduce standard bandwidth colour difference signals and l.f. luminance up to F_{sc}.

Figure 2.54 shows an ESP decoder. The ESP signal is band split at F_{sc} using phase segregation. The high band is demodulated in a conventional but wide-band quadrature demodulator. The demodulator output is then fed to a band splitter. The low band output is colour difference and the high band output is h.f. luma which is added back to the l.f. luma.

Chapter 3

Digital video

Increasingly, television equipment is adopting digital technology in almost every area possible. This chapter considers the principles of digital video and illustrates why it has become so popular.

3.1 Why digital?

There are two main answers to this question, and it is not possible to say which is the most important, as it will depend on one's standpoint.

(a) The quality of reproduction of a well engineered digital video system is independent of the storage or transmission medium and depends only on the quality of the conversion and compression processes.
(b) The conversion of video to the digital domain allows tremendous opportunities which were denied to analog signals.

Someone who is only interested in picture quality will judge the former the most relevant. If good quality converters can be obtained, all of the shortcomings of analog recording and transmission can be eliminated to great advantage. One's greatest effort is expended in the design of converters, whereas those parts of the system which handle data need only be workmanlike. Timebase error, tape noise, print-through, dropouts, and moiré are all history. When a digital recording is copied, the same numbers appear on the copy: it is not a dub, it is a clone. If the copy is indistinguishable from the original, there has been no generation loss. Digital recordings can be copied indefinitely without loss of quality.

In the real world everything has a cost, and one of the greatest strengths of digital technology is low cost. If copying causes no quality loss, recorders do not need to be far better than necessary in order to withstand generation loss. They need only be adequate on the first generation, whose quality is then maintained. There is no need for the great size and extravagant tape consumption of professional analog recorders. When the information to be recorded is discrete numbers, they can be packed densely on the medium without quality loss. Should some bits be in error because of noise or dropout, error correction can restore the original value. Digital recordings take up less space than analog recordings for the same or better quality. Tape costs are far less and storage costs are reduced.

Digital circuitry costs less to manufacture. Switching circuitry which handles binary can be integrated more densely than analog circuitry. More functionality can be put in the same chip. Analog circuits are built from a host of different component types which have a variety of shapes and sizes and are costly to assemble and adjust. Digital circuitry uses standardized component outlines and is easier to assemble on automated equipment. Little if any adjustment is needed.

Once video is in the digital domain, it becomes data, and as such is indistinguishable from any other type of data. Systems and techniques developed in other industries for other purposes can be used for video. Computer equipment is available at low cost because the volume of production is far greater than that of professional audio equipment. Disk drives and memories developed for computers can be put to use in video products. A word processor adapted to handle video samples becomes a workstation. There seems to be little point in waiting for a tape to wind when a disk head can access data in milliseconds.

Communications networks developed to handle data can happily carry digital video and accompanying audio over indefinite distances without quality loss. Digital TV broadcasting makes use of these techniques to eliminate the interference, fading and multipath reception problems of analog broadcasting. At the same time, more efficient use is made of available bandwidth.

Digital equipment can have self-diagnosis programmes built in. The machine points out its own failures. The days of chasing a signal with an oscilloscope are over. Even if a faulty component in a digital circuit could be located with such a primitive tool, it is well-nigh impossible to replace a chip having 60 pins soldered through a six-layer circuit board. The cost of finding the fault may be more than the board is worth. Routine, mind-numbing adjustment of analog circuits to counteract drift is no longer needed. The cost of maintenance falls. A small operation may not need maintenance staff at all – a service contract is sufficient. A larger organization will still need maintenance staff, but they will be fewer in number and their skills will be oriented more to systems than devices.

3.2 What is digital video?

One of the vital concepts to grasp is that digital video is simply an alternative means of carrying the same video information. An ideal digital video system has the same characteristics as an ideal analog system: both of them are totally transparent and reproduce the original applied waveform without error. One need only compare high quality analog and digital equipment side by side with the same signals to realize how transparent modern equipment can be. Needless to say, in the real world ideal conditions seldom prevail, so analog and digital equipment both fall short of the ideal. Digital equipment simply falls short of the ideal by a smaller distance than does analog and at lower cost; or, if the designer chooses, one can have the same performance as analog at much lower cost.

Although there are a number of ways in which video waveforms can be represented digitally, there is one system, known as Pulse Code Modulation (PCM), which is in virtually universal use. Figure 3.1 shows how PCM works. Instead of being continuous, the time axis is represented in a discrete, or stepwise manner. The waveform is not carried by continuous representation, but by measurement at regular intervals. This process is called sampling and the frequency with which samples are taken is called the sampling rate or sampling frequency F_s. As was shown in Chapter 1, sampling is an analog process. Each sample still varies infinitely as the original waveform did. To complete the conversion to PCM, each sample is then represented to finite accuracy by a discrete number in a process known as quantizing.

In television systems the input image which falls on the camera sensor will be continuous in time, and continuous in two spatial dimensions corresponding to the height and width of the sensor. In analog video systems, the time axis is sampled into frames, and the vertical axis is sampled into lines. Digital video simply adds a third sampling process along the lines.

Whilst any sampling rate which is high enough could be used for video, it is common to make the sampling rate a whole multiple of the line rate. Samples are then taken in the same place on every line. If this is done, a monochrome digital image is a rectangular array of points at which the brightness is stored as a

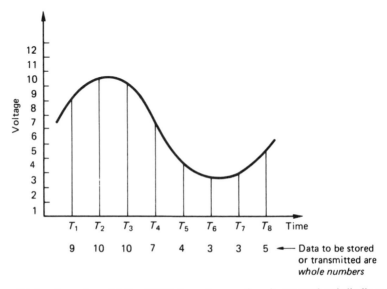

Figure 3.1 In pulse code modulation (PCM) the analog waveform is measured periodically at the sampling rate. The voltage (represented here by the height) of each sample is then described by a whole number. The whole numbers are stored or transmitted rather than the waveform itself.

number. The points are known as picture cells, generally abbreviated to pixels, although sometimes the abbreviation is more savage and they are known as pels. As shown in Figure 3.2(a), the array will generally be arranged with an even spacing between pixels, which are in rows and columns. By placing the pixels close together, it is hoped that the observer will perceive a continuous image. Obviously the finer the pixel spacing, the greater the resolution of the picture will be, but the amount of data needed to store one picture will increase as the square of the resolution, and with it the costs.

If it is desired to convey a coloured image, then it will be seen from Figure 3.2(b) that each image consists of three superimposed layers of samples, one for each component. The pixel is no longer a single number representing a scalar brightness value, but a vector which describes in some way the brightness, hue and saturation of that point in the picture. In *RGB*, the pixels contain three unipolar numbers representing the proportion of each of the three primary colours at that point in the picture. In colour difference working, each pixel again contains three numbers, but one of these is a unipolar number representing the

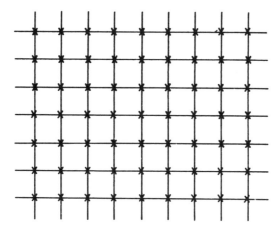

Figure 3.2(a) A picture can be stored digitally by representing the brightness at each of the above points by a binary number. For a colour picture each point becomes a vector and has to describe the brightness, hue and saturation of that part of the picture. Samples are usually but not always formed into regular arrays of rows and columns, and it is most efficient if the horizontal and vertical spacings are the same.

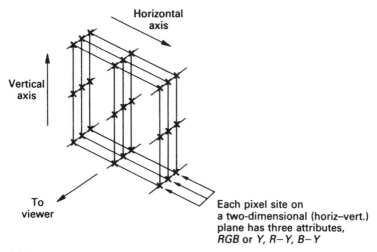

Figure 3.2(b) In the case of component video, each pixel site is described by three values and so the pixel becomes a vector quantity.

luminance and the other two are bipolar numbers representing the colour difference values.

In order to produce moving pictures, the current approach is simply to provide a mechanism where the value of every pixel can be updated periodically. This effectively results in a three-dimensional array, where two of the axes are spatial and the third is temporal.

Since it is possible to represent any analog waveform digitally, composite video can also be digitized. Owing to the critical nature of chroma phase, the sampling rate will generally be locked to subcarrier so that it can be readily created from burst. It should be stressed that digital composite is simply another way of conveying composite video, and all of the attributes of composite, such as colour framing sequences, are still present in the resulting data.

At the ADC (analog-to-digital converter), every effort is made to rid the sampling clock of jitter, or time instability, so every sample is taken at an exactly even time step. Clearly if there is any subsequent timebase error, the instants at which samples arrive will be changed and the effect can be detected. If samples arrive at some destination with an irregular timebase, the effect can be eliminated by storing the samples temporarily in a memory and reading them out using a stable, locally generated clock. This process is called timebase correction and all properly engineered digital video systems must use it. Clearly timebase error is not reduced – it is totally eliminated. As a result there is little point measuring the timebase stability of a digital recorder.

Those who are not familiar with digital principles often worry that sampling takes away something from a signal because it is not taking notice of what happened between the samples. This would be true in a system having infinite bandwidth, but no analog signal can have infinite bandwidth. All analog signal sources from cameras, VTRs and so on have a resolution or frequency response limit, as indeed do devices such as CRTs and human vision. When a signal has finite bandwidth, the rate at which it can change is limited, and the way in which it changes becomes predictable. When a waveform can only change between samples in one way, it is then only necessary to convey the samples and the original waveform can be reconstructed from them.

As stated, the magnitude of each sample is also discrete, or represented in a stepwise manner. The length of the sample, which will be proportional to the voltage of the video signal, is represented by a whole number. This process is known as quantizing and results in an approximation, but the size of the error can be controlled until it is negligible. If, for example, we were to measure the height of humans to the nearest metre, virtually all adults would register two metres high and obvious difficulties would result. These are generally overcome by measuring height to the nearest centimetre. Clearly there is no advantage in going further and expressing our height in a whole number of millimetres or even micrometres. The point is that an appropriate resolution can also be found for video signals, and a higher figure is not beneficial. The advantage of using whole numbers is that they are not prone to drift. If a whole number can be carried from one place to another without numerical error, it has not changed at all. By describing video waveforms numerically, the original information has been expressed in a way which is better able to resist unwanted changes.

Essentially, digital video carries the original waveform numerically. The number of the sample is an analog of time, which itself is an analog of position across the screen, and the magnitude of the sample is (in the case of luminance) an analog of the brightness at the appropriate point in the image. In fact the succession of samples in a digital system is actually *an analog* of the original waveform. This sounds like a contradiction and as a result some authorities prefer the term 'numerical video' to 'digital video' and in fact the French word is 'numérique'. The term 'digital' is so well established that it is unlikely to change.

As both axes of the digitally represented waveform are discrete, the waveform can be accurately restored from numbers as if it were being drawn on graph paper. If we require greater accuracy, we simply choose paper with smaller squares. Clearly more numbers are then required and each one could change over a larger range.

In simple terms, the video waveform is conveyed in a digital recorder as if the voltage had been measured at regular intervals with a digital meter and the readings had been written down on a roll of paper. The rate at which the measurements were taken and the accuracy of the meter are the only factors which determine the quality, because once a parameter is expressed as a discrete number, a series of such numbers can be conveyed unchanged. Clearly in this example the handwriting used and the grade of paper have no effect on the information. The quality is determined only by the accuracy of conversion and is independent of the quality of the signal path.

3.3 Why binary?

Humans insist on using numbers expressed to the base of ten, having evolved with that number of digits. Other number bases exist, and most people are familiar with the duodecimal system which uses the dozen and the gross. The most minimal system is binary, which has only two digits, 0 and 1. BInary digiTS are universally contracted to bits. These are readily conveyed in switching circuits by an 'on' state and an 'off' state. With only two states, there is little chance of error.

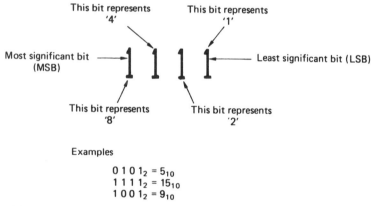

Examples

$0\ 1\ 0\ 1_2 = 5_{10}$
$1\ 1\ 1\ 1_2 = 15_{10}$
$1\ 0\ 0\ 1_2 = 9_{10}$

Figure 3.3 In a binary number, the digits represent increasing powers of two from the LSB. Also defined here are MSB and wordlength. When the wordlength is 8 bits, the word is a byte. Binary numbers are used as memory addresses, and the range is defined by the address wordlength. Some examples are shown here.

In decimal systems, the digits in a number (counting from the right, or least significant end) represent ones, tens, hundreds, thousands, etc. Figure 3.3 shows that in binary the bits represent one, two, four, eight, sixteen, etc. A multidigit binary number is commonly called a word, and the number of bits in the word is called the wordlength. The right-hand bit is called the Least Significant Bit (LSB) and the bit on the left-hand end of the word is called the Most Significant Bit (MSB). Clearly more digits are required in binary than in decimal, but they are more easily handled. A word of eight bits is called a byte. The capacity of memories and storage media is measured in bytes, but to avoid large numbers, kilobytes, megabytes and gigabytes are often used. As memory addresses are themselves binary numbers, the wordlength limits the address range. The range is found by raising two to the power of the wordlength. Thus a four-bit word has sixteen combinations, and could address a memory having sixteen locations. A ten-bit word has 1024 combinations, which is close to one thousand. In digital terminology, 1K = 1024, so a kilobyte of memory contains 1024 bytes. A megabyte (1MB) contains 1024 kilobytes and a gigabyte contains 1024 megabytes.

In a digital video system, the whole number representing the length of the sample is expressed in binary. The signals sent have two states, and change at predetermined times according to some stable clock. Figure 3.4 shows the consequences of this form of transmission. If the binary signal is degraded by noise, this will be rejected by the receiver, which judges the signal solely by whether it is above or below the half-way threshold, a process known as slicing.

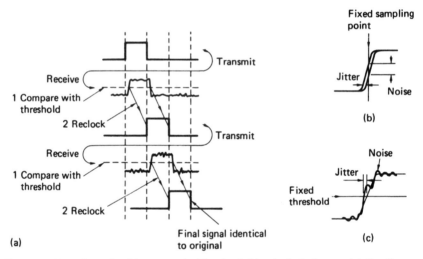

Figure 3.4 (a) A binary signal is compared with a threshold and relocked on receipt; thus the meaning will be unchanged. (b) Jitter on a signal can appear as noise with respect to fixed timing. (c) Noise on a signal can appear as jitter when compared with a fixed threshold.

The signal will be carried in a channel with finite bandwidth, and this limits the slew rate of the signal; an ideally upright edge is made to slope. Noise added to a sloping signal can change the time at which the slicer judges that the level passed through the threshold. This effect is also eliminated when the output of the slicer is reclocked. However many stages the binary signal passes through, it still comes out the same, only later.

Video samples which are represented by whole numbers can be reliably carried from one place to another by such a scheme, and if the number is correctly received, there has been no loss of information *en route*. There are two ways in which binary signals can be used to carry samples; these are shown in Figure 3.5. When each digit of the binary number is carried on a separate wire this is called parallel transmission. The state of the wires changes at the sampling rate. Using multiple wires is cumbersome, particularly where a long wordlength is in use, and a single wire can be used where successive digits from each sample are sent

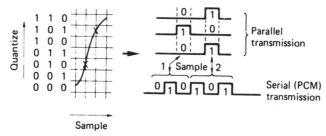

Figure 3.5 When a signal is carried in numerical form, either parallel or serial, the mechanisms of Figure 3.4 ensure that the only degradation is in the conversion process.

serially. This is the definition of Pulse Code Modulation. Clearly the clock frequency must now be higher than the sampling rate. Whilst the transmission of video by such a scheme is advantageous in that noise and timebase error have been eliminated, there is a penalty that a high quality colour difference signal requires around two hundred million bits per second. Clearly digital video could only become commonplace when such a data rate could be handled economically. Further applications become possible when means to reduce the data rate become economic.

3.4 Introduction to conversion

There are a number of ways in which a video waveform can be digitally represented, but the most useful and therefore most common is Pulse Code Modulation or PCM which was introduced above. The input is a continuous-time, continuous-voltage video waveform, and this is converted into a discrete-time, discrete-voltage format by a combination of sampling and quantizing. As these two processes are orthogonal (at right angles to one another) they are totally independent and can be performed in either order. Figure 3.6(a) shows an analog sampler preceding a quantizer, whereas Figure 3.6(b) shows an asynchronous quantizer preceding a digital sampler. Ideally, both will give the same results; in practice each has different advantages and suffers from different deficiencies. Both approaches will be found in real equipment.

The independence of sampling and quantizing allows each to be discussed quite separately. Whilst sampling an analog video waveform takes place in the time domain in an electrical ADC, this is because the analog waveform is the result of scanning an image. In reality the image has been spatially sampled in two dimensions (lines and pixels) and temporally sampled into fields along a third dimension. Sampling theory was considered in Chapter 1 in connection with analog video and that theory is equally valid here.

3.5 Choice of sampling rate: component

The sampling rate of a system need only satisfy the requirements of sampling theory and filter design. Any rate which does so can, in principle, be used to convey a video signal from one place to another. In practice, however, there are a number of practical restraints which limit the choice of sampling rate considerably.

It should be borne in mind that a video signal represents a series of two-dimensional images. If a video signal is sampled at an arbitrary frequency, samples in successive lines will be in different places. If it is sampled at a rate which is a multiple of line rate the result will be that samples on successive lines will be in the same place and the picture will be converted to a neat array having vertical columns of samples. This allows for the vertical spatial filtering necessary in DVEs and standards converters and for concealment in DVTRs. A line locked sampling rate can be conveniently obtained by multiplying the frequency of H-sync using a phase locked loop. The position of samples along the line is then determined by the leading edge of sync.

Whilst the bandwidth required by 525/59.94 is less than that required by 625/50, and a lower sampling rate might have been used, again practicality suggested a common sampling rate. The benefit of a standard sampling rate for component video is that the design of standards converters is simplified and

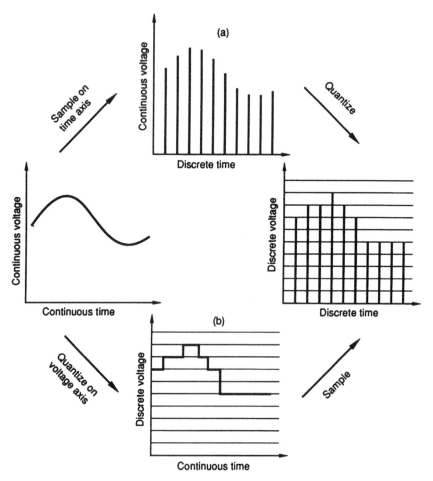

Figure 3.6 Since sampling and quantizing are orthogonal, the order in which they are performed is not important. In (a) sampling is performed first and the samples are quantized. This is common in audio converters. In (b) the analog input is quantized into an asynchronous binary code. Sampling takes place when this code is latched on sampling clock edges. This approach is universal in video converters.

DVTRs have a constant data rate independent of standard. This was the goal of CCIR Recommendation 601, which combined the 625/50 input of EBU Doc. Tech. 3246 and 3247 with the 525/59.94 input of SMPTE RP 125.

CCIR 601 recommends the use of certain sampling rates which are based on integer multiples of the carefully chosen fundamental frequency of 3.375 MHz. This frequency is normalized to 1 in the document.

In order to sample 625/50 luminance signals without quality loss, the lowest multiple possible is 4, which represents a sampling rate of 13.5 MHz. This frequency line locks to give 858 samples per line in 525/59.94 and 864 samples per line in 625/50. The spectra of such sampled luminance are shown in Figure 3.7.

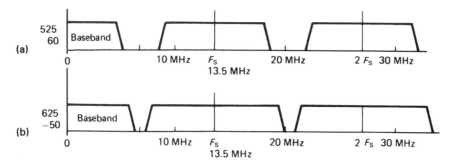

Figure 3.7 Spectra of video sampled at 13.5 MHz. In (a) the baseband 525/60 signal at left becomes the sidebands of the sampling rate and its harmonics. In (b) the same process for the 625/50 signal results in a smaller gap between baseband and sideband because of the wider bandwidth of the 625 system. The same sampling rate for both standards results in a great deal of commonality between 50 Hz and 60 Hz equipment.

In the component analog domain, the colour difference signals typically have one-half the bandwidth of the luminance signal. Thus a sampling rate multiple of 2 is used and results in 6.75 MHz. This sampling rate allows respectively 429 and 432 samples per line.

Component video sampled in this way has a 4:2:2 format. Figure 3.8 shows the spatial arrangement given by 4:2:2 sampling. Luminance samples appear at half the spacing of colour difference samples, and every other luminance sample is co-sited with a pair of colour difference samples. Co-siting is important because it allows all attributes of one picture point to be conveyed with a three-sample vector quantity. Modification of the three samples allows such techniques as colour correction to be performed. This would be difficult without co-sited information.

For lower bandwidths, multiples of 1 and 3 can also be used for colour difference and luminance respectively. 4:1:1 delivers colour bandwidth in excess of the composite formats. 3:1:1 meets 525 line bandwidth requirements. The factors of 3 and 1 do not, however, offer a columnar structure and are inappropriate for quality post production. For full bandwidth *RGB* working, 4:4:4 can be used.

Although these other sampling factors are included in CCIR 601, it is only the 4:2:2 subset which has become popular. The D-1, D-5, Digital Betacam and Digital-S format DVTRs record video sampled in the 4:2:2 subset, and this is the only subset for which standard interfaces are available.

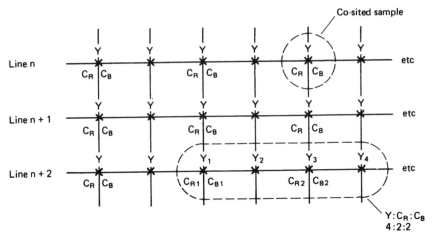

Figure 3.8 In CCIR-601 sampling mode 4:2:2, the line synchronous sampling rate of 13.5 MHz results in samples having the same position in successive lines, so that vertical columns are generated. The sampling rates of the colour difference signals C_r, C_b are one-half of that of luminance, i.e. 6.75 MHz, so that there are alternate Y-only samples and co-sited samples which describe Y, C_r and C_b. In a run of four samples, there will be four Y samples, two C_2 samples and two C_b samples, hence 4:2:2.

Figure 3.8 shows that in 4:2:2 there is one luminance signal sampled at 13.5 MHz and two colour difference signals sampled at 6.75 MHz. Three separate signals with different clock rates are inconvenient and so multiplexing can be used. If the colour difference signals are multiplexed into one channel, then two 13.5 MHz channels will be required. If these channels are multiplexed into one, a 27 MHz clock will be required. The word order will be:

C_b, Y, C_r, Y, etc.

In order unambiguously to deserialize the samples, the first sample in the line is always C_b.

3.6 Choice of sampling rate: composite

When composite video is to be digitized, the input will be a single waveform having spectrally interleaved luminance and chroma. Any sampling rate which allows sufficient bandwidth would convey composite video from one point to another. However, if processing in the digital domain is contemplated, there will be less choice.

In the composite digital colour processor it will be necessary to decode the composite signal, which will require some kind of digital filter. Whilst it is possible to construct filters with any desired response, it is a fact that a digital filter whose response is simply related to the sampling rate will be much less complex to implement. This is the reasoning which has led to the near universal use of four times subcarrier sampling rate. Figure 3.9 shows the spectra of PAL and NTSC sampled at $4F_{sc}$. It will be evident that there is a considerable space between the edge of the baseband and the lower sideband. This allows the anti-aliasing and reconstruction filters to have a more gradual cut-off, so that ripple in the passband can be reduced. This is particularly important for composite digital recorders, since they are digital devices which often operate in an analog environment, and signals may have been converted to and from the digital domain many times in the course of production.

A subcarrier multiple sampling clock is easily obtained by gating burst to a phase locked loop. In NTSC there is no burst swing, whereas at $4F_{sc}$ the burst swing of PAL moves burst crossings by exactly one sample period and so the phase relationship between burst crossings and $4F_{sc}$ clock is unaffected by burst swing.

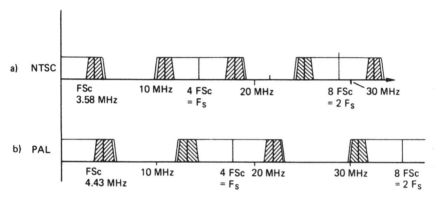

Figure 3.9 The spectra of NTSC in (a) and of PAL in (b) where both are sampled at four times the frequency of their respective subcarriers. The high sampling rate is unnecessary to satisfy sampling theory, and so both are oversampled systems. The advantages are in the large spectral gap between baseband and sideband which allows a more gentle filter slope to be employed, and in the relative ease of colour processing at a sampling rate related to subcarrier.

In NTSC, siting of samples along the line is affected by ScH phase. In addition to that, in PAL the presence of the 25 Hz component of subcarrier means that samples are not in exactly the same place from one line to the next. The columns lean over slightly such that at the bottom of a field there is a displacement of two samples with respect to the top.

3.7 Sampling clock jitter

The instants at which samples are taken in an ADC and the instants at which DACs make conversions must be evenly spaced, otherwise unwanted signals can be added to the video. Figure 3.10 shows the effect of sampling clock jitter on a sloping waveform. Samples are taken at the wrong times. When these samples have passed through a system, the timebase correction stage prior to the DAC will remove the jitter, and the result is shown in Figure 3.10(b). The magnitude of the unwanted signal is proportional to the slope of the waveform and so the amount of jitter which can be tolerated falls at 6 dB per octave. As the resolution of the system is increased by the use of longer sample wordlength, tolerance to jitter is further reduced. The nature of the unwanted signal depends on the spectrum of the jitter. If the jitter is random, the effect is noise-like and relatively benign unless the amplitude is excessive. Figure 3.11 shows the effect of

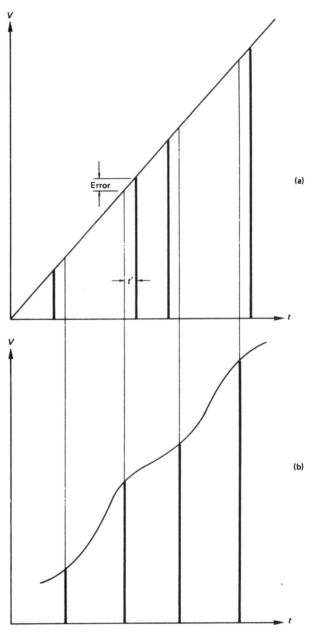

Figure 3.10 The effect of sampling timing jitter on noise. In (a) a sloping signal sampled with jitter has error proportional to the slope. When jitter is removed by reclocking, the result in (b) is noise.

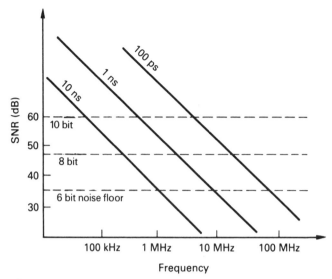

Figure 3.11 The effect of sampling clock jitter on signal-to-noise ratio at various frequencies, compared with the theoretical noise floors with different wordlengths.

differing amounts of random jitter with respect to the noise floor of various wordlengths. Note that even small amounts of jitter can degrade a 10 bit converter to the performance of a good 8 bit unit. There is thus no point in upgrading to higher resolution converters if the clock stability of the system is insufficient to allow their performance to be realized.

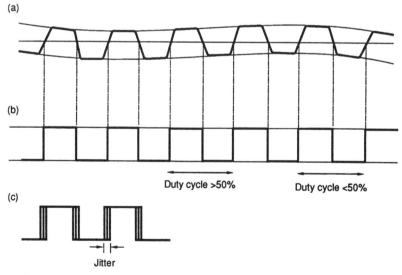

Figure 3.12 Crosstalk in transmission can result in unwanted signals being added to the clock waveform. It can be seen here that a low frequency interference signal affects the slicing of the clock and causes a periodic jitter.

Clock jitter is not necessarily random. Figure 3.12 shows that one source of clock jitter is crosstalk or interference on the clock signal, although a balanced clock line will be more immune to such crosstalk. The unwanted additional signal changes the time at which the sloping clock signal appears to cross the threshold voltage of the clock receiver. This is simply the same phenomenon as that of Figure 3.12 but in reverse. The threshold itself may be changed by ripple on the clock receiver power supply. There is no reason why these effects should be random; they may be periodic and potentially visible.

The allowable jitter is measured in picoseconds, as shown in Figure 3.12, and clearly steps must be taken to eliminate it by design. Converter clocks must be generated from clean power supplies which are well decoupled from the power used by the logic because a converter clock must have a signal-to-noise ratio of the same order as that of the signal. Otherwise noise on the clock causes jitter which in turn causes noise in the video. The same effect will be found in digital audio signals, which are perhaps more critical.

3.8 Quantizing

Quantizing is the process of expressing some infinitely variable quantity by discrete or stepped values. Quantizing turns up in a remarkable number of everyday guises. Figure 3.13 shows that an inclined ramp enables infinitely variable height to be achieved, whereas a step-ladder allows only discrete heights. A step-ladder quantizes height. When accountants round off sums of

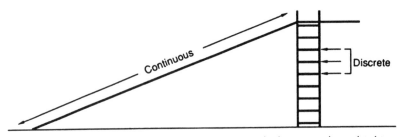

Figure 3.13 An analog parameter is continuous whereas a quantized parameter is restricted to certain values. Here the sloping side of a ramp can be used to obtain any height whereas a ladder only allows discrete heights.

money to the nearest pound or dollar they are quantizing. Time passes continuously, but the display on a digital clock changes suddenly every minute because the clock is quantizing time.

In video and audio the values to be quantized are infinitely variable voltages from an analog source. Strict quantizing is a process which operates in the voltage domain only. For the purpose of studying the quantizing of a single sample, time is assumed to stand still. This is achieved in practice either by the use of a track-hold circuit or the adoption of a quantizer technology such as a flash converter which operates before the sampling stage.

Figure 3.14(a) shows that the process of quantizing divides the voltage range up into quantizing intervals Q, also referred to as steps S. In applications such as telephony these may advantageously be of differing size, but for digital audio the

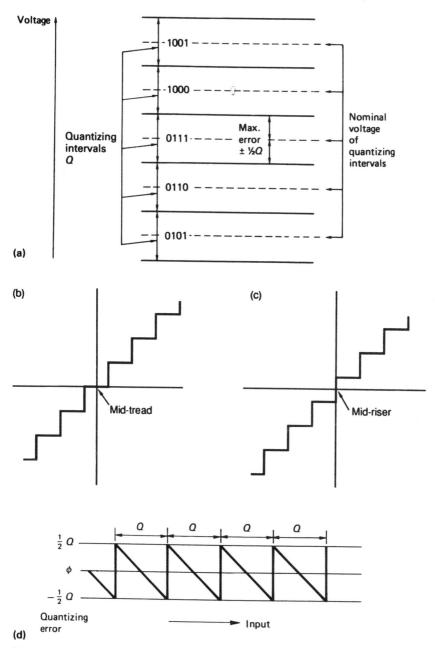

Figure 3.14 Quantizing assigns discrete numbers to variable voltages. All voltages within the same quantizing interval are assigned the same number which causes a DAC to produce the voltage at the centre of the intervals shown by the dashed lines in (a). This is the characteristic of the mid-tread quantizer shown in (b). An alternative system is the mid-riser system shown in (c). Here 0 volts analog falls between two codes and there is no code for zero. Such quantizing cannot be used prior to signal processing because the number is no longer proportional to the voltage. Quantizing error cannot exceed $\pm\tfrac{1}{2}Q$ as shown in (d).

quantizing intervals are made as identical as possible. If this is done, the binary numbers which result are truly proportional to the original analog voltage, and the digital equivalents of mixing and gain changing can be performed by adding and multiplying sample values. If the quantizing intervals are unequal this cannot be done. When all quantizing intervals are the same, the term uniform quantizing is used. The term linear quantizing will be found, but this is, like military intelligence, a contradiction in terms.

The term LSB (least significant bit) will also be found in place of quantizing interval in some treatments, but this is a poor term because quantizing works in the voltage domain. A bit is not a unit of voltage and can only have two values. In studying quantizing, voltages within a quantizing interval will be discussed, but there is no such thing as a fraction of a bit.

Whatever the exact voltage of the input signal, the quantizer will locate the quantizing interval in which it lies. In what may be considered a separate step, the quantizing interval is then allocated a code value which is typically some form of binary number. The information sent is the number of the quantizing interval in which the input voltage lay. Whereabouts that voltage lay within the interval is not conveyed, and this mechanism puts a limit on the accuracy of the quantizer. When the number of the quantizing interval is converted back to the analog domain, it will result in a voltage at the centre of the quantizing interval as this minimizes the magnitude of the error between input and output. The number range is limited by the wordlength of the binary numbers used. In an 8 bit system, 256 different quantizing intervals exist, although in digital video the ones at the extreme ends of the range are reserved for synchronizing.

3.9 Quantizing error

It is possible to draw a transfer function for such an ideal quantizer followed by an ideal DAC, and this is also shown in Figure 3.14. A transfer function is simply a graph of the output with respect to the input. In electronics when the term linearity is used, this generally means the overall straightness of the transfer function. Linearity is a goal in video and audio, yet it will be seen that an ideal quantizer is anything but linear.

Figure 3.14(b) shows that the transfer function is somewhat like a staircase, and blanking level is half-way up a quantizing interval, or on the centre of a tread. This is the so-called mid-tread quantizer which is universally used in video and audio. Figure 3.14(c) shows the alternative mid-riser transfer function which causes difficulty because it does not have a code value at blanking level and as a result the numerical code value is not proportional to the analog signal voltage.

Quantizing causes a voltage error in the video sample which is given by the difference between the actual staircase transfer function and the ideal straight line. This is shown in Figure 3.14(d) to be a sawtooth-like function which is periodic in Q. The amplitude cannot exceed $\pm\frac{1}{2}Q$ peak-to-peak unless the input is so large that clipping occurs.

Quantizing error can also be studied in the time domain where it is better to avoid complicating matters with the aperture effect of the DAC. For this reason it is assumed here that output samples are of negligible duration. Then impulses from the DAC can be compared with the original analog waveform and the difference will be impulses representing the quantizing error waveform. This has been done in Figure 3.15. The horizontal lines in the drawing are the boundaries

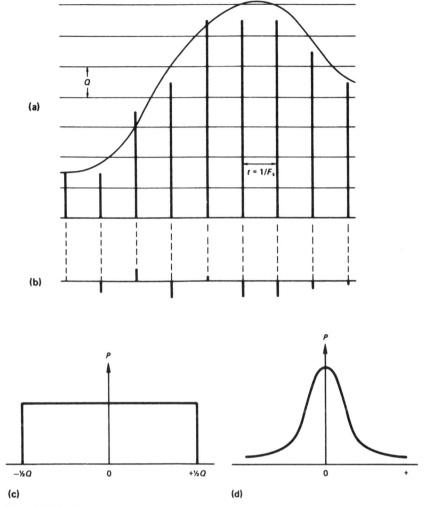

Figure 3.15 In (a) an arbitrary signal is represented to finite accuracy by PAM needles whose peaks are at the centre of the quantizing intervals. The errors caused can be thought of as an unwanted signal (b) added to the original. In (c) the amplitude of a quantizing error needle will be from $-\frac{1}{2}Q$ to $+\frac{1}{2}Q$ with equal probability. Note, however, that white noise in analog circuits generally has Gaussian amplitude distribution, shown in (d).

between the quantizing intervals, and the curve is the input waveform. The vertical bars are the quantized samples which reach to the centre of the quantizing interval. The quantizing error waveform shown in Figure 3.15(b) can be thought of as an unwanted signal which the quantizing process adds to the perfect original. If a very small input signal remains within one quantizing interval, the quantizing error *is* the signal.

As the transfer function is non-linear, ideal quantizing can cause distortion. As a result practical digital video equipment deliberately uses non-ideal quantizers to achieve linearity. As the magnitude of the quantizing error is limited, its effect can be minimized by making the signal larger. This will require more quantizing intervals and more bits to express them. The number of quantizing intervals multiplied by their size gives the quantizing range of the converter. A signal outside the range will be clipped. Provided that clipping is avoided, the larger the signal the less will be the effect of the quantizing error.

Where the input signal exercises the whole quantizing range and has a complex waveform (such as from a contrasty, detailed scene), successive samples will have widely varying numerical values and the quantizing error on a given sample will be independent of that on others. In this case the size of the quantizing error will be distributed with equal probability between the limits. Figure 3.15(c) shows the resultant uniform probability density. In this case the unwanted signal added by quantizing is an additive broadband noise uncorrelated with the signal, and it is appropriate in this case to call it quantizing noise. Unfortunately, at low depths of modulations, and particularly with flat fields or simple pictures, this is not the case.

At low modulation depth, quantizing error ceases to be random, and becomes a function of the input waveform and the quantizing structure as Figure 3.15 showed. Once an unwanted signal becomes a deterministic function of the wanted signal, it has to be classed as a distortion rather than a noise. Distortion can also be predicted from the non-linearity, or staircase nature, of the transfer function. With a large signal, there are so many steps involved that we must stand well back, and a staircase with 256 steps appears to be a slope. With a small signal there are few steps and they can no longer be ignored.

The effect can be visualized readily by considering a television camera viewing a uniformly painted wall. The geometry of the lighting and the coverage of the lens mean that the brightness is not absolutely uniform, but falls slightly at the ends of the TV lines. After quantizing, the gently sloping waveform is replaced by one which stays at a constant quantizing level for many sampling periods and then suddenly jumps to the next quantizing level. The picture then consists of areas of constant brightness with steps between, resembling nothing more than a contour map, hence the use of the term *contouring* to describe the effect.

Needless to say the occurrence of contouring precludes the use of an ideal quantizer for high quality work. There is little point in studying the adverse effects further as they should be and can be eliminated completely in practical equipment by the use of dither. The importance of correctly dithering a quantizer cannot be emphasized enough, since failure to dither irrevocably distorts the converted signal: there can be no process which will subsequently remove that distortion.

3.10 Introduction to dither

At high signal levels, quantizing error is effectively noise. As the depth of modulation falls, the quantizing error of an ideal quantizer becomes more strongly correlated with the signal and the result is distortion, visible as contouring. If the quantizing error can be decorrelated from the input in some way, the system can remain linear but noisy. Dither performs the job of decorrelation by making the action of the quantizer unpredictable and gives the system a noise floor like an analog system.

In one approach, pseudo-random noise is added to the input signal prior to quantizing, but was subtracted after reconversion to analog. This is known as subtractive dither, and has the advantage that the amplitude is non-critical. The noise has full statistical independence from the signal and has the same level as the quantizing error in the large signal undithered case. Unfortunately subtractive dither suffers from practical drawbacks, since the original noise waveform must accompany the samples or must be synchronously re-created at the DAC. This is virtually impossible in a system where the signal may have been edited or where its level has been changed by processing, as the noise needs to remain synchronous and be processed in the same way. All practical digital video systems use non-subtractive dither where the dither signal is added prior to quantization and no attempt is made to remove it at the DAC. The introduction of dither prior to a conventional quantizer inevitably causes a slight reduction in the signal-to-noise ratio attainable, but this reduction is a small price to pay for the elimination of non-linearities.

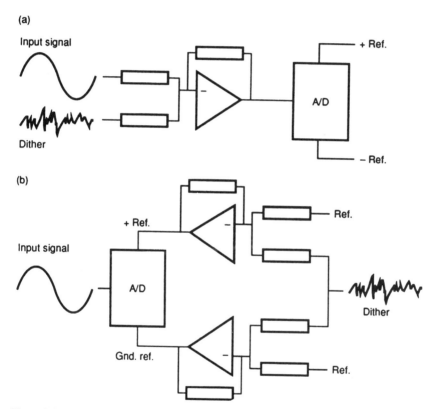

Figure 3.16 Dither can be applied to a quantizer in one of two ways. In (a) the dither is linearly added to the analog input signal, whereas in (b) it is added to the reference voltages of the quantizer.

The ideal (undithered) quantizer of Figure 3.14 has fixed quantizing intervals and must always produce the same quantizing error from the same signal. In Figure 3.16 it can be seen that an ideal quantizer can be dithered by linearly adding a controlled level of noise either to the input signal or to the reference voltage which is used to derive the quantizing intervals. There are several ways of considering how dither works, all of which are equally valid.

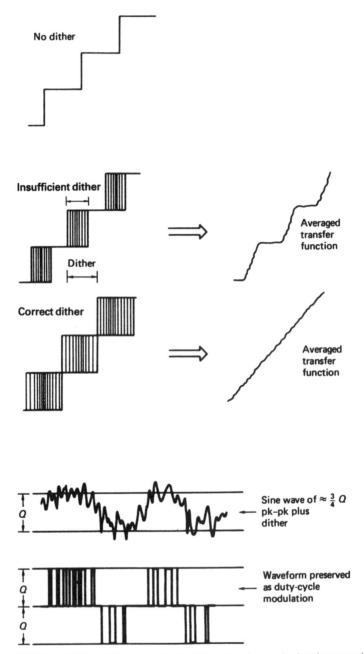

Figure 3.17 Wideband dither of the appropriate level linearizes the transfer function to produce noise instead of distortion. This can be confirmed by spectral analysis. In the voltage domain, dither causes frequent switching between codes and preserves resolution in the duty cycle of the switching.

The addition of dither means that successive samples effectively find the quantizing intervals in different places on the voltage scale. The quantizing error becomes a function of the dither, rather than a predictable function of the input signal. The quantizing error is not eliminated, but the subjectively unacceptable distortion is converted into a broadband noise which is subjectively more benign.

Some alternative ways of looking at dither are shown in Figure 3.17. Consider the situation where a low level input signal is changing slowly within a quantizing interval. Without dither, the same numerical code is output for a number of sample periods, and the variations within the interval are lost. Dither has the effect of forcing the quantizer to switch between two or more states. The higher the voltage of the input signal within a given interval, the more probable it becomes that the output code will take on the next higher value. The lower the input voltage within the interval, the more probable it is that the output code will take the next lower value. The dither has resulted in a form of duty cycle modulation, and the resolution of the system has been extended indefinitely instead of being limited by the size of the steps.

Dither can also be understood by considering what it does to the transfer function of the quantizer. This is normally a perfect staircase, but in the presence of dither it is smeared horizontally until with a certain amplitude the average transfer function becomes straight.

3.11 Requantizing and digital dither

Recent ADC technology allows the resolution of video samples to be raised from 8 bits to 10 or even 12 bits. The situation then arises that an existing 8 bit device such as a digital VTR needs to be connected to the output of an ADC with greater wordlength. The words need to be shortened in some way.

When a sample value is attenuated, in, for example, a digital vision mixer, the extra low-order bits which come into existence below the radix point preserve the resolution of the signal and the dither in the least significant bit(s) which linearizes the system. The same word extension will occur in any process involving multiplication, such as digital filtering. It will subsequently be necessary to shorten the wordlength. Low-order bits must be removed in order to reduce the resolution whilst keeping the signal magnitude the same. Even if the original conversion was correctly dithered, the random element in the low-order bits will now be some way below the end of the intended word. If the word is simply truncated by discarding the unwanted low-order bits or rounded to the nearest integer the linearizing effect of the original dither will be lost.

Shortening the wordlength of a sample reduces the number of quantizing intervals available without changing the signal amplitude. As Figure 3.18 shows, the quantizing intervals become larger and the original signal is *requantized* with the new interval structure. This will introduce requantizing distortion having the same characteristics as quantizing distortion in an ADC. It then is obvious that when shortening the wordlength of a 10 bit converter to 8 bits, the two low-order bits must be removed in a way that displays the same overall quantizing structure as if the original converter had been only of 8 bit wordlength. It will be seen from Figure 3.18 that truncation cannot be used because it does not meet the above requirement but results in signal-dependent offsets because it always rounds in the same direction. Proper numerical rounding is essential in video applications because it accurately simulates analog quantizing to the new interval size.

Unfortunately the 10 bit converter will have a dither amplitude appropriate to quantizing intervals one-quarter the size of an 8 bit unit and the result will be highly non-linear.

In practice, the wordlength of samples must be shortened in such a way that the requantizing error is converted to noise rather than distortion. One technique which meets this requirement is to use digital dithering prior to rounding. This is directly equivalent to the analog dithering in an ADC.

Digital dither is a pseudo-random sequence of numbers. If it is required to simulate the analog dither signal of Figures 3.16 and 17, then it is obvious that the noise must be bipolar so that it can have an average voltage of zero. Two's complement coding must be used for the dither values.

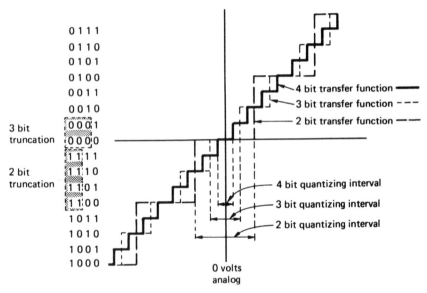

Figure 3.18 Shortening the wordlength of a sample reduces the number of codes which can describe the voltage of the waveform. This makes the quantizing steps bigger, hence the term requantizing. It can be seen that simple truncation or omission of the bits does not give analogous behaviour. Rounding is necessary to give the same result as if the larger steps had been used in the original conversion.

Figure 3.19 shows a simple digital dithering system (i.e. one without noise shaping) for shortening sample wordlength. The output of a two's complement pseudo-random sequence generator of appropriate wordlength is added to input samples prior to rounding. The most significant of the bits to be discarded is examined in order to determine whether the bits to be removed sum to more or less than half a quantizing interval. The dithered sample is either rounded down, i.e. the unwanted bits are simply discarded, or rounded up, i.e. the unwanted bits are discarded but 1 is added to the value of the new short word. The rounding process is no longer deterministic because of the added dither which provides a linearizing random component.

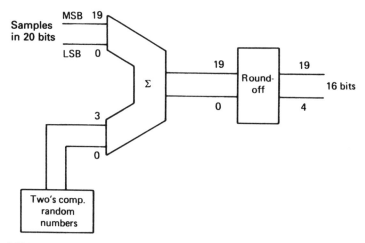

Figure 3.19 In a simple digital dithering system, two's complement values from a random number generator are added to low-order bits of the input. The dithered values are then rounded up or down according to the value of the bits to be removed. The dither linearizes the requantizing.

If this process is compared with that of Figure 3.16 it will be seen that the principles of analog and digital dither are identical; the processes simply take place in different domains using two's complement numbers which are rounded or voltages which are quantized as appropriate. In fact quantization of an analog dithered waveform is identical to the hypothetical case of rounding after bipolar digital dither where the number of bits to be removed is infinite, and remains identical for practical purposes when as few as eight bits are to be removed. Analog dither may actually be generated from bipolar digital dither (which is no more than random numbers with certain properties) using a DAC.

3.12 Coding standards

In the same way that analog video signals require standardized voltages for interchange, digital video signals must have standardized relationships between the code value and the analog signal voltage. In this way, when code values are interchanged they are interpreted correctly at the receiving device.

Figure 3.20 shows the standard coding scheme used for digital component video. The 0.7 volt luminance signal almost fills the quantizing range. The numbering for 10 bit systems is shown with figures for 8 bits in brackets. Black is at a level of 64_{10} (16_{10}) and peak white is at 940_{10} (235_{10}) so that there is some tolerance of imperfect analog signals. The sync pulse will clearly go outside the quantizing range, but this is of no consequence as conventional syncs are not transmitted in component digital. The visible voltage range fills the quantizing range and this gives the best possible resolution.

The colour difference signals use offset binary, where 512_{10} (128_{10}) is the equivalent of blanking voltage. The $\pm350\,mV$ peak analog limits are reached at 64_{10} (16_{10}) and 960_{10} (240_{10}) respectively, allowing once more some latitude for maladjusted analog inputs.

Note that the code values corresponding to the eight most significant bits being all ones or all zeros (i.e. the two extreme ends of the quantizing range in 8 bit data) are not allowed to occur in the active line as they are reserved for synchronizing. Converters must be followed by circuitry which catches these values and forces the LSB to a different value if out of range analog inputs are applied.

The peak-to-peak amplitude of Y is 880 (220) quantizing intervals, whereas for the colour difference signals it is 900 (225) intervals. There is thus a small gain difference between the signals. This will be cancelled out by the opposing gain difference at any future DAC, but must be borne in mind when digitally converting to other standards.

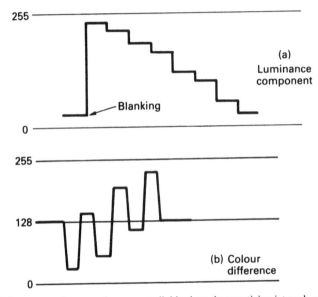

Figure 3.20 In component, sync pulses are not digitized, so the quantizing intervals can be smaller as in (a). An offset of half scale is used for colour difference signals (b).

The instantaneous voltage of composite video can go below blanking on dark saturated colours, and above peak white on bright colours. As a result the quantizing ranges need to be stretched in comparison with component in order to accommodate all possible voltage excursions. Sync tip can be accommodated at the low end and peak white is some way below the end of the scale. It is not so easy to determine when overload clipping will take place in composite as the sample sites are locked to subcarrier. The degree of clipping depends on the chroma phase. When samples are taken either side of a chroma peak, clipping will be less likely to occur than when the sample is taken at the peak. Advantage is taken of this phenomenon in PAL as the peak analog voltage of a 100 per cent yellow bar goes outside the quantizing range. The sampling phase is such that samples are sited either side of the chroma peak and remain within the range.

The quantizing range of digital PAL is shown in Figure 3.21. Blanking level is at 256_{10} (64_{10}) and sync tip is the lowest allowable code of 4 (1) as 0 is reserved for digital synchronizing. Peak white is 844_{10} (211_{10}).

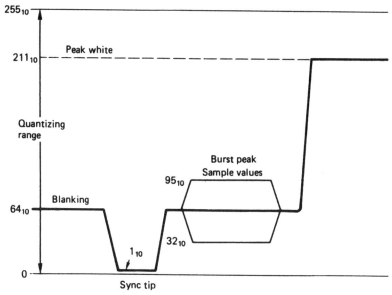

Figure 3.21 The composite PAL signal fits into the quantizing range as shown here. Note that there is sufficient range to allow the instantaneous voltage to exceed that of peak white in the presence of saturated bright colours. Values shown are decimal equivalents in a 10 or 8 bit system. In a 10 bit system the additional 2 bits increase resolution, not magnitude, so they are below the radix point and the decimal equivalent is unchanged. PAL samples in phase with burst, so the values shown are on the burst peaks and are thus also the values of the envelope.

Figure 3.22 shows how the NTSC waveform fits into the quantizing structure. Blanking is at 240_{10} (60_{10}) and peak white is at 800_{10} (200_{10}), so that 1 IRE unit is the equivalent of $1.4Q$. These different values are due to the different sync/vision ratio of NTSC. PAL is 7:3 whereas NTSC is 10:4 (see Section 1.2).

3.13 Basic digital-to-analog conversion

This direction of conversion will be discussed first, since ADCs often use embedded DACs in feedback loops. The purpose of a digital-to-analog converter is to take numerical values and reproduce the continuous waveform that they represent. Figure 3.23 shows the major elements of a conventional conversion subsystem, i.e. one in which oversampling is not employed. The jitter in the clock needs to be removed with a VCO or VCXO. Sample values are buffered in a latch and fed to the converter element which operates on each cycle of the clean clock. The output is then a voltage proportional to the number for at least a part of the sample period. A resampling stage may be found next, in order to remove switching transients, reduce the aperture ratio or allow the use of a converter which takes a substantial part of the sample period to operate. The resampled waveform is then presented to a reconstruction filter which rejects frequencies above the audio band.

This section is primarily concerned with the implementation of the converter element. The most common way of achieving this conversion is to control binary-weighted currents and sum them in a virtual earth. Figure 3.24 shows the

D.L.I.A.D.T.
Library

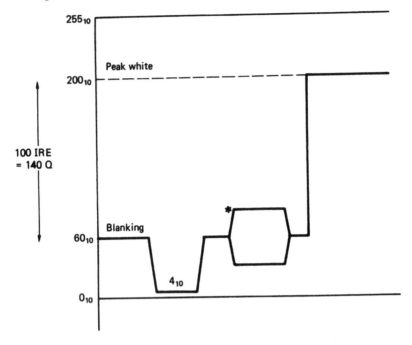

Figure 3.22 The composite NTSC signal fits into the quantizing range as shown here. Note that there is sufficient range to allow the instantaneous voltage to exceed peak white in the presence of saturated, bright colours. Values shown are decimal equivalents in an 8 or 10 bit system. In a 10 bit system the additional 2 bits increase resolution, not magnitude, so they are below the radix point and the decimal equivalent is unchanged. *Note that, unlike PAL, NTSC does not sample on burst phase and so values during burst are not shown here. See Fig. 4.30 for burst sample details.

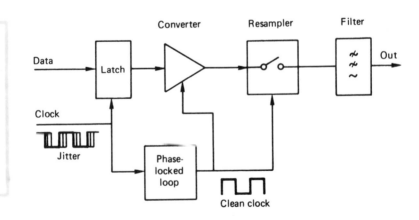

Figure 3.23 The components of a conventional converter. A jitter-free clock drives the voltage conversion, whose output may be resampled prior to reconstruction.

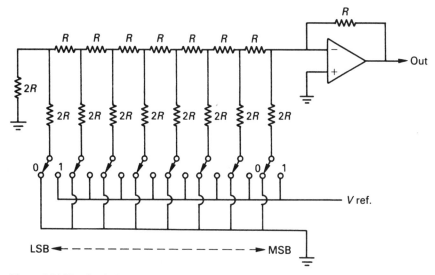

Figure 3.24 The classical R–2R DAC requires precise resistance values and 'perfect' switches.

classical *R–2R* DAC structure. This is relatively simple to construct, but the resistors have to be extremely accurate. To see why this is so, consider the example of Figure 3.25. In Figure 3.25(a) the binary code is about to have a major overflow, and all the low-order currents are flowing. In Figure 3.25(b), the binary input has increased by one, and only the most significant current flows. This current must equal the sum of all the others plus 1. The accuracy must be such that the step size is within the required limits. In this 8 bit example, if the step size needs to be a rather casual 10 per cent accurate, the necessary accuracy is only one part in 2560, but for a 10 bit system it would become one part in 10 240. This degree of accuracy is difficult to achieve and maintain in the presence of ageing and temperature change.

3.14 Basic analog-to-digital conversion

The general principle of a quantizer is that different quantized voltages are compared with the unknown analog input until the closest quantized voltage is

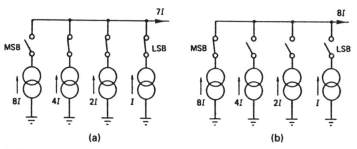

(a)   **(b)**

Figure 3.25 In (a) current flow with an input of 0111 is shown. In (b) current flow with input code one greater is shown.

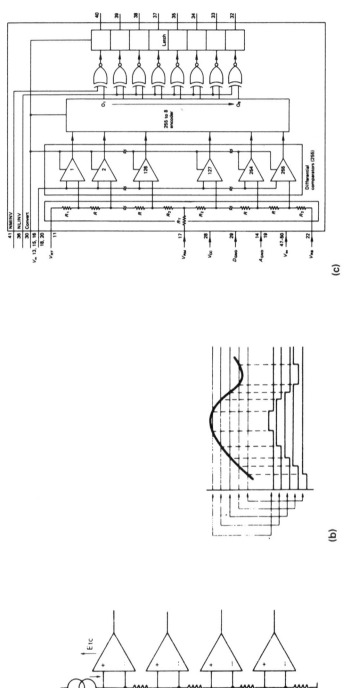

Figure 3.26 The flash converter. In (a) each quantizing interval has its own comparator, resulting in waveforms of (b). A priority encoder is necessary to convert the comparator outputs to a binary code. Shown in (c) is a typical 8 bit flash converter primarily intended for video applications. (Courtesy TRW).

found. The code corresponding to this becomes the output. The comparisons can be made in turn with the minimal amount of hardware, or simultaneously with more hardware.

The flash converter is probably the simplest technique available for PCM video conversion. The principle is shown in Figure 3.26. The threshold voltage of every quantizing interval is provided by a resistor chain which is fed by a reference voltage. This reference voltage can be varied to determine the sensitivity of the input. There is one voltage comparator connected to every reference voltage, and the other input of all of the comparators is connected to the analog input. A comparator can be considered to be a one-bit ADC. The input voltage determines how many of the comparators will have a true output. As one comparator is necessary for each quantizing interval, then, for example, in an 8 bit system there will be 255 binary comparator outputs, and it is necessary to use a priority encoder to convert these to a binary code. Note that the quantizing stage is asynchronous: comparators change state as and when the variations in the input waveform result in a reference voltage being crossed. Sampling takes place when the comparator outputs are clocked into a subsequent latch. This is an example of quantizing before sampling as was illustrated in Figure 3.6. Although the device is simple in principle, it contains a lot of circuitry and can only be practicably implemented on a chip. The analog signal has to drive a lot of inputs, which results in a significant parallel capacitance, and a low-impedance driver is essential to avoid restricting the slewing rate of the input. The extreme speed of a flash converter is a distinct advantage in oversampling. Because computation of all bits is performed simultaneously, no track/hold circuit is required, and droop is eliminated. Figure 3.26(c) shows a flash converter chip. Note the resistor ladder and the comparators followed by the priority encoder. The MSB can be selectively inverted so that the device can be used either in offset binary or two's complement mode.

The flash converter is ubiquitous in digital video because of the high speed necessary.

3.15 Temporal oversampling

Oversampling means using a sampling rate which is greater (generally substantially greater) than that required by sampling theory. Neither this nor quantizing theory *require* oversampling to be used to obtain a given signal quality, but normal rate conversion places extremely high demands on component accuracy when a converter is implemented. Oversampling allows a given signal quality to be reached without requiring very close tolerance, and therefore expensive components.

Figure 3.27 shows the main advantages of oversampling. In Figure 3.27(a) it will be seen that the use of a sampling rate considerably above the Nyquist rate allows the anti-aliasing and reconstruction filters to be realized with a much more gentle cut-off slope. There is then less likelihood of phase linearity and ripple problems in the passband.

Figure 3.27(b) shows that information in an analog signal is two dimensional and can be depicted as an area which is the product of bandwidth and the linearly expressed signal-to-noise ratio. The figure also shows that the same amount of information can be conveyed down a channel with a SNR of half as much (6 dB less) if the bandwidth used is doubled, with 12 dB less SNR if bandwidth is quadrupled, and so on, provided that the modulation scheme used is perfect.

The information in an analog signal can be conveyed using some analog modulation scheme in any combination of bandwidth and SNR which yields the appropriate channel capacity. If bandwidth is replaced by sampling rate and SNR is replaced by a function of wordlength, the same must be true for a digital signal as it is no more than a numerical analog. Thus raising the sampling rate potentially allows the wordlength of each sample to be reduced without information loss.

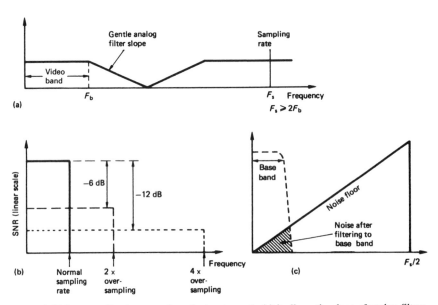

Figure 3.27 Oversampling has a number of advantages. In (a) it allows the slope of analog filters to be relaxed. In (b) it allows the resolution of converters to be extended. In (c) a *noise-shaped* converter allows a disproportionate improvement in resolution.

Oversampling is highly effective in converter technology where it gives specific advantages in implementation. The storage or transmission system will usually employ PCM, where the sampling rate is a little more than twice the input bandwidth. Figure 3.28 shows a digital VTR using oversampling converters. The ADC runs at *n* times the Nyquist rate, but once in the digital domain the rate needs to be reduced in a type of digital filter called a *decimator*. The output of this is conventional Nyquist rate PCM, according to the tape format, which is then recorded. On replay the sampling rate is raised once more in a further type of digital filter called an *interpolator*. The system now has the best of both worlds: using oversampling in the converters overcomes the shortcomings of analog anti-aliasing and reconstruction filters and the wordlength of the converter elements is reduced making them easier to construct; the recording is made with Nyquist rate PCM which minimizes tape consumption.

Oversampling is a method of overcoming practical implementation problems by replacing a single critical element or bottleneck by a number of elements whose overall performance is what counts. Oversampling overlaps the operations which are quite distinct in a conventional converter. In earlier sections of this

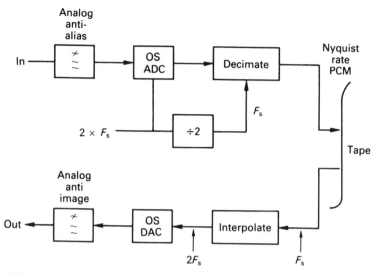

Figure 3.28 An oversampling DVTR. The converters run faster than sampling theory suggests to ease analog filter design. Sampling-rate reduction allows efficient PCM recording on tape.

chapter, the vital subjects of filtering, sampling, quantizing and dither have been treated almost independently. Figure 3.29(a) shows that it is possible to construct an ADC of predictable performance by taking a suitable anti-aliasing filter, a sampler, a dither source and a quantizer and assembling them like building bricks. The bricks are effectively in series and so the performance of each stage can only limit the overall performance. In contrast Figure 3.29(b) shows that with

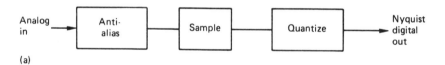

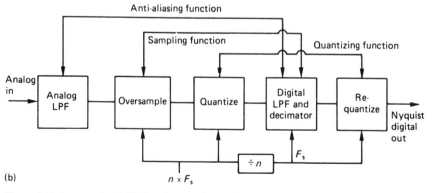

Figure 3.29 A conventional ADC performs each step in an identifiable location as in (a). With oversampling, many of the steps are distributed as shown in (b).

oversampling the overlap of operations allows different processes to augment one another, allowing a synergy which is absent in the conventional approach.

If the oversampling factor is n, the analog input must be bandwidth limited to $nF_s/2$ by the analog anti-aliasing filter. This unit need only have flat frequency response and phase linearity within the baseband. Analog dither of an amplitude compatible with the quantizing interval size is added prior to sampling at nF_s and quantizing.

Next, the anti-aliasing function is completed in the digital domain by a low-pass filter which cuts off at $F_s/2$. Using an appropriate architecture this filter can be absolutely phase linear and implemented to arbitrary accuracy. Such filters were discussed in Chapter 2. The filter can be considered to be the demodulator of Figure 3.27 where the SNR improves as the bandwidth is reduced. The wordlength can be expected to increase. As Chapter 2 illustrated, the multiplications taking place within the filter extend the wordlength considerably more than the bandwidth reduction alone would indicate. The analog filter serves only to prevent aliasing into the baseband at the oversampling rate; the signal spectrum is determined with greater precision by the digital filter.

With the information spectrum now Nyquist limited, the sampling process is completed when the rate is reduced in the decimator. One sample in n is retained. The excess wordlength extension due to the anti-aliasing filter arithmetic must then be removed. Digital dither is added, completing the dither process, and the quantizing process is completed by requantizing the dithered samples to the appropriate wordlength which will be greater than the wordlength of the first quantizer. Alternatively, noise shaping may be employed.

Figure 3.30(a) shows the building brick approach of a conventional DAC. The Nyquist rate samples are converted to analog voltages and then a steep-cut analog low pass filter is needed to reject the sidebands of the sampled spectrum. Figure 3.30(b) shows the oversampling approach. The sampling rate is raised in an

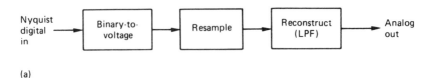

(a)

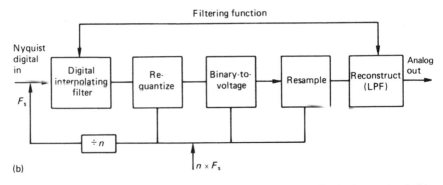

(b)

Figure 3.30 A conventional DAC in (a) is compared with the oversampling implementation in (b).

interpolator which contains a low-pass filter which restricts the baseband spectrum to the bandwidth shown. A large frequency gap now exists between the baseband and the lower sideband. The multiplications in the interpolator extend the wordlength considerably and this must be reduced within the capacity of the DAC element by the addition of digital dither prior to requantizing.

3.16 Filters

Filtering is inseparable from digital video and audio. Analog or digital filters, and sometimes both, are required in ADCs, DACs, in the data channels of digital recorders and transmission systems and in sampling rate converters and equalizers. Optical systems used in disk recorders also act as filters. There are many parallels between analog, digital and optical filters, which this section treats as a common subject. The main difference between analog and digital filters is that in the digital domain very complex architectures can be constructed at low cost in LSI and that arithmetic calculations are not subject to component tolerance or drift.

Filtering may modify the frequency response of a system, and/or the phase response. Every combination of frequency and phase response determines the impulse response in the time domain. Figure 3.31 shows that impulse response

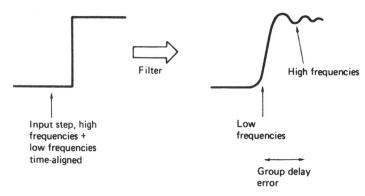

Figure 3.31 Group delay time-displaces signals as a function of frequency.

testing tells a great deal about a filter. In a perfect filter, all frequencies should experience the same time delay. If some groups of frequencies experience a different delay to others, there is a group-delay error. As an impulse contains an infinite spectrum, a filter suffering from group-delay error will separate the different frequencies of an impulse along the time axis.

A pure delay will cause a phase shift proportional to frequency, and a filter with this characteristic is said to be phase-linear. The impulse response of a phase-linear filter is symmetrical. If a filter suffers from group-delay error it cannot be phase-linear. It is almost impossible to make a perfectly phase-linear analog filter, and many filters have a group-delay equalization stage following them which is often as complex as the filter itself. In the digital domain it is straightforward to make a phase-linear filter, and phase equalization becomes unnecessary.

Because of the sampled nature of the signal, whatever the response at low frequencies may be, all digital channels (and sampled analog channels) act as low-pass filters cutting off at the Nyquist limit, or half the sampling frequency.

Figure 3.32(a) shows a simple *RC* network and its impulse response. This is the familiar exponential decay due to the capacitor discharging through the resistor (in series with the source impedance which is assumed here to be negligible). The figure also shows the response to a squarewave (Figure 3.32(b)). These responses can be calculated because the inputs involved are relatively simple. When the input waveform and the impulse response are complex functions, this approach becomes almost impossible.

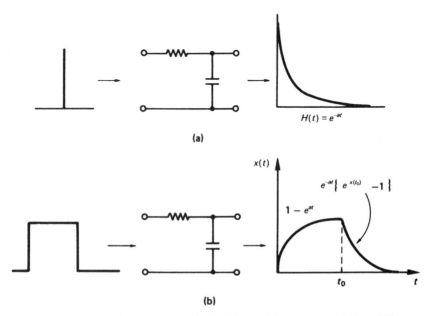

Figure 3.32 (a) The impulse response of a simple *RC* network is an exponential decay. This can be used to calculate the response to a square wave, as in (b).

In any filter, the time domain output waveform represents the convolution of the impulse response with the input waveform. Convolution can be followed by reference to a graphic example in Figure 3.33. Where the impulse response is asymmetrical, the decaying tail occurs *after* the input. As a result it is necessary to reverse the impulse response in time so that it is mirrored prior to sweeping it through the input waveform. The output voltage is proportional to the shaded area shown where the two impulses overlap.

The same process can be performed in the sampled, or discrete, time domain as shown in Figure 3.34. The impulse and the input are now a set of discrete samples which clearly must have the same sample spacing. The impulse response only has value where impulses coincide. Elsewhere it is zero. The impulse response is therefore stepped through the input one sample period at a time. At each step, the area is still proportional to the output, but as the time steps are of uniform width, the area is proportional to the impulse height and so the output is obtained by adding up the lengths of overlap. In mathematical terms, the output

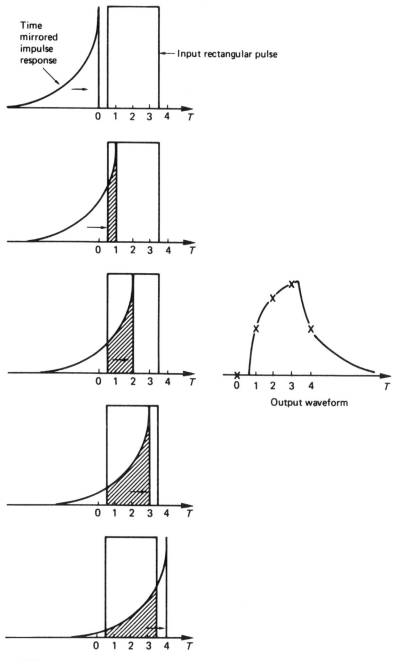

Figure 3.33 In the convolution of two continuous signals (the impulse response with the input), the impulse must be time reversed or mirrored. This is necessary because the impulse will be moved from left to right, and mirroring gives the impulse the correct time-domain response when it is moved past a fixed point. As the impulse response slides continuously through the input waveform, the area where the two overlap determines the instantaneous output amplitude. This is shown for five different times by the crosses on the output waveform.

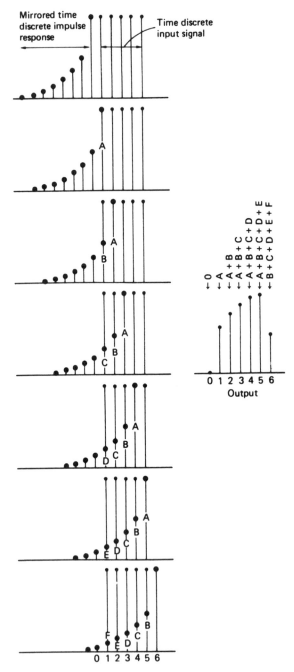

Figure 3.34 In time discrete convolution, the mirrored impulse response is stepped through the input one sample period at a time. At each step, the sum of the cross-products is used to form an output value. As the input in this example is a constant height pulse, the output is simply proportional to the sum of the coincident impulse response samples. This figure should be compared with Figure 3.33.

samples represent the convolution of the input and the impulse response by summing the coincident cross-products.

As a digital filter works in this way, perhaps it is not a filter at all, but just a mathematical simulation of an analog filter. This approach is quite useful in visualizing what a digital filter does.

Somewhere between the analog filter and the digital filter is the switched capacitor filter. This uses analog quantities, namely the charges on capacitors, but the time axis is discrete because the various charges are routed using electronic switches which close during various phases of the sampling rate clock. Switched capacitor filters have the same characteristics as digital filters with infinite precision. They are often used in preference to continuous time analog filters in integrated circuit converters because they can be implemented with the same integration techniques. Figure 3.35(a) shows a switched capacitor delay. There

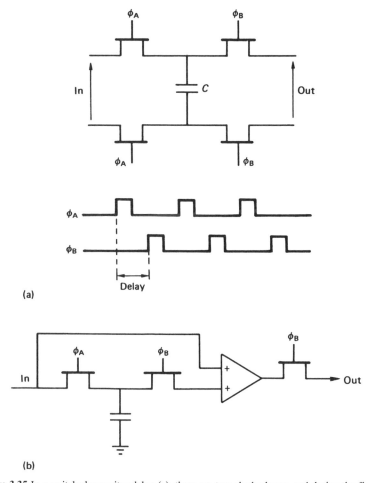

(a)

(b)

Figure 3.35 In a switched capacitor delay (a), there are two clock phases, and during the first the input voltage is transferred to the capacitor. During the second phase the capacitor voltage is transferred to the output. (b) A simple switched capacitor filter. The delay causes a phase shift which is dependent on frequency and the resultant frequency response is sinusoidal.

are two clock phases and during the first the input voltage is transferred to the capacitor. During the second phase the capacitor voltage is transferred to the output. Combining delay with operational amplifier summation allows frequency-dependent circuitry to be realized. Figure 3.35(b) shows a simple switched capacitor filter. The delay causes a phase shift which is dependent on frequency. The frequency response is sinusoidal.

3.17 Transforms

Convolution is a lengthy process to perform on paper. It is much easier to work in the frequency domain. Figure 3.36 shows that if a signal with a spectrum or frequency content a is passed through a filter with a frequency response b the result will be an output spectrum which is simply the product of the two. If the frequency responses are drawn on logarithmic scales (i.e. calibrated in dB) the two can simply be added because the addition of logs is the same as multiplication. Whilst

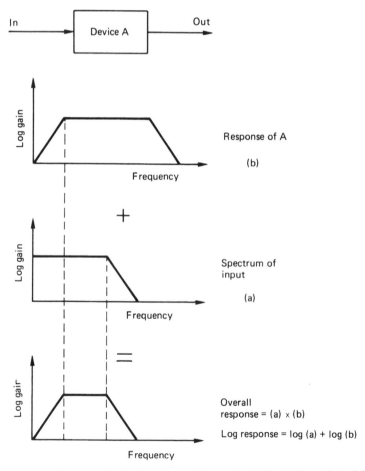

Figure 3.36 In the frequency domain, the response of two series devices is the product of their individual responses at each frequency. On a logarithmic scale the responses are simply added.

frequency in video has traditionally meant temporal frequency measured in Hertz, frequency in optics can also be spatial and measured in lines per millimetre (mm^{-1}). Multiplying the spectra of the responses is a much simpler process than convolution.

In order to move to the frequency domain or spectrum from the time domain or waveform, it is necessary to use the Fourier Transform, or in sampled systems, the discrete Fourier Transform (DFT). Fourier analysis holds that any waveform can be reproduced by adding together an arbitrary number of harmonically related sinusoids of various amplitudes and phases. Figure 3.37 shows how a square wave can be built up of harmonics. The spectrum can be drawn by plotting the amplitude of the harmonics against frequency. It will be seen that this gives a spectrum which is a decaying wave. It passes through zero at all even multiples of the fundamental. The shape of the spectrum is a $\sin x/x$ curve. If a square wave has a $\sin x/x$ spectrum, it follows that a filter with a rectangular impulse response will have a $\sin x/x$ spectrum.

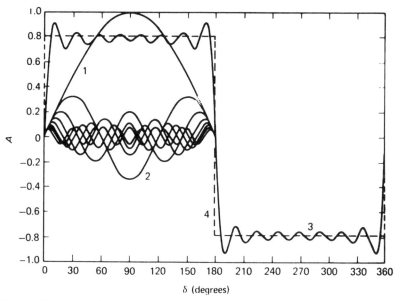

Figure 3.37 Fourier analysis of a square wave into fundamental and harmonics. A, amplitude; δ, phase of fundamental wave in degrees; 1, first harmonic (fundamental); 2, odd harmonics 3–15; 3, sum of harmonics 1–15; 4, ideal square wave.

A low-pass filter has a rectangular spectrum, and this has a $\sin x/x$ impulse response. These characteristics are known as a transform pair. In transform pairs, if one domain has one shape of the pair, the other domain will have the other shape. Thus a squarewave has a $\sin x/x$ spectrum and a $\sin x/x$ impulse has a square spectrum. Figure 3.38 shows a number of transform pairs. Note the pulse pair. A time domain pulse of infinitely short duration has a flat spectrum. Thus a flat waveform, i.e. DC, has only zero in its spectrum. Interestingly, the transform of a Gaussian response is still Gaussian. The impulse response of the optics of a laser disk has a $\sin^2 x/x^2$ function, and this is responsible for the triangular falling frequency response of the pickup.

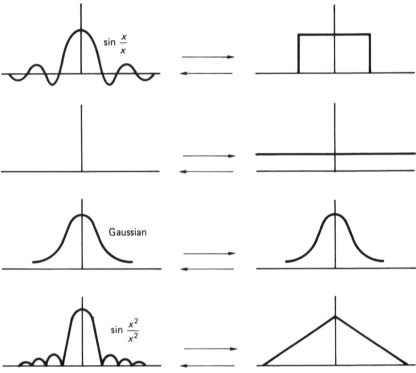

Figure 3.38 The concept of transform pairs illustrates the duality of the frequency (including spatial frequency) and time domains.

3.18 FIR and IIR filters compared

Filters can be described in two main classes, as shown in Figure 3.39, according to the nature of the impulse response. Finite-impulse response (FIR) filters are always stable and, as their name suggests, respond to an impulse once, as they have only a forward path. In the temporal domain, the time for which the filter

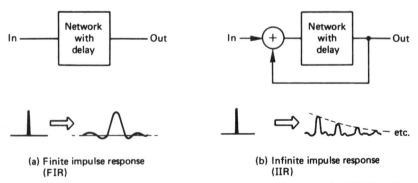

(a) Finite impulse response
(FIR)

(b) Infinite impulse response
(IIR)

Figure 3.39 An FIR filter (a) responds only to an input, whereas the output of an IIR filter (b) continues indefinitely rather like a decaying echo.

responds to an input is finite, fixed and readily established. The same is therefore true about the distance over which an FIR filter responds in the spatial domain. FIR filters can be made perfectly phase linear if required. Most filters used for sampling rate conversion and oversampling fall into this category.

Infinite-impulse response (IIR) filters respond to an impulse indefinitely and are not necessarily stable, as they have a return path from the output to the input. For this reason they are also called recursive filters. As the impulse response is not symmetrical, IIR filters are not phase linear.

3.19 FIR filters

An FIR filter works by graphically constructing the impulse response for every input sample. It is first necessary to establish the correct impulse response. Figure 3.40(a) shows an example of a low-pass filter which cuts off at $\frac{1}{4}$ of the sampling rate. The impulse response of a perfect low-pass filter is a $\sin x/x$ curve, where the time between the two central zero crossings is the reciprocal of the cut-off frequency. According to the mathematics, the waveform has always existed, and carries on for ever. The peak value of the output coincides with the input impulse. This means that the filter is not causal, because the output has changed before the input is known. Thus in all practical applications it is necessary to truncate the extreme ends of the impulse response, which causes an aperture effect, and to introduce a time delay in the filter equal to half the duration of the truncated impulse in order to make the filter causal. As an input impulse is shifted through the series of registers in Figure 3.40(b), the impulse response is created, because at each point it is multiplied by a coefficient as in Figure 3.40(c). These coefficients are simply the result of sampling and quantizing the desired impulse response. Clearly the sampling rate used to sample the impulse must be the same as the sampling rate for which the filter is being designed. In practice the coefficients are calculated, rather than attempting to sample an actual impulse response. The coefficient wordlength will be a compromise between cost and performance. Because the input sample shifts across the system registers to create the shape of the impulse response, the configuration is also known as a transversal filter. In operation with real sample streams, there will be several consecutive sample values in the filter registers at any time in order to convolve the input with the impulse response.

Simply truncating the impulse response causes an abrupt transition from input samples which matter and those which do not. Truncating the filter superimposes a rectangular shape on the time domain impulse response. In the frequency domain the rectangular shape transforms to a $\sin x/x$ characteristic which is superimposed on the desired frequency response as a ripple. One consequence of this is known as Gibb's phenomenon: a tendency for the response to peak just before the cut-off frequency. As a result, the length of the impulse which must be considered will depend not only on the frequency response, but also on the amount of ripple which can be tolerated. If the relevant period of the impulse is measured in sample periods, the result will be the number of points or multiplications needed in the filter. Figure 3.41 compares the performance of filters with different numbers of points. Video filters may use as few as eight points whereas a high quality digital audio FIR filter may need as many as 96 points.

Rather than simply truncate the impulse response in time, it is better to make a smooth transition from samples which do not count to those that do. This can be done by multiplying the coefficients in the filter by a window function which peaks in the centre of the impulse. In the example of Figure 3.42, the low-pass filter of Figure 3.40 is shown with a Bartlett window. Acceptable ripple determines the number of significant sample periods embraced by the impulse. This determines in turn both the number of points in the filter, and the filter delay. As the impulse is symmetrical, the delay will be half the impulse period. The

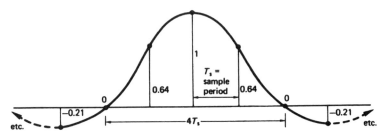

Figure 3.40(a) The impulse response of an LPF is a sin x/x curve which stretches from $-\infty$ to $+\infty$ in time. The ends of the response must be neglected, and a delay introduced to make the filter causal.

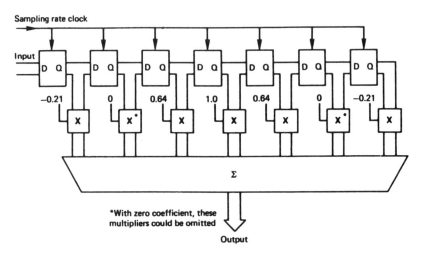

Figure 3.40(b) The structure of an FIR LPF. Input samples shift across the register and at each point are multiplied by different coefficients.

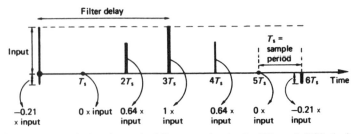

Figure 3.40(c) When a single unit sample shifts across the circuit of Figure 3.40(b), the impulse response is created at the output as the impulse is multiplied by each coefficient in turn.

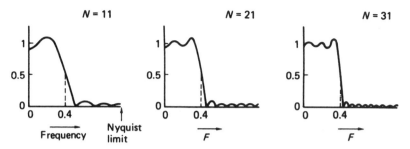

Figure 3.41 The truncation of the impulse in an FIR filter caused by the use of a finite number of points (*N*) results in ripple in the response. Shown here are three different numbers of points for the same impulse response. The filter is an LPF which rolls off at 0.4 of the fundamental interval. (Courtesy *Philips Technical Review*.)

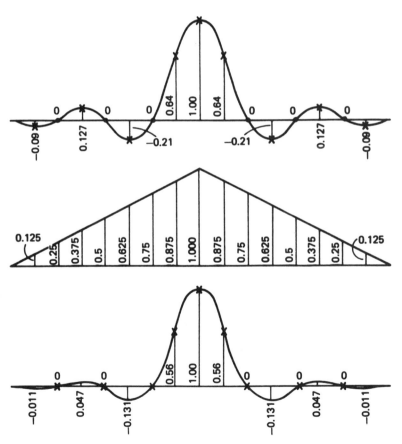

Figure 3.42 A truncated sin *x/x* impulse (top) is multiplied by a Bartlett window function (centre) to produce the actual coefficients used (bottom).

impulse response is a $\sin x/x$ function, and this has been calculated in the figure. The $\sin x/x$ response is next multiplied by the window function to give the windowed impulse response.

If the coefficients are not quantized finely enough, it will be as if they had been calculated inaccurately, and the performance of the filter will be worse than expected. Figure 3.43 shows an example of quantizing coefficients. Conversely, raising the wordlength of the coefficients increases cost.

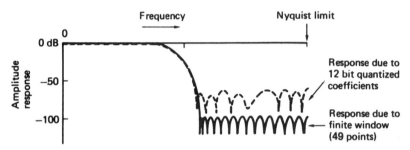

Figure 3.43 Frequency response of a 49 point transversal filter with infinite precision (solid line) shows ripple due to finite window size. Quantizing coefficients to 12 bits reduces attenuation in the stopband. (Responses courtesy *Philips Technical Review.*)

The FIR structure is inherently phase linear because it is easy to make the impulse response absolutely symmetrical. The individual samples in a digital system do not know in isolation what frequency they represent, and they can only pass through the filter at a rate determined by the clock. Because of this inherent phase-linearity, an FIR filter can be designed for a specific impulse response, and the frequency response will follow.

The frequency response of the filter can be changed at will by changing the coefficients. A programmable filter only requires a series of PROMs to supply the coefficients; the address supplied to the PROMs will select the response. The frequency response of a digital filter will also change if the clock rate is changed, so it is often less ambiguous to specify a frequency of interest in a digital filter in terms of a fraction of the fundamental interval rather than in absolute terms. The configuration shown in Figure 3.40 serves to illustrate the principle. The units used on the diagrams are sample periods and the response is proportional to these periods or spacings, and so it is not necessary to use actual figures.

Where the impulse response is symmetrical, it is often possible to reduce the number of multiplications, because the same product can be used twice, at equal distances before and after the centre of the window. This is known as folding the filter. A folded filter is shown in Figure 3.44.

FIR filters can be used for interpolation, which in its most general sense is the computation of a sample value which lies somewhere between existing samples. Interpolation is an important enabling technology on which a large number of practical digital video devices are based. There are three basic but related categories of interpolation as shown in Figure 3.45. The most straightforward (a) changes the sample spacing by an integer ratio, up or down. The timing of the system is thus simplified because all samples (input and output) are present on edges of the higher-rate sampling clock. Such a system is generally adopted for

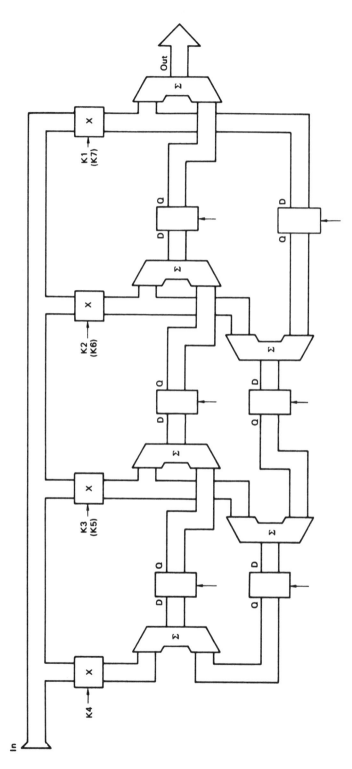

Figure 3.44 A seven-point folded filter for a symmetrical impulse response. In this case K1 and K7 will be identical, and so the input sample can be multiplied once, and the product fed into the output shift system in two different places. The centre coefficient K4 appears once. In an even-numbered filter the centre coefficient would also be used twice.

oversampling converters; the exact sampling rate immediately adjacent to the analog domain is not critical, and will be chosen to make the filters easier to implement.

Next in order of difficulty is the category shown in Figure 3.45(b) where the rate is changed by the ratio of two small integers. Samples in the input periodically time-align with the output. Such devices can be used for converting from $4F_{sc}$ to $3F_{sc}$, in the vertical processing of standards converters, or between the various rates of CCIR-601.

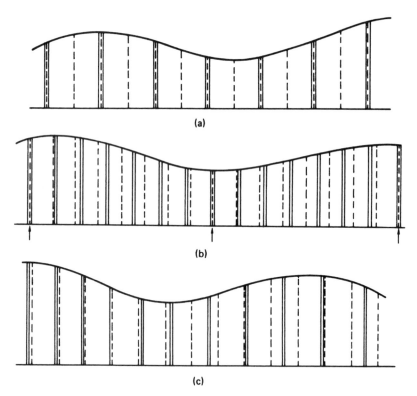

(a)

(b)

(c)

Figure 3.45 Categories of rate conversion. (a) Integer-ratio conversion, where the lower-rate samples are always coincident with those of the higher rate. There are a small number of phases needed. (b) Fractional-ratio conversion, where sample coincidence is periodic. A larger number of phases is required. Example here is conversion from 50.4 kHz to 44.1 kHz (8/7). (c) Variable-ratio conversion, where there is no fixed relationship, and a large number of phases are required.

The most complex interpolation category is where there is no simple relationship between input and output sampling rates, and in fact they may vary. This situation shown in Figure 3.45(c) is known as variable-ratio conversion. The temporal or spatial relationship of input and output samples is arbitrary. This problem will be met in effects machines which zoom or rotate images and in motion-compensated standards converters.

In considering how interpolators work it should be recalled that, according to sampling theory, all sampled systems have finite bandwidth. An individual digital sample value is obtained by sampling the instantaneous voltage of the original analog waveform, and because it has zero duration, it must contain an infinite spectrum. However, such a sample can never be seen or heard in that form because of the reconstruction process, which limits the spectrum of the impulse to the Nyquist limit. After reconstruction, one infinitely short digital sample ideally represents a $\sin x/x$ pulse whose central peak width is determined by the response of the reconstruction filter, and whose amplitude is proportional to the sample value. This implies that, in reality, one sample value has meaning over a considerable timespan, rather than just at the sample instant. If this were not true, it would be impossible to build an interpolator.

As in rate reduction, performing the steps separately is inefficient. The bandwidth of the information is unchanged when the sampling rate is increased; therefore the original input samples will pass through the filter unchanged, and it is superfluous to compute them. The combination of the two processes into an interpolating filter minimizes the amount of computation.

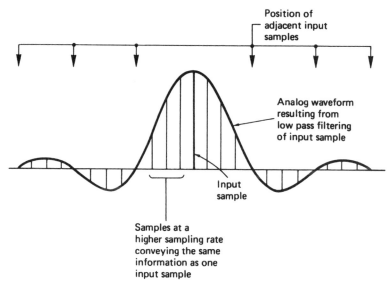

Figure 3.46 A single sample results in a $\sin x/x$ waveform after filtering in the analog domain. At a new, higher, sampling rate, the same waveform after filtering will be obtained if the numerous samples of differing size shown here are used. It follows that the values of these new samples can be calculated from the input samples in the digital domain in an FIR filter.

As the purpose of the system is purely to change the sample spacing, the filter must be as transparent as possible, and this implies that a linear-phase configuration is mandatory, suggesting the use of an FIR structure. Figure 3.46 shows that the theoretical impulse response of such a filter is a $\sin x/x$ curve which has zero value at the position of adjacent input samples. In practice this impulse cannot be implemented because it is infinite. The impulse response used will be truncated and windowed as described earlier. To simplify this discussion, assume that a $\sin x/x$ impulse is to be used. There is a strong parallel with the operation of a DAC where the analog voltage is returned to the time-continuous state by summing the analog impulses due to each sample. In a digital interpolating filter, this process is duplicated.

If, for example, the sampling rate is to be doubled, new samples must be interpolated exactly half-way between existing samples. The necessary impulse response is shown in Figure 3.47; it can be sampled at the *output* sample period

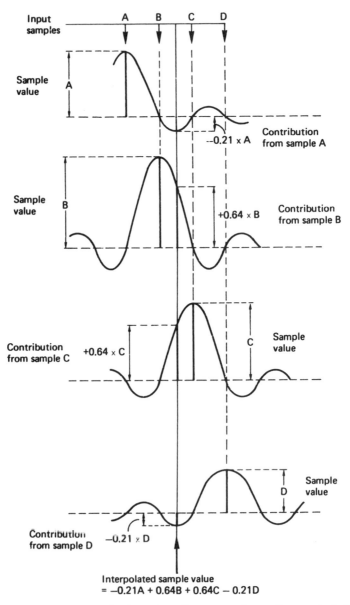

Figure 3.47 A two times oversampling interpolator. To compute an intermediate sample, the input samples are imagined to be sin x/x impulses, and the contributions from each at the point of interest can be calculated. In practice, rather more samples on either side need to be taken into account.

and quantized to form coefficients. If a single input sample is multiplied by each of these coefficients in turn, the impulse response of that sample at the new sampling rate will be obtained. Note that every other coefficient is zero, which confirms that no computation is necessary on the existing samples; they are just transferred to the output. The intermediate sample is computed by adding together the impulse responses of every input sample in the window. The figure shows how this mechanism operates.

In a variable-ratio interpolator, values will exist for the points at which input samples were made, but it is necessary to compute what the sample values would have been at absolutely any point between available samples. The general concept of the interpolator is the same as for the fractional-ratio converter, except that an infinite number of filter phases is ideally necessary. Since a realizable filter will have a finite number of phases, it is necessary to study the degradation this causes. The desired continuous temporal or spatial axis of the interpolator is quantized by the phase spacing, and a sample value needed at a particular point will be replaced by a value for the nearest available filter phase. The number of phases in the filter therefore determines the accuracy of the interpolation. The effects of calculating a value for the wrong point are identical to those of sampling with clock jitter, in that an error occurs proportional to the slope of the signal. The result is programme-modulated noise. The higher the noise specification, the greater the desired time accuracy and the greater the number of phases required. The number of phases is equal to the number of sets of coefficients available, and should not be confused with the number of points in the filter, which is equal to the number of coefficients in a set (and the number of multiplications needed to calculate one output value).

The sampling jitter accuracy necessary for 8 bit working is measured in picoseconds. This implies that something like 32 filter phases will be required for adequate performance in an 8 bit sampling-rate converter.

Chapter 4

Video interfacing

4.1 Introduction

Today's television installations generally contain a combination of analog and digital, component and composite equipment linked by routers, encoders, decoders and converters. The configuration may be redundant to allow continued use in the case of equipment failures, or expensive, special purpose devices may be shared between studios or edit suites. It will be seen here that the reconfiguration made possible by the use of routers places heavy demands on signal standardization. It does not matter whether the system is analog or digital – correct operation can only be ensured if all devices in a signal chain are designed and adjusted so that the meaning of the signal does not change with the configuration. Analog signals have standardized voltages and timings; digital signals have standardized code values and protocols. This chapter outlines the principles and practice of analog and digital video interfacing. To ensure that standards are met, various tests have been developed. These are described here along with the equipment and techniques needed to make them. The testing procedures for analog and digital equipment are quite different. However, in order to set up an ADC or a DAC correctly, both types of test may be needed together.

4.2 Routers

In a typical television installation, whether analog or digital, the signal may pass through a large number of different devices on its way from the camera to the final viewer. For practical reasons, not least the ability to carry on working if an individual item fails, most installations connect major signal processing blocks to a central switching device called a *router* which is essentially a telephone exchange for video, audio and control signals. Figure 4.1(a) shows a system without a router. As every device is effectively in a chain, the failure of one device breaks the chain and the whole system fails. The alternative is the system of Figure 4.1(b) in which the same equipment is connected to a router. It will be seen that the router contains a *crosspoint switch*, a device capable of connecting any vertical line to any horizontal line. The crosspoints selected in Figure 4.1(b) give exactly the same signal flow as in Figure 4.1(a). However, in the case of a failure, a rearrangement of the crosspoints will allow the signal through, bypassing the failed device. Obviously the router itself is expected to be extremely reliable. Generally the electronic switching circuits are fed from a dual power supply, each half of which is capable of delivering the entire power

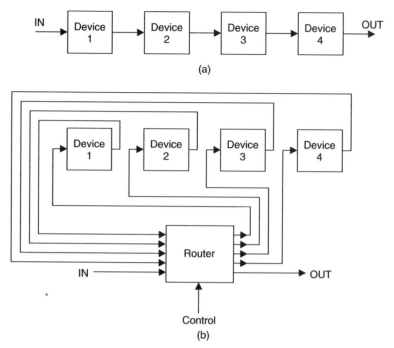

(a)

(b)

Figure 4.1 (a) Without a router, the system configuration can only be changed by rearranging interconnecting wiring. If a device fails, it cannot readily be bypassed. (b) With a router, the system configuration is flexible. Devices can be omitted from the chain for maintenance.

requirements. In the case of a power supply fault there is no interruption to the signal. It is normal practice to connect each power supply to a different phase of the electricity supply so that a single-phase failure cannot take out the router.

Whilst a breakdown in an edit suite causes delay, a breakdown in the on-air signal path leaves the viewers with blank screens and so systems are designed to be fault tolerant. Any equipment designed for use on-air must not only be designed for reliability, but also with the assumption that it will go wrong at some time. Figure 4.2 shows a device which contains a *bypass relay*. In the case of

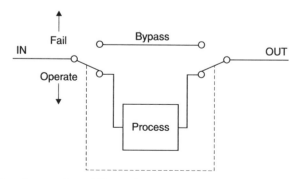

Figure 4.2 Using a bypass relay, a failing device can take itself out of service by connecting the input to the output.

power loss or an internally detected fault condition, the bypass relay will automatically connect the input direct to the output. The process performed by the unit will not now be available, but the signal path is not broken, except momentarily. In practice this is not as bad as it seems because, in practical installations, many signal processing stages are present in case an incoming signal is deficient in some way so that a correction can be made. Most of the time, many of these units do not alter the signal at all and so their omission from the signal path is of little consequence. The bypass relay allows the unit to pass a signal in the case of failure, but it does not allow the unit to be removed for

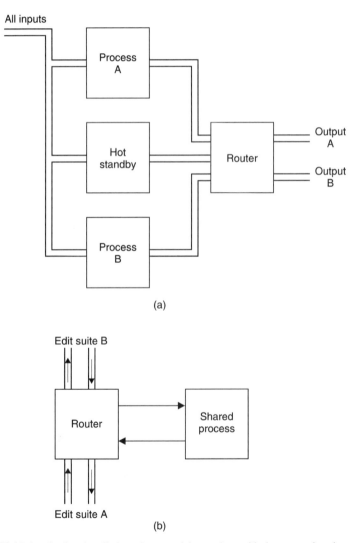

Figure 4.3 (a) A redundant installation where two jobs are done with three sets of equipment. In the case of a failure the hot spare is routed to the affected channel. (b) A shared installation where an expensive processing device can be assigned to whichever system needs it.

maintenance. In this case the router would be reconfigured to bypass the device and its wiring completely.

In large installations routers can be used to make the system more fault tolerant or more economical according to requirements. The two goals are usually exclusive and so the philosophy of the system must be clear at the design stage. In a critical installation, such as a presentation suite where television signals are actually connected live to the transmitter, multiple redundancy may be employed. Figure 4.3(a) shows a TV station which transmits two channels. Here the inputs of three routers are connected in parallel to all source signals. Three vision mixers are available, two of which will be on-air at any one time. A second, smaller, router determines which pair of vision mixers are on-air. Any one vision mixer or router can fail but the system will not be permanently affected.

Figure 4.3(b) shows a pair of edit suites which do not work on-air and can therefore tolerate failures. For economy, a single noise reducer is connected to the router. It can process signals from one suite or the other, but not both. A single device shared between systems in this way is said to be *assigned* to the system it is connected to.

4.3 Multilayer routers

A router does not necessarily just switch video signals. Generally it will also switch several audio channels and a number of control signals as well. Figure 4.4 shows a multilayer router having a common control system which is generally

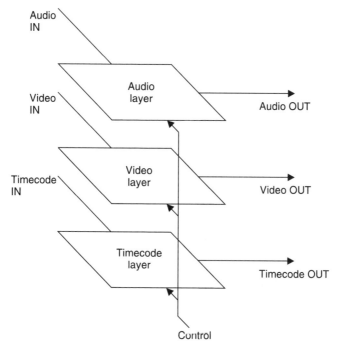

Figure 4.4 A multilayer router has switching for several kinds of signal: video, audio, timecode, etc., using a common control system.

programmed to switch every layer identically. In the case of a video recorder which can be assigned to two or more edit suites, the router will need to switch video, audio, timecode and the remote control signals which the edit controller uses to control the tape transport. In broadcast applications, one router layer may be for tally control. The tally signal starts at the feed to the transmitter as a DC voltage which travels in the opposite direction to the video signal. Figure 4.5 shows that at every stage where there is a routing decision, one layer of the router switches tally power towards the source of the selected signal. This process may be followed through several layers until the tally signal arrives at a signal source

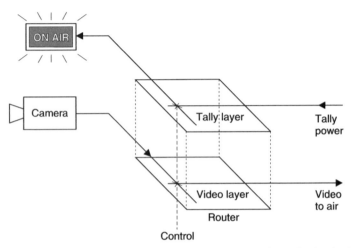

Figure 4.5 The tally system allows a control voltage to retrace the routing path taken by the video so that the 'on-air' lights reflect the camera or source which is currently live.

such as a camera or a playout VTR. The DC power causes the 'on-air' light to illuminate so that all concerned know that unit is in the transmission path. If a different source is selected, the tally routing will automatically illuminate a different 'on-air' light.

4.4 Video cable characteristics

Video signals produce a wide range of frequencies. Analog standard definition TV (SDTV) contains frequencies up to nearly 6 MHz. Analog HDTV contains frequencies up to 30 MHz. Parallel digital video runs at up to 36 Mbits/sec and serial digital video requires bit rates up to 360 Mbits/sec.

In all cases it is necessary to take into account the characteristics of cables. Figure 4.6 shows how the impedance of a cable changes with frequency. At DC and low frequencies a cable is effectively an open circuit. As frequency rises, eventually the dimensions and the dielectric constant of the insulating material dominate. At analog audio frequencies, cabling has effectively infinite impedance. The common 600 ohm analog audio interface only has such an impedance because of the load which the cable drives.

A change of impedance causes reflections in the energy flow and some of it heads back in the opposite direction. Constant impedance cables with fixed conductor spacing are necessary, and these must be suitably terminated.

As frequency rises still further, the energy travels less in the conductors and more in the insulation between them. Their composition becomes important and they begin to be called dielectrics. A poor dielectric like PVC absorbs high frequency energy and attenuates the signal. The response of a cable becomes proportional to the reciprocal of the square root of the frequency. At high frequencies, so-called low-loss dielectrics such as PTFE are used; one way of achieving low loss is to incorporate as much air in the dielectric as possible by making it in the form of a foam or extruding it with voids.

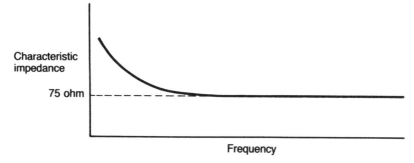

Figure 4.6 At low frequencies the impedance of a cable is very high and is determined primarily by the load impedance. However, as frequency rises the cable takes on a characteristic impedance resulting from the interplay of the cable inductance and capacitance.

At high frequencies, a cable must be considered a transmission line and signals travel down it as current loops which roll along. An example of pulse propagation is shown in Figure 4.7. If the pulse is positive, as it is launched along the line, it will charge the dielectric locally as in Figure 4.7(a). As the pulse moves along, it will continue to charge the local dielectric as in Figure 4.7(b). When the driver finishes the pulse, the trailing edge of the pulse follows the leading edge along the line. The voltage of the dielectric charged by the leading edge of the pulse is now higher than the voltage on the line, and so the dielectric discharges into the line as in Figure 4.7(c). The current flows forward as it is in fact the same current which is flowing into the dielectric at the leading edge. There is thus a loop of current rolling down the line flowing forward in the 'hot' wire and backwards in the return. The analogy with the tracks of a Caterpillar tractor is quite good. Individual plates in the track find themselves being lowered to the ground at the front and raised again at the back.

The constant to-ing and fro-ing of charge in the dielectric results in dielectric loss of signal energy. Dielectric loss increases with frequency and so a long transmission line acts as a filter. Thus the term 'low-loss' cable refers primarily to the kind of dielectric used.

Transmission lines which transport energy in this way have a characteristic impedance caused by the interplay of the inductance along the conductors with the parallel capacitance. One consequence of that transmission mode is that correct termination or matching is required between the line and both the driver and the receiver. When a line is correctly matched, the rolling energy rolls straight out of the line into the load and the maximum energy is available. If the impedance presented by the load is incorrect, there will be reflections from the mismatch. An open circuit will reflect all of the energy back in the same polarity as the original, whereas a short circuit will reflect all of the energy back in the opposite polarity. Thus impedances above or below the correct value will have a tendency toward reflections whose magnitude depends upon the degree of mismatch and whose polarity depends upon whether the load is too high or too low. In practice it is the need to avoid reflections which is the most important

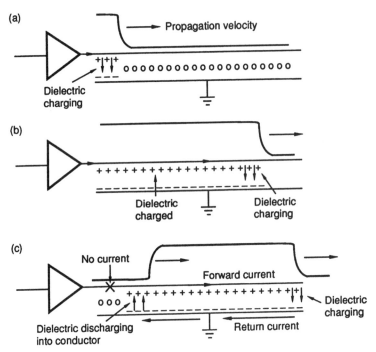

Figure 4.7 A transmission line conveys energy packets which appear to alternate with respect to the dielectric. In (a) the driver launches a pulse which charges the dielectric at the beginning of the line. As it propagates the dielectric is charged further along as in (b). When the driver ends the pulse, the charged dielectric discharges into the line (c). A current loop is formed where the current in the return loop flows in the opposite direction to the current in the 'hot' wire.

reason to correctly terminate. A signal reflected by mistermination at the receiver proceeds back towards the driver. This in itself does not cause any signal distortion. If the driver is also misterminated, a second reflection will take place such that the double-reflected signal now follows the original signal and is effectively added to it.

The return loss parameter is a measure of the degree of impedance matching obtained. The return loss is the ratio of the input and reflected signal voltages measured in dB. In analog video systems reflections should be at least 40 dB and preferably 50 dB below the signal level, implying that return loss at each end of the cable must be better than −20 to −25 dB. In practice quality equipment will perform better than these figures.

In professional video equipment both analog and digital video cables have an impedance of 75 Ω, but oddly employ 50 Ω BNC (Bayonet Neill-Concelman) connectors. The original BNC connector was available in 50 Ω and 75 Ω versions, but the 50 Ω version had a larger centre pin which was found to be more robust. This apparent mismatch does not cause any difficulty as the quality of termination is determined primarily by the impedance of the circuitry behind the connector. Figure 4.8(a) shows how a typical video transmission line works. The principles are the same for analog and digital systems. The drive amplifier usually incorporates negative feedback to improve linearity and frequency response and this has the effect of making the output impedance very small. In order to match the driver to the cable a series resistor is required between the

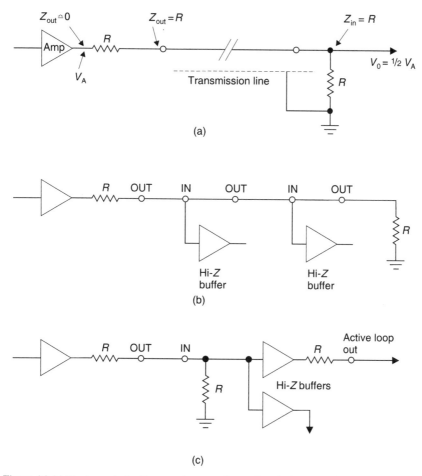

Figure 4.8 (a) The transmission line must be correctly terminated, thus the driver must have a series resistance which forms a potential divider with the load, causing a 6 dB loss. (b) In order to drive more than one load, loop-through is used where a termination is only provided at the last device. (c) The high frequencies of SDI require an active device if loop-through is needed.

driver and the socket. The terminator at the load is effectively in series with the source impedance and the received voltage is the result of a potential dividing process. With a correctly terminated line, the drive amplifier must produce twice the amplitude required across the termination. Terminators are subject to manufacturing tolerances and changing a terminator may result in a change of signal amplitude.

If the line is unterminated, the signal amplitude will roughly double. If two loads are connected to the same signal the amplitude will be drastically reduced and the system is said to be *double terminated*. In both cases the signal quality will be seriously impaired.

In analog video, most equipment is fitted with *loop-through* facilities as shown in Figure 4.8(b). The input socket is connected to an output socket and to a high impedance amplifier. If no further device is to be connected, the signal is terminated either by fitting a *terminator* (a BNC plug containing a 75 Ω resistance) to the output socket or by switching in a resistor. If several devices are fed from the same cable, only the last device is terminated to avoid double termination. The small capacitances of the amplifier inputs in a looped-through system do not cause a significant return loss problem in an analog system.

In serial digital systems, the frequencies involved are much higher and passive loop-through is considered to cause excessive reflection because a good return loss figure cannot be achieved. Figure 4.8(c) shows that, in digital video, the terminator is incorporated in the receiver. If loop-through is required, this will use an active buffer as shown.

The frequency-dependent losses caused by cables mean that some equalization will be needed in both analog and digital systems.

4.5 Introduction to analog testing

In the analog domain, the voltage of the signal directly represents the parameter being conveyed and the time at which signals arrive is critical. Thus any phenomenon which can disturb the signal voltage is undesirable. Gain errors, noise and baseline wander are obvious contenders; however, imperfect transmission channels may also distort the waveform. There are two types of distortion: linear and non-linear. Linear waveform distortion can be caused by an imperfect frequency response or by any phenomenon which changes the time of arrival of one frequency in the signal with respect to another. Non-linear distortion is caused by devices which do not have a straight transfer function; i.e. the gain is a function of signal level. Over the years, a number of tests have been developed, and those which have proved simple and reliable have been widely adopted.

4.6 Insertion loss testing

Practical video systems require the ability to be reconfigured using a router. If a recalibration is to be avoided on every change of configuration, all components must be accurately terminated with 75 Ω and the insertion loss must be made to have a value of unity. Figure 4.9 shows how insertion loss is measured. When the device under test is bypassed, the voltage across the terminator is exactly half that of the generator. When the device under test is *inserted*, the voltage on the terminator should not change. The ratio of the inserted voltage to the bypassed voltage is the insertion loss and is usually measured in dB.

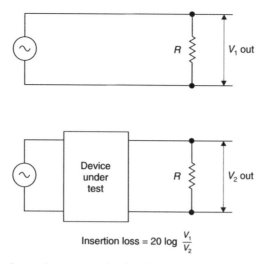

Insertion loss = $20 \log \dfrac{V_1}{V_2}$

Figure 4.9 Insertion loss testing compares the signal level with and without the device under test.

In practice, if it can be assumed that the input impedance of the device under test is correct, it can be left *in situ* and the insertion loss can be measured simply by comparing the input and output voltages.

4.7 Pulse and bar testing

Analog video signals contain a wide range of frequencies and are sensitive to distortion, particularly linear distortion. Linear distortion includes loss of high frequencies, which results in a soft or defocused picture, and group delay error, or lack of phase linearity, which causes smearing of vertical edges on the screen. Any device or transmission path through which a signal passes can potentially cause such distortion and so regular checking is necessary in order to maintain standards. These problems can be discovered using a rigorous process of measurement of frequency and phase response, but this is time consuming and expensive and the results need careful interpretation. What is needed is a simple yet effective test which is rapid enough to be performed routinely. The pulse and bar test signal is designed to fulfil that role. It is a signal which can be used to test paths carrying any type of analog video signal but only over the range of frequencies such a signal actually uses. This includes monochrome or luminance, and component colour signals. It can also test the luminance characteristics of composite video paths.

The pulse and bar signal is shown in Figure 4.10. It consists of a spike followed by a flat-topped bar which lasts for about half the line period. The signal is bandwidth limited to the required video system bandwidth, usually 5 MHz. Consequently the spike is not sharp; it is a $\sin^2$ impulse. Similarly the bar transitions are not vertical; they are in fact the integral of the impulse which is a slope.

In order to set the bandwidth to be tested, a parameter T is defined, such that:

Nominal video bandwidth $\times 2T = 1$

In 625 line SDTV, T is 100 ns whereas in 525 line SDTV it is 125 ns.

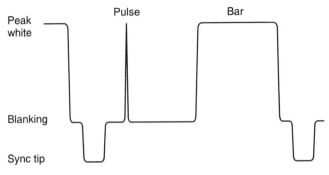

Figure 4.10 The common pulse and bar test signal.

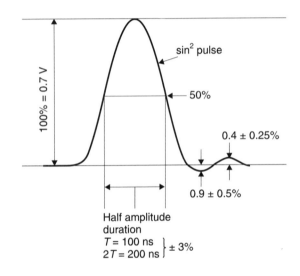

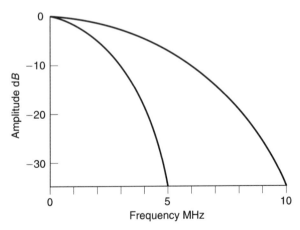

Figure 4.11 The waveform and spectrum of a 2*T* pulse. Frequencies beyond the normal video range are not tested.

Figure 4.11 shows that if T represents the time from the peak of the impulse to the half-amplitude point, the spectrum of the pulse will be contained within the nominal bandwidth. Consequently a $2T$ pulse has the ideal characteristic for testing only over the required bandwidth. The falling spectrum parallels the falling sensitivity of human vision to distortions as frequency rises. Consequently the top half of the video band is not tested very stringently. If a more stringent test is required a $1T$ pulse can be used, although this requires more care as its spectrum goes beyond the nominal video bandwidth.

Clearly the amplitude of the $2T$ pulse will be affected by h.f. loss, but the pulse will also become broader and will contain pre- and post-rings. These rings will be asymmetrical unless the system is phase-linear. The bar contains more low frequency energy and consequently will reveal distortions up to a few hundred

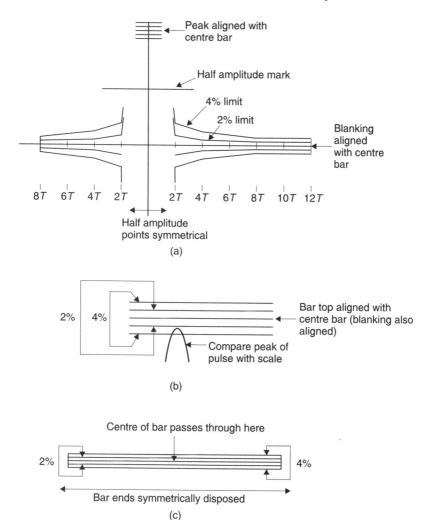

Figure 4.12 K-factor testing with a pre-engraved graticule. (a) K_p measurement. (b) K_{pb} measurement. (c) K_b measurement.

kilohertz in the shape of the top of the bar. High frequency losses will not affect the top of the bar, and so it can be used as a reference level for insertion loss testing. Consequently the amplitude of the pulse is made identical to the amplitude of the bar at the test generator. Should the two amplitudes differ after emerging from the system under test it can be seen at a glance that a problem exists.

Whilst the distortions of the pulse and bar waveform could be analysed mathematically, this is inappropriate for everyday testing. Instead the pulse and bar waveform has been standardized so that a special test graticule can be fitted to a waveform monitor. This is engraved with lines which allow the distortions to be assessed in terms of percentage K-factors. There are three K-factors, and the K-rating of the system under test is the largest (i.e. the worst) of the three.

K-factor of the pulse K_p is measured by aligning the received pulse with the graticule shown in Figure 4.12(a). The gain and vertical shift controls must be adjusted to normalize the amplitude by aligning the baseline and the peak with horizontal lines. The trace speed of the waveform monitor must be such that the T markings are correct. Normally this will correspond to 200 ns/cm. The half-amplitude points must be symmetrical about the centreline. Any pre- or post-rings indicating bandwidth impairment will cause the waveform to approach or cross the percentage-calibrated lines and the K-factor can be estimated.

The K-factor of the pulse-to-bar ratio, K_{pb} is measured by aligning the bar with the baseline and top lines. Figure 4.12(b) shows that the K-factor of the peak of the pulse with respect to the bar can then be read from the calibrated lines.

The K-factor of the bar, K_b is measured by aligning the baseline and the centre of the bar as before. The K-factor is measured by taking the maximum deviation of the bar top with respect to the centre as in Figure 4.12(c).

4.8 Noise testing

Noise is an unwanted signal which has superimposed itself on the wanted signal. It may be caused by interference or crosstalk from other equipment or signals, or the origin may be thermal noise in circuitry, or one of the many forms of noise which are experienced in magnetic recording. Broad-band random noise gives the picture a 'snowy' appearance, and extreme noise lifts black level to grey because of the rectifying action of tube gamma. Periodic noise causes diagonal bars or 'herring-bone' patterning on the screen.

For convenience, noise is divided into two broad classifications: frequencies below line rate and frequencies above. This is simply because superimposed signals below line rate can successfully be removed with a black-level clamp. Figure 4.13(a) shows a band-splitting filter used to classify the noise. The CCIR recommended crossover frequency is 10 KHz because the original line rate concerned was the 10.25 KHz of the now obsolete UK 405 line system. The exact frequency is sufficiently non-critical that when newer standards were introduced it was not worthwhile to change.

High frequency noise should only be measured within the nominal video bandwidth, otherwise out-of-band noise which cannot be reproduced may give misleading results. Consequently a second, low-pass, filter is required to band-limit the h.f. noise. Figure 4.13(b) shows a low-pass filter designed for 625 line systems.

A signal-to-noise measurement carried out with the above filters is an engineering measurement which does not convey how the viewer will perceive

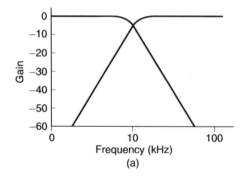

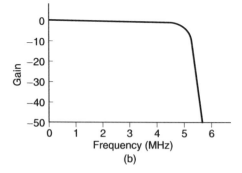

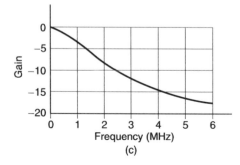

Figure 4.13 (a) Band-splitting or junction filter divides noise about the 10 kHz crossover. (b) Low-pass filter prevents noise beyond the video band affecting measurements. (c) Weighting filter measures noise in a way which parallels the subjective impairment.

any impairment. As the human visual system is less sensitive to high frequency noise, it follows that an impairment-based measurement must weight the signal to be tested. Figure 4.13(c) shows the psycho-optically weighted filter which has been developed for that purpose.

It is impossible to assess the amplitude or level of noise on a waveform monitor as it becomes a subjective function of brightness and frequency distribution. Consequently accurate noise measurement requires an electronic instrument which can measure the noise power and from this derive the true rms amplitude.

The signal-to-noise ratio is defined as follows:

$$SNR = 20 \log_{10} \frac{\text{pk-pk signal amplitude}}{\text{rms noise amplitude}}$$

As noise is statistical and has no peak amplitude, the rms equivalent derived from the power is all that can be measured. However, the rms amplitude is close to the most probable pk–pk amplitude. The pk–pk signal amplitude is taken to be the black–white picture component of the video signal, i.e. 0.7 volts or 0.714 volts as only this range is displayed. Naturally the kind of filtering used affects the result. Consequently a SNR quoted without a description of the filter used is quite meaningless.

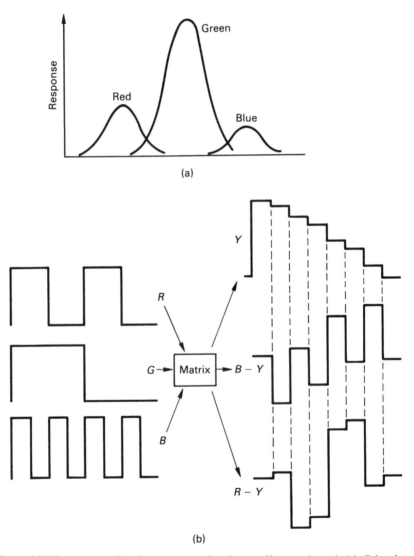

Figure 4.14 The response of the human eye to colour is not uniform as shown in (a). Colour bars originate as three square waves in RGB, but luminance obtained by weighted adding follows an irregular staircase shown in (b).

4.9 Colour bars

Colour bars are useful for checking colour encoding and decoding equipment and for calibrating levels in component systems to ensure that hue and saturation errors are avoided. They cannot reveal transmission distortions and do not replace tests such as pulse and bar, which should be carried out before colour alignment is attempted.

The origin of the common colour bar test signal is shown in Figure 4.14. *R*, *G* and *B* are matrixed together to form a luminance (and monochrome compatible) signal *Y* which has full bandwidth. The eye is not equally sensitive to the three primary colours, as can be seen in Figure 4.14(a) and so the luminance signal is a weighted sum. Full-amplitude binary *RGB* signals are produced, having one, two and four cycles per screen width. When these are added together as in Figure 4.14(b), an eight-level luminance staircase results because of the unequal weighting. The matrix also produces two colour difference signals, $R - Y$ and $B - Y$, causing each step to appear a different colour.

The bars described above are full-amplitude, otherwise known as 100.0.100.0 bars or just 100 per cent bars. These are popular in the UK, but elsewhere other types are found. Figure 4.14(c) shows 100.0.100.25 bars in which the peak white luminance level is retained, but the saturation is reduced to 95 per cent by having the *RGB* signals go down only to 25 per cent of scale instead of 0 per cent. Another approach is the EBU or 100.0.75.0 bars, or just 75 per cent bars (Figure 4.14(d)), where saturation remains 100 per cent but the amplitude is reduced to 75 per cent except for the white bar. In NTSC countries a 75 per cent bar signal may be found in which the white bar is also made 75 per cent of peak. Such a signal may also have a pedestal.

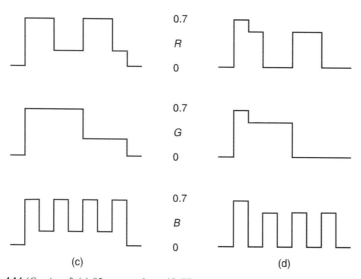

(c)   (d)

Figure 4.14 (*Continued*) (c) 95 per cent bars. (d) 75 per cent EBU bars.

4.10 Testing colour difference signals

The three analog components of a colour difference signal set are carried by separate coaxial cables and it is possible for each component to encounter different losses and delays. Signal voltage errors result in saturation or hue errors, and relative timing errors result in rainbow fringes at vertical transitions. As was mentioned above, terminator tolerance can result in signal levels changing and it is common to specify close tolerance terminators in component systems.

In order to check that signals are received with correct amplitudes, often called *insertion gain* measurement, a colour bar generator and a component waveform monitor are required. In 'parade' mode, the waveform monitor may display selected parts of all three components (such as one line) side by side. This display makes it easy to tell which trace results from which signal and to detect obvious or gross errors.

A more accurate way of portraying component signals is the 'lightning' display developed by Tektronix. Figure 4.15(a) shows that in the lightning display the screen is divided into two halves. The upper half displays $B - Y$ horizontally against Y vertically upwards, whereas the lower half displays $R - Y$ horizontally against Y vertically downwards. The *graticule* is marked with boxes in which the display dots should fall for an ideal colour bar signal. If a colour difference signal gain is wrong, the dots will miss the boxes horizontally; if the luminance gain is wrong the dots will miss the boxes vertically.

Colour difference signals are often displayed simultaneously on a vectorscope as shown in Figure 4.15(b). The horizontal deflection of the vectorscope spot is controlled by the P_b signal and the vertical deflection by the P_r signal.

Note that the white bar and the black bar are not colours and so the colour difference signals have a value of zero in those bars, resulting in a central spot. There are six remaining colours, each of which results in a spot on the perimeter of the vectorscope display. Once more a graticule will be provided which indicates the ideal positions of the vector dots so that it is possible to tell at a glance if one of the signals is incorrect as a gain error in P_b will displace the spot horizontally whereas a gain error in P_r will displace the spot vertically.

The relative timing of the components can be checked using colour bars with a lightning display. The test relies upon the fact that all three components contain a transition at the green/magenta boundary in the centre of the active line. If the components are time aligned, the centre of the trace joining the green and magenta dots lies on a straight line joining the dots. If, for example, the $B - Y$ signal is lagging the luminance signal, the trace leaving the green dot will be deflected down by the luminance transition before it is deflected right by the $B - Y$ transition and it will appear bowed towards the screen centre. A graticule between the green and magenta boxes displays the degree of bowing. Note that the colour dots must be correctly centred in their boxes before this test can be made. Figure 4.16 shows the principle.

A very accurate measure of intersignal delay can be made using a special signal known as the 'bowtie' test signal. During the active line, the luminance signal carries a burst of 500 kHz sine wave. In the colour difference signals, a co-sited burst of a slightly higher frequency is used. The frequency is chosen so that there is exactly one extra cycle in the colour difference bursts. The phasing is

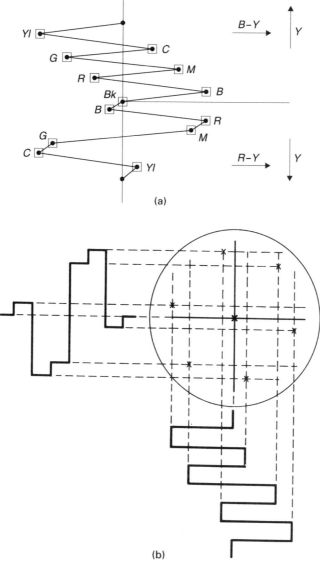

Figure 4.15 (a) The 'lightning' display shows each colour difference signal with respect to luminance. (b) Colour difference signals can be shown two-dimensionally on a vectorscope.

such that the three bursts are in phase at the ends but the colour difference bursts are phase reversed with respect to luminance in the centre. The waveform monitor displays $Y + (B - Y)$ and $Y + (R - Y)$. Figure 4.17(a) shows that in a system with ideal gains and timing the display shows a centred null in the summed waveforms, which resemble bowties. If a gain is wrong, the depth of the null will fall as in Figure 4.17(b). If there is a relative timing error, the null will move away from the centre as shown in Figure 4.17(c).

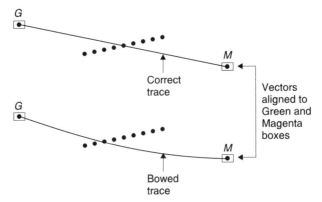

Figure 4.16 Intercomponent timing can be checked with the green/magenta transition which will bow or bend if the transitions do not coincide.

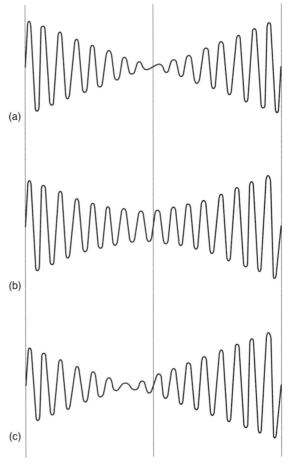

Figure 4.17 (a) Ideal bowtie display. (b) Bowtie showing gain error preventing a null. (c) Timing error displaces null from centre.

4.11 Errors in composite video

Most coding errors can be detected using an accurate colour bar test signal and a composite vectorscope to display the output of the unit under test with respect to a reference subcarrier. Figure 4.18(a) shows that the vectorscope will be provided with a standard graticule showing where ideal vectors should lie on the tube face. In the case of NTSC colour bars there should be six colour vectors radially disposed, two central vectors corresponding to the black and white bars

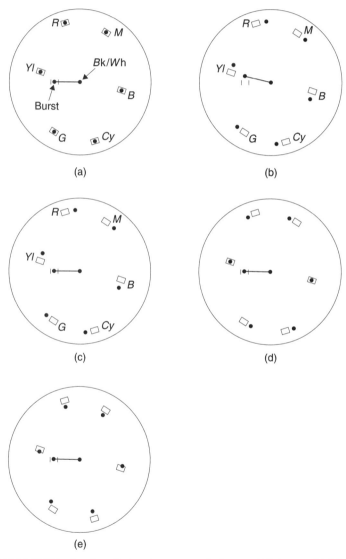

Figure 4.18 (a) NTSC colour bars display six vectors and a burst at 180 degrees. (b) Subcarrier phase error rotates the entire display. (c) Chroma phase error rotates vectors with respect to burst. (d) Quadrature error causes some vectors to be rotated more than others. (e) Level error prior to quadrature encoder causes shift in one dimension only.

and one vector pointing to the left representing the burst which in NTSC is inverted subcarrier.

Phase errors cause the display to rotate. Figure 4.18(b) shows that if the entire display is rotated, including the burst vector, the cause is a subcarrier phase error. A subcarrier phase error will not prevent a self-synchronized monitor from displaying correct colours, because the burst and the active line have the correct relative phase. However, it will prevent the signal being mixed with another. The error can be rectified by adjusting the phase of the encoder subcarrier with respect to reference until the burst vector lies in its graticule box.

If the burst phase is correct but the six colour bar vectors are rotated with respect to burst as shown in Figure 4.18(c), the cause is a chroma phase error. Chroma phase error will cause incorrect colours on a monitor because the decoder reference phase obtained from burst will be inappropriate. Correction requires the phase of the colour bars to be adjusted with respect to burst phase.

It is also possible for an encoder to suffer quadrature error in which the two subcarriers are not at exactly 90 degrees to one another. In this case the vectorscope reveals some bars having phase errors and some which do not, according to which axis is incorrect. Figure 4.18(d) shows an example.

Whilst phase errors rotate the vectorscope display, amplitude errors change the vector radius. One obvious error in the output of an encoder is where the level of one of the colour difference inputs is incorrect. Figure 4.18(e) shows that this causes the vectors to miss the boxes in one axis only. In this case the correct action is to adjust the gain of the appropriate signal *before* the chroma modulator.

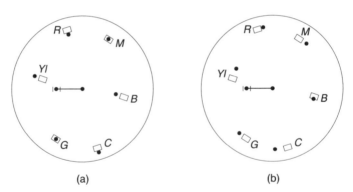

(a)   (b)

Figure 4.19 (a) Differential gain; chroma amplitude is affected by luminance level. (b) Differential phase; chroma phase is affected by luminance level.

There are two slightly more obscure sources of error in composite signals which must be considered. These are known as *differential gain* and *differential phase* errors. Figure 4.19(a) shows a differential gain error. A test signal with a fixed chroma amplitude and a varying luminance level is used. If such a signal passes through a unit which causes the chroma amplitude to vary as a function of the luminance level, the symptom is called a differential gain error. The result on real programme material is that the colour saturation varies with brightness. This is not highly visible and is the least serious of the two errors.

Figure 4.19(b) shows differential phase error. As the luminance level changes, the signal delay may also change resulting in the chroma phase becoming a function of luminance. This effect was particularly problematical in early transmitters, causing the hue to vary with brightness, although later transmitter designs have reduced the effect. Differential phase error is serious as it cannot be adjusted out as changing the burst phase will only alter which hues are correct and which are wrong.

Differential gain and phase errors are easily seen on a composite vectorscope as Figure 4.19 shows. If there is a fixed chroma gain error, all of the vectors will miss the graticule boxes by the same radial error. Adjustment to the chroma gain will result in all vectors entering the boxes. However, if there is a differential gain error, vectors corresponding to bright colours, like yellow, may have excessive radius, whereas vectors corresponding to dark colours, like blue, may have insufficient radius. This is shown in Figure 4.19(a). Clearly a chroma gain adjustment cannot rectify the problem. It is important to ensure that level errors in the colour difference signals prior to the chroma modulator are not misinterpreted as differential gain. In the case of a differential phase error, shown in Figure 4.19(b), the vectors miss the boxes by a varying amount, and cannot all be adjusted by setting the chroma phase.

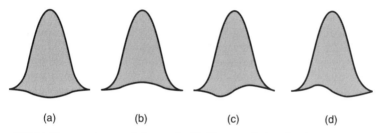

Figure 4.20 (a) Chroma gain exceeds luma gain. (b) Chroma gain less than luma gain. (c) Chroma leads luma. (d) Chroma lags luma.

A composite version of the pulse and bar signal can be used for composite signal path testing. Figure 4.20 shows how the signal is obtained by adding chroma to a conventional luminance signal. This pulse and bar plus chroma signal can be used to make a number of useful tests. The figure shows how the relative amplitude and timing of the luminance and chroma can be verified.

4.12 Digital video interfaces

Standards or advanced proposals now exist for both 4:2:2 component and $4F_{sc}$ composite digital in both 525/59.94 and 625/50 and in both parallel and serial forms. There are also interfaces for 16:9 signals in both standard and high definition.

Digital interfaces require to be standardized in the following areas: connectors, to ensure plugs mate with sockets; pinouts; electrical signal specification, to ensure that the correct voltages and timing are transferred; and protocol, to ensure that the meaning of the data words conveyed is the same to both devices. As digital video of any type is only data, it follows that the same physical and electrical standards can be used for a variety of protocols.

The parallel interface uses common connectors, pinouts and electrical levels for both line standards in both the component and composite versions. The same is true for the serial interfaces. Thus there are only two electrical interfaces: parallel and serial. The type of video being transferred is taken care of in the protocol differences.

4.13 The parallel electrical interface

Composite digital signals use the same electrical and mechanical interface as is used for 4:2:2 component working. This means that it is possible to erroneously plug a component signal into a composite machine. Whilst this cannot possibly work, no harm will be done because the signal levels and pinouts are the same.

A 25 pin D-type connector to ISO 2110–1989 is specified. Equipment always has female connectors, cables always have male connectors. Metal or metallized backshells are recommended with screened cables for optimum shielding. Equipment has been seen using ribbon cables and IDC (insulation displacement) connectors, but is it not clear whether such cables would meet the newer more stringent EMC (electromagnetic compatibility) regulations. It should be borne in mind that the ninth and eighteenth harmonics of 13.5 MHz are both emergency frequencies for aircraft radio.

Whilst equipment may produce or accept only 8 bit data, cables must contain conductors for all 10 bits. Connector latching is by a pair of 4–40 (an American thread) screws, with suitable posts provided on the female connector. It is important that the screws are used as the multicore cable is quite stiff and can eventually unseat the plug if it is not secured. Some early equipment had slidelocks instead of screw pillars, but these proved to be too flimsy. During the changeover from slidelocks to 4–40 screws, some equipment was made with metric screw pillars and these will need to be changed to attach modern cables.

When unscrewing the locking screws from a D-connector it is advisable to check that the lock screw is actually unscrewing from the pillar. It is not unknown for the pillar to rotate instead. If this is not noticed, the pillar fixings may become detached inside the equipment which will then have to be dismantled.

Each signal in the interface is carried by a balanced pair using ECL (emitter coupled logic) drive levels. The cable has a nominal impedance of 110 ohms and must be correctly terminated. ECL runs from a power supply of nominally -5.2 V and the logic states are -0.8 V for a 'high' and -1.85 V for a 'low'. As ECL is primarily a current-driven system, the signal amplitude is quite low compared with other logic families.

Figure 4.21 shows the pinouts used. Whilst it is not obvious from the figure, the numbering of the D-connector is such that signal pairs are on physically adjacent pins. Originally most equipment used 8 bit data while 10 bit working was viewed as an option, and this was reflected in the wording of the first standards. However, in order to reflect the increasing quantity of 10 bit equipment now in use, the wording of later standards has subtly changed to describe a 10 bit system in which only eight bits may be used.

In the old specification shown in Figure 4.21(a), there are eight signal pairs and two optional pairs, so that extension to a 10 bit word can be accommodated. The optional signals were used to add bits at the least significant end of the word. Adding bits in this way extends resolution rather than increasing the magnitude. It will be seen from the figure that the optional bits are called Data–1 and Data–2

Old 8-bit system	Connector pin number	New 10-bit system
Clock	1	Clock
System ground A	2	System ground A
Data 7 (MSB)	3	Data 9 (MSB)
Data 6	4	Data 8
Data 5	5	Data 7
Data 4	6	Data 6
Data 3	7	Data 5
Data 2	8	Data 4
Data 1	9	Data 3
Data 0	10	Data 2
Data A	11	Data 1
Data B	12	Data 0
Cable shield	13	Cable shield
Clock return	14	Clock return
System ground B	15	System ground B
Data 7 return	16	Data 9 return
Data 6 return	17	Data 8 return
Data 5 return	18	Data 7 return
Data 4 return	19	Data 6 return
Data 3 return	20	Data 5 return
Data 2 return	21	Data 4 return
Data 1 return	22	Data 3 return
Data 0 return	23	Data 2 return
Data A return	24	Data 1 return
Data B return	25	Data 0 return

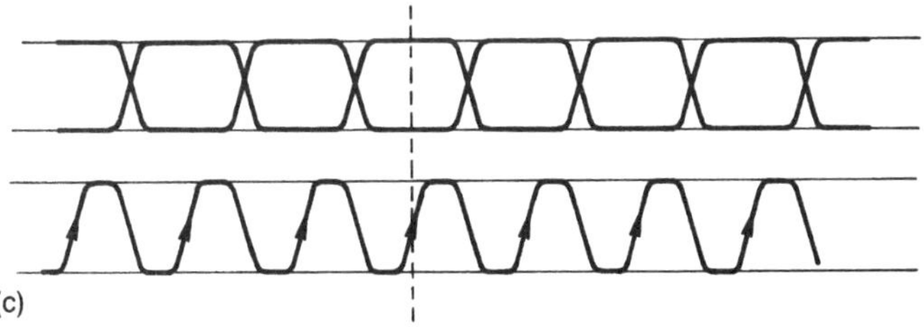

(a)

(b)

(c)

Figure 4.21 The parallel interface was originally specified as in (a) with eight bits expandable to ten. Later documents specify a 10 bit system (b) in which the bottom two bits may be unused. Clock timing in (c) is arranged so that a clock transition occurs between data transitions to allow maximum settling time.

where the −1 and −2 refer to the power of two represented, i.e. 2^{-1} and 2^{-2}. The 8 bit word describes 256 levels and ends in a radix point. The extra bits below the radix point represent the half and quarter quantizing intervals. In this way a degree of compatibility exists between 10 and 8 bit systems, as the correct magnitude will always be obtained when changing wordlength, and all that is lost is a degree of resolution in shortening the wordlength when the bits below the radix point are lost. The same numbering scheme can be used for both wordlengths; the longer wordlength simply has a radix point and an extra digit in any number base. Converting to the 8 bit equivalent is then simply a matter of deleting the extra digit and retaining the integer part.

However, the later specification shown in Figure 4.21(b) renumbers the bits from 0 to 9 and assumes a system with 1024 levels. Thus all standard levels defined in the old 8 + 2 bit documents have to be multiplied by four to convert them to the levels in the new 10 bit documents. Thus a level of 16 decimal or 10 hex in the 8 bit system becomes 64 decimal or 40 hex in the 10 bit system. Figure 4.22 shows that 8 + 2 schemes may use hexadecimal numbering in the XYZ or XYLo format where two hex digits X and Y represent the most significant eight bits and the remaining two bits are represented by the Z or Lo symbol. 10 bit schemes are numbered with three hex digits PQR where P only has two meaningful bits.

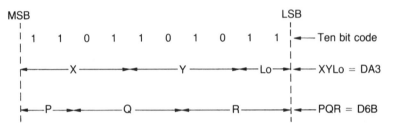

Figure 4.22 As there are two ways to parse ten bits into hexadecimal, there are two numbering schemes in use. In the XYLo system the parsing begins from the MSB down and the Lo parameter is expressed in quarters. In the PQR system the parsing starts from the LSB and so the P parameter has a maximum value of 3.

A separate clock signal pair and a number of grounding and shielding pins complete the connection. Figure 4.21 also shows the relationship between the clock and the data. A positive-going clock edge is used to sample the signal lines after the level has settled between transitions. In component, the clock will be line locked 27 MHz or 36 MHz irrespective of the line standard, whereas in composite digital the clock will be four times the frequency of PAL or NTSC subcarrier.

The parallel interface is suitable for distances of up to 50 metres (27 MHz) or 40 metres (36 MHz). Beyond this distance equalization is likely to be necessary and skew or differential delay between signals may become a problem. Equalization of such a large number of signals is not economically viable and for longer distances a serial interface is a better option.

4.14 The component parallel interface

It is not necessary to digitize analog sync pulses in component systems, since the only useful video data are those sampled during the active line. As the sampling rate is derived from sync, it is only necessary to standardize the size and position of a digital active line and all other parts of the video waveform can be re-created at a later time. The position is specified as a given number of sampling clock periods from the leading edge of sync, and the length is simply a standard number of samples. The component digital active line with 13.5 MHz sampling is 720 luminance samples long. This is somewhat longer than the analog active line and allows for some drift in the line position of the analog input. Ideally some of the first and last samples of the digital active line will represent blanking level.

Figure 4.23 shows that in 625 line systems the control system waits for 132 sample periods after an analog sync edge before commencing sampling the line. Then 720 luminance samples and 360 of each type of colour difference sample are taken: 1440 samples in all. A further 12 sample periods will elapse before the next sync edge, making $132 + 720 + 12 = 864$ sample periods. In 525 line systems, the analog active line is in a slightly different place and so the controller

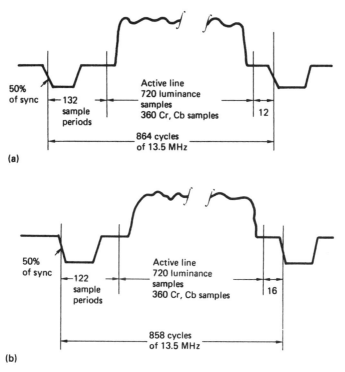

Figure 4.23 (a) In 625 line systems to CCIR-601, with 4:2:2 sampling, the sampling rate is exactly 864 times line rate, but only the active line is sampled, 132 sample periods after sync. (b) In 525 line systems to CCIR-601, with 4:2:2 sampling, the sampling rate is exactly 858 times line rate, but only the active line is sampled, 122 sample periods after sync. The active line contains exactly the same quantity of data as for 50 Hz systems.

waits 122 sample periods before taking the same digital active line samples as before. There will then be 16 sample periods before the next sync edge, making $122 + 720 + 16 = 858$ sample periods.

For 16:9 aspect ratio working, the line and field rate remain the same, but the luminance sampling rate may be raised to 18 MHz and the colour difference sampling rates are raised to 9 MHz. This results in the sampling structure shown for 625 lines in Figure 4.24(a) and for 525 lines in Figure 4.24(b). There are now 960 luminance pixels and 2 × 480 colour difference pixels per active line. The parallel interface remains the same except that the clock rate rises to 36 MHz.

When converting analog signals to digital it is important that the analog unblanked picture should be correctly positioned within the line. In this way the analog line will be symmetrically disposed within the digital active line. If this is the case, when converting the data back to the analog domain, no additional blanking will be needed as the blanking at the ends of the original analog line will be re-created from the data. The DAC can pass the whole of the digital active line for conversion and the result will be a correctly timed analog line with blanking edges in the right position.

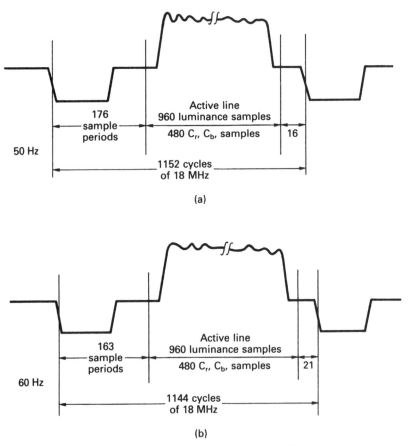

Active line
960 luminance samples

176
sample
periods

480 C_r, C_b, samples   16

50 Hz

1152 cycles
of 18 MHz

(a)

Active line
960 luminance samples

163
sample
periods

480 C_r, C_b, samples   21

60 Hz

1144 cycles
of 18 MHz

(b)

Figure 4.24 In 16:9 working with an 18 MHz sampling rate the sampling structure shown here results.

However, if the original analog timing was incorrect, the unblanked analog line may be too long or off-centre in the digital active line. In this case a DAC may apply digital blanking to the line data prior to conversion. Some equipment gives the user the choice of using blanking in the data or locally applied blanking prior to conversion.

In addition to specifying the location of the samples, it is also necessary to standardize the relationship between the absolute analog voltage of the waveform and the digital code value used to express it so that all machines will interpret the numerical data in the same way. These relationships were shown in Section 3.12 and are in the voltage domain and therefore independent of the scanning standard used.

The component interface carries a multiplex of luminance and colour difference samples and it is necessary to synchronize the demultiplexing process at the receiver so that the components are not inadvertently transposed. As conventional analog syncs are discarded, horizontal and vertical synchronizing must also be provided. These functions are performed by special bit patterns known as timing reference signals (TRS) sent with each line. Immediately before the digital active line location is the *SAV* (start of active video) TRS pattern, and immediately after is the *EAV* (end of active video) TRS pattern. These unique patterns occur on every line and continue throughout the vertical interval.

Each TRS pattern consists of four symbols; three of these form a sync pattern for demultiplexing and one is an information symbol which replaces the analog sync signals. As the parallel interface must work with 8 or 10 bit data, the sync pattern can only be specified for the eight most significant bits as the other two may not be present. The first symbol is eight ones and the next two are eight zeros. As these cannot occur in active video, their detection reliably indicates a sync pattern and is sufficient to enable unambiguous location of the information symbol and demultiplexing of the components. Ten-bit sources should output ten ones and ten zeros during the TRS.

The fourth symbol is a data byte which contains three data bits, *H*, *F* and *V*. These bits are protected by four redundancy bits which form a 7 bit Hamming codeword. Figure 4.25(a) shows how the Hamming code is generated. Single bit errors can be corrected and double bit errors can be detected according to the decoding table in Figure 4.25(b).

Figure 4.26(a) shows the structure of the TRS. The data bits have the following meanings:

- *H* is used to distinguish between *SAV*, where it is set to 0, and *EAV* where it is set to 1.
- *F* defines the state of interlace and is 0 during the first field and 1 during the second field. *F* is only allowed to change at *EAV*. In interlaced systems, one field begins at the centre of a line, but there is no sync pattern at that location so the field bit changes at the end of the line in which the change took place.
- *V* is 1 during vertical blanking and 0 during the active part of the field. It can only change at *EAV*.

Figure 4.26(b) (top) shows the relationship between the sync pattern bits and 625 line analog timing, whilst below is the relationship for 525 lines.

As only the active line is transmitted in component digital systems, DACs will need to have some additional logic which allows them to recreate analog syncs. As the sampling clock is horizontally locked only a small number of different sync edges need be stored and the memory requirements are minimal.

D.L.I.A.D.T. Library

4.15 Component ancillary data

Only the active line is transmitted and this leaves a good deal of spare capacity. The two line standards differ on how this capacity is used. In 625 lines, only the

Bit	9	8 F	7 V	6 H	5 P3	4 P2	3 P1	2 P0	1	0
	1	0	0	0	0	0	0	0	0	0
	1	0	0	1	1	1	0	1	0	0
	1	0	1	0	1	0	1	1	0	0
	1	0	1	1	0	1	1	0	0	0
	1	1	0	0	0	1	1	1	0	0
	1	1	0	1	1	0	1	0	0	0
	1	1	1	0	1	1	0	0	0	0
	1	1	1	1	0	0	0	1	0	0

Data — Check bits

(a)

Received P3 – P0	Received bits 8, 7, and 6 (F, V, and H)							
	000	001	010	011	100	101	110	111
0000	000	000	000	*	000	*	*	111
0001	000	*	*	111	*	111	111	111
0010	000	*	*	011	*	101	*	*
0011	*	*	010	*	100	*	*	111
0100	000	*	*	011	*	*	110	*
0101	*	001	*	*	100	*	*	111
0110	*	011	011	011	100	*	*	011
0111	100	*	*	011	100	100	100	*
1000	000	*	*	*	*	101	110	*
1001	*	001	010	*	*	*	*	111
1010	*	101	010	*	101	101	*	101
1011	010	*	010	010	*	101	010	*
1100	*	001	110	*	110	*	110	110
1101	001	001	*	001	*	001	010	*
1110	*	*	*	011	*	101	110	*
1111	*	001	010	*	100	*	*	*

(b)

Figure 4.25 The data bits in the TRS are protected with a Hamming code which is calculated according to the table in (a). Received errors are corrected according to the table in (b) where a dot shows an error detected but not correctable.

active line period may be used on lines 20 to 22 and 333 to 335. Lines 20 and 333 are reserved for equipment self-testing.

In 525 lines there is considerably more freedom and ancillary data may be inserted anywhere there is no active video, either during horizontal blanking where it is known as HANC, vertical blanking where it is known as VANC, or both.

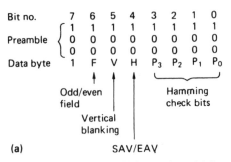

Figure 4.26(a) The 4 byte synchronizing pattern which precedes and follows every active line sample block has this structure.

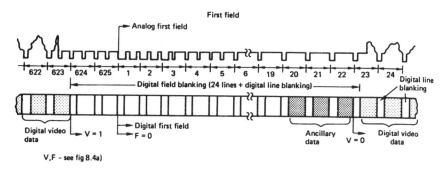

First field

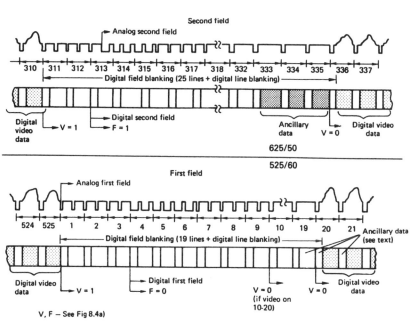

625/50

525/60

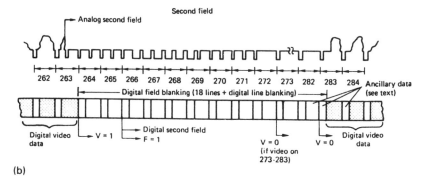

(b)

Figure 4.26(b) The relationships between analog video timing and the information in the digital timing reference signals for 625/50 (above) and 525/60 (below).

The all zeros and all ones codes are reserved for synchronizing, and cannot be allowed to appear in ancillary data. In practice only seven bits of the 8 bit word can be used as data; the eighth bit is redundant and gives the byte odd parity. As all ones and all zeros are even parity, the sync pattern cannot then be generated accidentally.

Ancillary data are always prefaced by a different four-symbol TRS which is the inverse of the video TRS in that it starts with all zeros and then has two symbols of all ones followed by the information symbol. See Section 4.22 for details of embedded audio in SDI.

4.16 The composite digital parallel interface

Composite digital samples at four times subcarrier frequency, and so there will be major differences between the standards. Whilst the component interface transmits only active lines and special sync patterns, the composite interfaces carry the entire composite waveform: syncs, burst and active line. Although ancillary data may be placed in sync tip, the rising and falling sync edges must be present. In the absence of ancillary data, the data on the parallel interface is essentially the continuous stream of samples from a converter which is digitizing a normal analog composite signal. Virtually all that is necessary to return to the analog domain is to strip out ancillary data and substitute sync tip values prior to driving a DAC and a filter. One of the reasons for this different approach is that the sampling clock in composite video is subcarrier locked. The sample values during sync can change with ScH phase in NTSC and PAL and change with the position in the frame in PAL due to the 25 Hz component. It is simpler to convey sync sample values on the interface than to go to the trouble of re-creating them later.

The PAL and NTSC versions of the composite digital interface will be described separately. The electrical interface is the same for both, and was described in Section 4.13.

4.17 PAL interface

The coding range of PAL was specified in Section 3.12. In PAL, the composite digital interface samples at $4F_{sc}$ with sample phase aligned with burst phase. PAL burst swing results in burst phases of ±135 degrees, and samples are taken at these phases and at ±45 degrees, precisely half-way between the U and V axes. This sampling phase is easy to generate from burst and avoids premature clipping of chroma. It is most important that samples are taken exactly at the points specified, since any residual phase error in the sampling clock will cause the equivalent of a chroma phase error when samples from one source are added to samples from a different source in a switcher. A digital switcher can only add together pairs of samples from different inputs, but if these samples were not taken at the same instants with respect to their subcarriers, the samples represent different vectors and cannot be added.

Figure 4.27 shows how the sampling clock may be derived. The incoming sync is used to derive a burst gate, during which the samples of burst are analysed. If the clock is correctly phased, the sampled burst will give values of 380_{10} (95_{10}), 256_{10} (64_{10}), 128_{10} (32_{10}), 256_{10} (64_{10}), repeated, whereas if a phase error exists, the values at the burst crossings will be above or below 256_{10} (64_{10}). The difference between the sample values and blanking level can be used to drive a DAC which

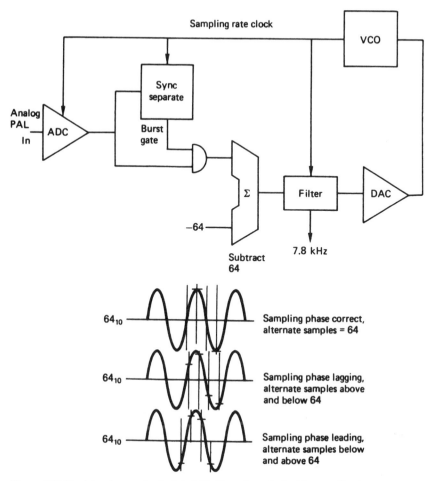

Figure 4.27 Obtaining the sample clock in PAL. The values obtained by sampling burst are analysed. When phase is correct, burst will be sampled at zero crossing and sample value will be 64_{10} or blanking level. If phase is wrong, sample will be above or below blanking. Filter must ignore alternate samples at burst peaks and shift one sample every line to allow for burst swing. It also averages over several burst crossings to reduce jitter. Filter output drives DAC and thus controls sampling clock VCO.

controls the sampling VCO. In this way any phase errors in the ADC are eliminated, because the sampling clock will automatically servo its phase to be identical to digital burst. Burst swing causes the burst peak and burst crossing samples to change places, so a phase comparison is always possible during burst. DC level shifts can be removed by using both positive and negative burst crossings and averaging the results. This also has the effect of reducing the effect of noise.

In PAL, the subcarrier frequency contains a 25 Hz offset, and so $4F_{sc}$ will contain a 100 Hz offset. The sampling rate is not h-coherent, and the sampling structure is not quite orthogonal. As subcarrier is given by:

$$F_{sc} = 283\frac{3}{4}F_h + F_v/2$$

the sampling rate will be given by:

$$F_s = 1135F_h + 2F_v$$

This results in 709 379 samples per frame, and there will not be a whole number of samples in a line. In practice, 1135 sample periods, numbered 0 to 1134, are defined as one digital line, with an additional 2 sample periods per field which are included by having 1137 samples, numbered 0 to 1136, in lines 313 and 625. Figure 4.28(a) shows the sample numbering scheme for an entire line. Note that the sample numbering begins at 0 at the start of the digital active line

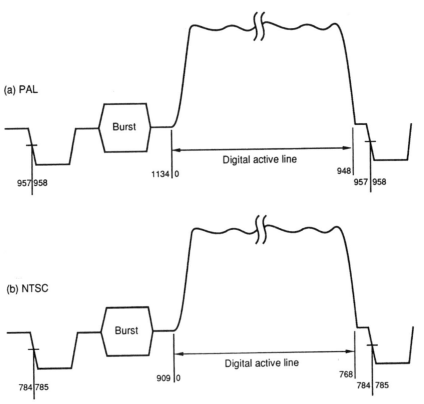

Figure 4.28 (a) Sample numbering in digital PAL. There are defined to be 1135 sample periods per line of which 948 are the digital active line. This is longer than the analog active line. Two lines per frame have two extra samples to compensate for the 25 Hz offset in subcarrier. NTSC is shown in (b). Here there are 910 samples per line of which 768 are the digital active line.

so that the horizontal blanking area is near the end of the digital line and the sample numbers will be large. The digital active line is 948 samples long and is longer than the analog active line. This allows the digital active line to move with 25 Hz whilst ensuring the entire analog active line is still conveyed.

Since sampling is not h-coherent, the position of sync pulses will change relative to the sampling points from line to line. The relationship can also be changed by the ScH phase of the analog input. Zero ScH is defined as coincidence between sync and zero degrees of subcarrier phase at line one of field one. Since composite digital samples on burst phase, not on subcarrier phase, the definition of zero ScH will be as shown in Figure 4.29, where it will be seen that two samples occur at exactly equal distances either side of the 50 per cent sync point. If the input is not zero ScH, the samples conveying sync will have different values. Measurement of these values will allow ScH phase to be computed. In a DVTR installation, non-standard ScH is only a problem on the

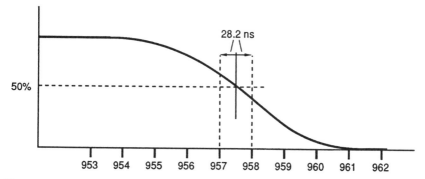

Figure 4.29 As PAL is sampled half-way between the colour axes, sample sites will fall either side of 50 per cent sync at the zero ScH measurement line.

initial conversion from analog because composite DVTRs do not record sync, and will regenerate zero ScH syncs on replay. If non-zero ScH is input to a DVTR the output will be shifted horizontally on playback. Many composite digital VTRs are less tolerant of ScH phase variation than analog machines.

4.18 NTSC interface

Although they have some similarities, PAL and NTSC are quite different when analysed at the digital sample level. The coding range was specified in Section 3.12. Subcarrier in NTSC has an exact half-line offset, so there will be an integer number of cycles of subcarrier in two lines. F_{sc} is simply $227.5F_h$, and as sampling is at $4F_{sc}$, there will be $227.5 \times 4 = 910$ samples per line period, and the sampling will be orthogonal. Figure 4.28(b) shows that the digital active line consists of 768 samples numbered 0 to 767. Horizontal blanking follows the digital active line in sample numbers 768 to 909.

The sampling phase is chosen to facilitate encoding and decoding in the digital domain. In NTSC there is a phase shift of 123 degrees between subcarrier and the I axis. As burst is gated, inverted, subcarrier there is a phase shift of 57 degrees between burst and the I axis (see Section 2.8). Composite digital NTSC does not sample in phase with burst, but on the I and Q axes at 57, 147, 237 and 327 degrees with respect to burst.

Figure 4.30 shows how this approach works in relation to sync and burst. Zero ScH is defined as zero degrees of subcarrier at the 50 per cent point on sync, but the 57 degree sampling phase means that the sync edge is actually sampled 25.6 ns ahead of, and 44.2 ns after, the 50 per cent point. Similarly, when the burst is reached, the phase shift means that burst sample values (in an 8 bit system) will be 46_{10}, 83_{10}, 74_{10} and 37_{10} repeating. The phase locked loop which produces the sampling clock will digitally compare the samples of burst with the values given here. Since it is not sampling burst at a zero crossing, the slope will be slightly less, so the gain of the phase error detector will also be less, and more prone to burst noise than in the PAL process. The phase error can, however, be averaged over several burst samples to overcome this problem.

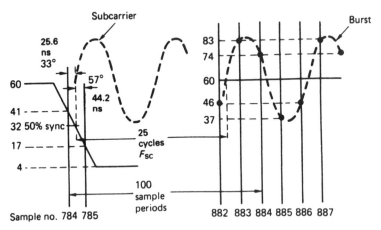

Figure 4.30 NTSC ScH phase. Sampling is not performed in phase with burst as in PAL, but on the I and Q axes. Since in NTSC there is a phase angle of 57 degrees between burst and I, this will also be the phase at which burst samples should be taken. If ScH phase is zero, then phase of subcarrier taken at 50% sync will be zero, and the samples will be taken 33 degrees before and 57 degrees after sync; 25 cycles of subcarrier or 100 samples later, during burst, the sample values will be obtained. Note that in NTSC burst is inverted subcarrier, so sample 785 is positive, but sample 885 is negative.

As in PAL, if the analog input does not have zero ScH phase, the sync pulse values will change, but burst values will not. As in PAL, NTSC DVTRs do not record syncs or burst, and will regenerate burst and zero ScH syncs on replay.

4.19 Serial interfacing

Serial digital interfaces use the same transmission line principles which were introduced in Section 4.4. In principle there is no difference between an analog and a digital signal. The difference is solely in the way in which the signals are interpreted. In a digital system the received signal is interpreted as discrete data, whereas in an analog system the signal is continuous. The cable does not know what interpretation will be put on the signal it carries. Consequently a square pulse representing data may be sent down a cable, but it will not be square on arrival.

A perfectly square pulse contains an indefinite series of harmonics, but the higher ones suffer progressively more loss. A square pulse at the driver becomes less and less square with distance, as Figure 4.31 shows. The harmonics are progressively lost until in the extreme case all that is left is the fundamental. A transmitted square wave is received as a sine wave. Fortunately data can still be recovered from the fundamental signal component.

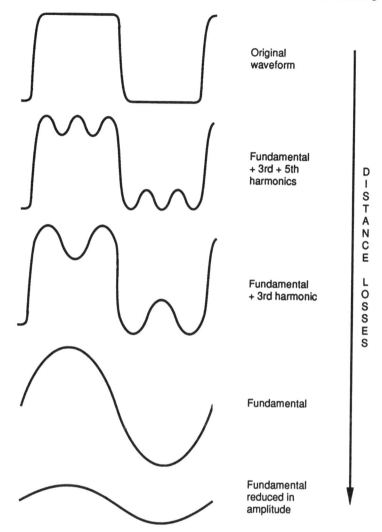

Figure 4.31 A signal may be square at the transmitter, but losses increase with frequency and as the signal propagates, more of the harmonics are lost until only the fundamental remains. The amplitude of the fundamental then falls with further distance.

Once all the harmonics have been lost, further losses cause the amplitude of the fundamental to fall. The effect worsens with distance and it is necessary to ensure that data recovery is still possible from a signal of unpredictable level.

Figure 4.32 shows that an initial step in data recovery at the receiver is the slicing process. The received signal voltage is compared with the mid-way voltage, known as the baseline or slicing level, using a comparator. If the signal voltage is above the baseline, the comparator outputs a high level; if below, a low level results.

In Figure 4.32(a) the signal to be sliced was transmitted with an uneven duty cycle. The DC component, or average level, of the signal is received with high amplitude, but the pulse amplitude falls as the pulse gets shorter. Eventually the waveform cannot be sliced.

In Figure 4.32(b) the opposite duty cycle is shown. The signal level drifts to the opposite polarity and once more slicing is impossible. The phenomenon is called baseline wander and will be observed with any signal whose average voltage is not the same as the slicing level.

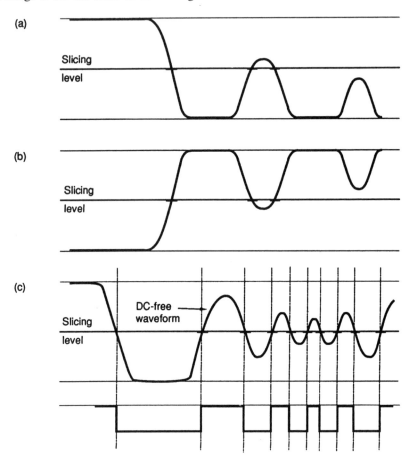

Figure 4.32 Slicing a signal which has suffered losses works well if the duty cycle is even. If the duty cycle is uneven, as in (a), timing errors will become worse until slicing fails. With the opposite duty cycle, the slicing fails in the opposite direction as (b). If, however, the signal is DC free, correct slicing can continue even in the presence of serious losses, as (c) shows.

In Figure 4.32(c) it will be seen that if the transmitted waveform has a relatively constant average voltage, slicing remains possible up to high frequencies even in the presence of serious loss, because the received waveform remains symmetrical about the baseline.

It is clearly not possible to simply serialize data in a shift register for so-called direct transmission, because successful slicing can only be obtained if the number of ones is equal to the number of zeros; there is little chance of this happening consistently with real data.

Instead, a modulation code or channel code is necessary. This converts the data into a waveform which is DC-free or nearly so for the purpose of transmission.

In digital circuitry the signals are generally accompanied by a separate clock signal. A further problem with transmission is that provision of a separate clock is not feasible except over short distances. A separate clock line would not only raise cost, but is impractical because at high frequency it is virtually impossible to ensure that the clock cable propagates signals at the same speed as the data cable. Propagation speed differences are called skew.

In certain serial digital video interfaces, the bit rate is 270 Mbits/sec. Each bit lasts for 3.7 ns. Assuming a 100 metre cable, there will be around 70 bits actually in the cable. If there were a separate clock, there would be roughly the same number of cycles in the clock cable, but no guarantee that they would propagate at the same speed or arrive in phase.

The solution is to use a self-clocking waveform. A further essential function of the channel code is to create a waveform which carries its own clock content. Clearly direct transmission does not have this characteristic. If all the data bits are the same, for example all zeros, there is no clock when they are serialized.

The characteristics of most transmission lines are that signal loss occurs which increases with frequency. This has the effect of slowing down rise times and thereby sloping off edges. If a signal with sloping edges is sliced, the time at which the waveform crosses the slicing level will be changed, and this causes jitter which will be exaggerated in the presence of baseline wander.

On a long cable, high frequency roll-off can cause sufficient jitter to move a transition into an adjacent bit period. This is called intersymbol interference and the effect becomes worse in signals which have greater asymmetry, i.e. short pulses alternating with long ones. The effect can be reduced by the application of equalization, which is typically a high frequency boost, and by choosing a channel code which has restricted asymmetry.

Ideally equalization ought to be applied at the transmitting end of a cable as this would result in better noise figures than if the equalization were applied at the receiver. Unfortunately it is not generally possible to know how much equalization to apply at the transmitter and so in practice equalization is done at the receiver. The adjustment may be manual or, in more recent equipment, automatic. If the spectrum of the coded signal is fairly constant, it is possible to assess the degree of equalization necessary by comparing the signal level at two different frequencies.

The squared-up waveform at the output of the slicer will be a replica of the transmitted waveform, except for the addition of jitter or time uncertainty in the position of the edges due to noise, baseline wander, intersymbol interference and imperfect equalization. In the same way that binary circuits reject noise by using two voltage levels which are spaced further apart than the uncertainty due to noise, digital transmission combats time uncertainty by using events, known as transitions, spaced apart at integer multiples of some basic time period, called a detent, which is larger than the typical time uncertainty. Figure 4.33 shows how this jitter-rejection mechanism works.

As ideal transitions occur at multiples of a basic period, an oscilloscope, which is repeatedly triggered on a channel coded signal carrying random data, will show an eye pattern if connected to the output of the equalizer. Study of the eye pattern reveals how well the coding used suits the channel. With a short cable, the losses will be small, and the eye opening will be virtually square except for some

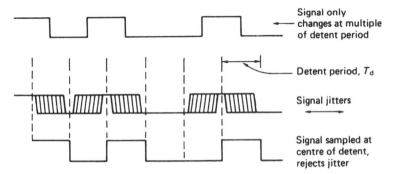

Figure 4.33 A certain amount of jitter can be rejected by changing the signal at multiples of the basic detent period T_{d}.

edge sloping due to cable capacitance. As cable length increases, the harmonics are lost and the remaining fundamental gives the eyes a diamond shape. Noise closes the eyes in a vertical direction, and jitter closes the eyes in a horizontal direction, as in Figure 4.34. If the eyes remain sensibly open, this will be possible. Clearly more jitter can be tolerated if there is less noise, and vice versa. If the equalizer is adjustable, the optimum setting will be where the greatest eye opening is obtained.

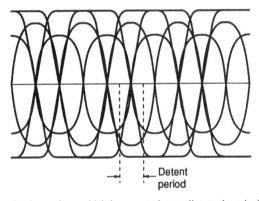

Figure 4.34 A transmitted waveform which is generated according to the principle of Figure 4.33 will appear like this on an oscilloscope as successive parts of the waveform are superimposed on the tube. When the waveform is rounded off by losses, diamond-shaped eyes are left in the centre, spaced apart by the detent period.

In the centre of the eyes, at regular intervals, the receiver must make binary decisions about the state of the signal, high or low, using the slicer output. The receiver is in fact sampling the output of the slicer, and it needs to have a sampling clock in order to do that. The clock edges which operate the sampler must be in the centre of the eyes.

A fixed frequency clock would be of no use as, even if it was sufficiently stable, it would not know what phase to run at. The only way in which the sampling clock can be obtained is to use a phase locked loop to regenerate it from the clock content of the self-clocking channel coded waveform. In phase locked loops, the voltage-controlled oscillator is driven by a phase error measured between the output and some reference, such that the oscillator eventually runs at the same frequency as the reference. If a divider is placed between the VCO and the phase comparator, as in Figure 4.35, the VCO frequency can be made to be a multiple of the reference. This also has the effect of making the loop more heavily damped. If a channel coded waveform is used as a reference to a PLL, the loop will be able to make a phase comparison whenever a transition arrives, but when there are several detents between transitions, the loop will flywheel at the last known frequency and phase until it can rephase at a subsequent transition. Once the loop is locked, clock edges will be phased with the average

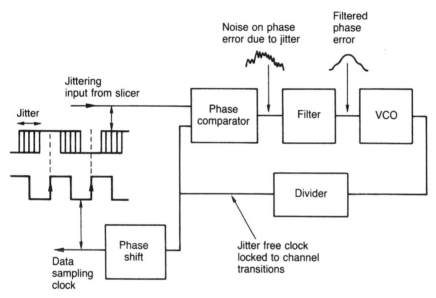

Figure 4.35 In a phase-locked loop data receiver the VCO frequency is synchronized to the clock content of the transmitted waveform so the clock can continue when transitions are omitted to send data. The filter in the phase error removes jitter from the VCO. A suitable phase shift produces sampling edges which are used to measure the incoming signal level between transitions so that jitter is rejected.

phase of the jittering edges of the input waveform. If, for example, falling edges of the clock are phased to input transitions, then rising edges will be in the centre of the eyes and can be used to operate the sampling process in such a way that the maximum jitter is rejected. Cycles of the VCO can be counted to measure the number of detents between transitions and hence to decode the information. Figure 4.36 illustrates this mechanism.

Clearly data cannot be separated if the PLL is not locked, but it cannot be locked until it has seen transitions for a reasonable period. In recorders, which have discontinuous recorded blocks to allow editing, the solution is to precede each data block with a pattern of transitions whose sole purpose is to provide a timing reference for synchronizing the phase locked loop. This pattern is known

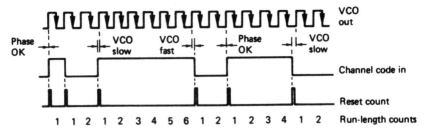

Figure 4.36 In order to reconstruct the channel patterns, a phase-locked loop is fed with the channel code and freewheels between transitions, correcting its phase at each one. Counting the low-going VCO edges between transitions reconstructs the channel bits. If the data rate changes the VCO will track. If the maximum run length is too long, the VCO will not be able to phase-correct often enough and may miscount channel bits in the presence of jitter.

as a preamble. In interfaces, the transmission can be continuous and there is no difficulty remaining in lock indefinitely. There will simply be a short delay on first applying the signal before the receiver locks to it.

It is important for reliable data reception that the phase locked loop in a receiver is correctly centred. This means that the free running frequency of the oscillator is very close to the frequency at which it will run when the loop is locked. If the VCO is not centred, a static control voltage will be required to pull it back to the correct frequency. This can only be obtained with a static phase error. This phase error means that the incoming waveform is not being sampled in the centres of the eyes, but with an offset, resulting in the ability to reject jitter being impaired.

In summary, it is not practicable simply to serialize raw data in a shift register for the purpose of transmission except over relatively short distances. Practical systems require the use of a modulation scheme, known as a channel code, which expresses the data as waveforms which are self-clocking in order to reject jitter,

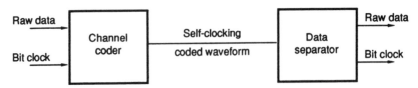

Figure 4.37 Channel coding requires a coder at the transmitter which combines a bit clock with the serial data to produce a channel-coded waveform. The receiver has a data separator which extracts the clock content of the waveform and decodes it to serial data.

separate the received bits and to avoid skew on separate clock lines. The coded waveforms should further be DC-free or nearly so to enable slicing in the presence of losses and have a narrower spectrum than the raw data to make equalization possible.

Figure 4.37 shows that a channel coder is necessary prior to the record stage, and that a decoder, known as a data separator, is necessary after the replay stage.

4.20 Serial digital interface (SDI)

The interface described here has been developed to allow up to ten-bit samples of component or composite digital video to be communicated serially. The interface allows ancillary data including conveyance of AES/EBU digital audio channels.

SDI uses a coding technique known as convolutional randomizing, which is simpler to implement in a cable installation because no separate synchronizing of the randomizing is needed.

In convolutional randomizing, the signal sent down the channel is the serial data waveform which has been convolved with the impulse response of a digital filter. On reception the signal is deconvolved to restore the original data. Figure 4.38(a) shows that the filter is an infinite-impulse response (IIR) filter which has recursive paths from the output back to the input. As it is a one-bit filter its output cannot decay, and, once excited, it runs indefinitely. The filter is followed by a transition generator which consists of a one-bit delay and an exclusive-or gate. An input 1 results in an output transition on the next clock edge. An input 0 results in no transition.

A result of the infinite impulse response of the filter is that frequent transitions are generated in the channel which result in sufficient clock content for the phase locked loop in the receiver.

Transitions are converted back to ones by a differentiator in the receiver. This consists of a one-bit delay with an exclusive-or gate comparing the input and the output. When a transition passes through the delay, the input and the output will be different and the gate outputs a 1 which enters the deconvolution circuit.

Figure 4.38(b) shows that in the deconvolution circuit a data bit is simply the exclusive-or of a number of channel bits at a fixed spacing. The deconvolution is implemented with a shift register having the exclusive-or gates connected in a reverse pattern to that in the encoder. The same effect as block randomizing is obtained, in that long runs are broken up and the DC content is reduced, but it has the advantage over block randomizing that no synchronizing is required to remove the randomizing, although it will still be necessary for deserialization.

It is a characteristic of the convolutional code described that if a bit in the channel (i.e. the cable) is corrupted, then it will cause more than one bit of data to be incorrect. This is known as error propagation. In the case of SDI, up to five data bits can be corrupted by a single channel error and so there is a strong possibility that errors will be visible.

Convolutional codes are also prone to data bit sequences which happen to replicate the feedback sequence at the input gate of the encoder. This results in a long run-length on the cable without transitions and makes it difficult for the receiving PLO to stay in lock, hence the term pathological sequence. Whilst pathological sequences are relatively rare in real programme material, they can be generated deliberately by reliability test equipment in order to stress equipment beyond its service conditions.

SDI operates with cable losses up to 30 dB. The losses increase with frequency and so the video standard in use and the grade of cable employed both affect the maximum distance which the signal will safely travel. Figure 4.39 gives some examples of cable lengths which can be used.

The components necessary for a composite serial link are shown in Figure 4.40. Parallel component or composite data having a wordlength of up to 10 bits

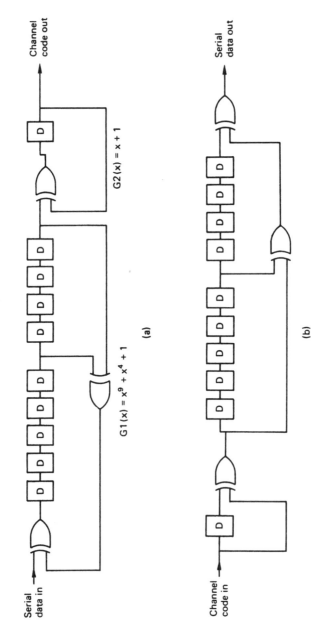

Figure 4.38 (a) A convolutional randomizing encoder transmits exclusive OR of 3 bits at a fixed spacing in the data. The 1 bit delay, far right, produces channel transitions from data ones. (b) The decoder has an opposing 1 bit delay to return from transitions to data levels, followed by an opposing shift register which exactly reverses the coding process.

form the input. These are fed to a 10 bit shift register which is clocked at ten times the input rate, which will be 360 MHz, 270 MHz or $40F_{sc}$. If there are only eight bits in the input words, the missing bits are forced to zero for transmission except for the all ones condition which will be forced to ten ones. The serial data emerge from the shift register LSB first and are then passed through the scrambler, in which a given bit is converted to the exclusive-or of itself and two bits which are five and nine clocks ahead. This is followed by another stage, which converts channel ones into transitions. The resulting logic level signal is converted to a waveform which is symmetrical about ground and has an amplitude of 800 mV pk–pk across a 75 Ω load. This signal can be fed down 75 Ω coaxial cable using BNC connectors. SDI is restricted to point-to-point links. Serial receivers contain correct termination which is permanently present and passive loop-through is not recommended. No attempt should be made to drive more than one load using T-pieces as this will result in signal reflections which seriously compromise the data integrity.

System	Clock	Fundamental	Crash knee length	Practical length
NTSC Composite	143 MHz	71.5 MHz	400 m	320 m
PAL Composite	177 MHz	88.5 MHz	360 m	290 m
Component 601	270 MHz	135 MHz	290 m	230 m
Component 16:9	360 MHz	180 MHz	210 m	170 m
CABLE: BICC TM3205, PSF1/2, BELDEN 8281 or any cable with a loss of 8.7 dB/100 m at 100 MHz				

Figure 4.39 Suggested maximum cable lengths as a function of cable type and data rate to give a loss of no more than 30 dB. It is unwise to exceed these lengths due to the 'crash knee' characteristic of SDI.

The scrambling process at the transmitter spreads the signal spectrum and makes that spectrum reasonably constant and independent of the picture content. It is possible to assess the degree of equalization necessary by comparing the energy in a low frequency band with that in higher frequencies. The greater the disparity, the more equalization is needed. Thus fully automatic cable equalization at the receiver is easily achieved. The receiver must generate a bit clock at 360 MHz, 270 MHz or $40F_{sc}$ from the input signal, and this clock drives the input sampler and slicer which converts the cable waveform back to serial binary. The local bit clock also drives a circuit which simply reverses the scrambling at the transmitter. The first stage returns transitions to ones, and the second stage is a mirror image of the encoder which reverses the exclusive-or calculation to output the original data. Since transmission is serial, it is necessary to obtain word synchronization, so that correct descrialization can take place.

In the component parallel input, the *SAV* and *EAV* TRS patterns are present and the all ones and all zeros bit patterns these contain can be detected in the shift

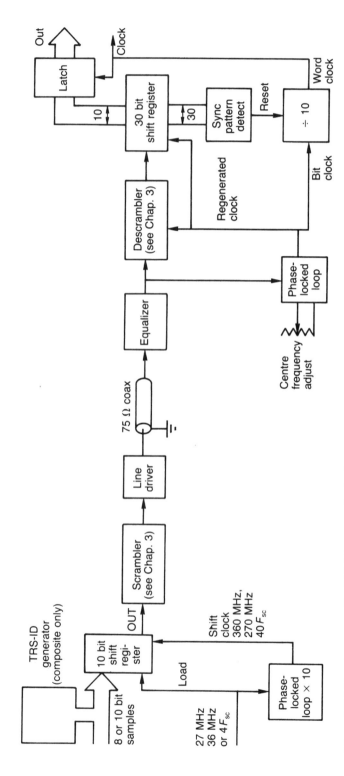

Figure 4.40 Major components of an SDI link; see text for details.

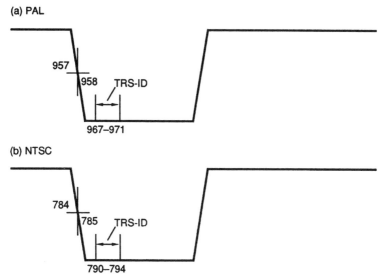

Figure 4.41 In composite digital it is necessary to insert a sync pattern during analog sync tip to ensure correct deserialization. The location of TRS-ID is shown in (a) for PAL and in (b) for NTSC.

register and used to teach the deserializer the location of word boundaries in the transmission.

In the composite parallel interface signal, there are no digital sync patterns and it is necessary to create an equivalent which can be inserted at the serializer and subsequently stripped out at a serial-to-parallel converter. The Timing Reference and Identification Signal (TRS-ID) is added during blanking, and the receiver can detect the patterns which it contains. TRS-ID consists of five words which are inserted just after the leading edge of video sync. Figure 4.41(a) shows the location of TRS-ID at samples 967–971 in PAL and Figure 4.41(b) shows the location at samples 790–794 in NTSC.

Out of the five words in TRS-ID, the first four are for synchronizing, and consist of a single word of all ones, followed by three words of all zeros. Note

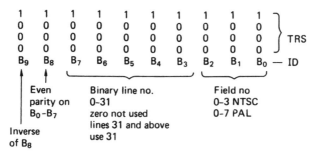

Figure 4.42 The contents of the TRS-ID pattern which is added to the transmission during the horizontal sync pulse just after the leading edge. The field number conveys the composite colour framing field count, and the line number carries a restricted line count intended to give vertical positioning information during the vertical interval. This count saturates at 31 for lines of that number and above.

that the composite TRS contains an extra word of zeros compared to the component TRS and this could be used for signal identification in multistandard devices. The fifth word is for identification, and carries the line and field numbering information shown in Figure 4.42. The field numbering is colour framing information which is useful for editing. In PAL the field numbering will go from zero to seven, whereas in NTSC it will only reach three.

On detection of the synchronizing symbols, a divide-by-ten circuit is reset, and the output of this will clock words out of the shift register at the correct times. This circuit will also provide the output word clock.

4.21 Digital video interfacing chipsets

Implementation of digital video systems is much easier now that specialized chips are available. Figure 4.43 shows a hypothetical 4:2:2 component system starting with analog signals and ending with the same to illustrate the processes which are necessary. The syncs on Y are separated and multiplied in a phase

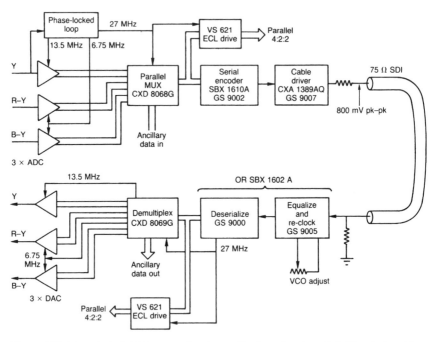

Figure 4.43 A hypothetical 4:2:2 system showing applications of various digital interfacing chips.

locked loop to produce a 27 MHz master clock. This is divided by 2 and by 4 to produce the sampling clocks for the converters. This results in three data streams, which can be multiplexed to form a parallel interface signal using a parallel encoder chip such as the Sony CXD8068G. This parallel signal may be output using a set of ECL line drivers. If it is required to convert the parallel signal to SDI, a serial encoder will be required. The Sony SBX1610A and the Gennum GS9002 contain all parallel-to-serial functions, but output logic level signals which require a CXA 1389AQ or a GS9007 cable driver to produce the 1.6 volt pk–pk SDI signal which will fall to the standard 0.8 volts after passing through the source terminating resistors.

At the receiving end of the cable the signal requires equalization, clock regeneration and deserializing. The Sony SBX1602A provides all of these functions in one device whereas the Gennum solution is to combine equalization and reclocking in the GS9005 and to perform deserialization in the GS9000. In both cases the output is parallel single-ended data which can be returned to the parallel interface specification using ECL drivers. Alternatively the parallel data may be sent directly to a parallel interface decoder such as the Sony CXD8069G which demultiplexes the 27 MHz data to provide separate outputs for driving three DACs.

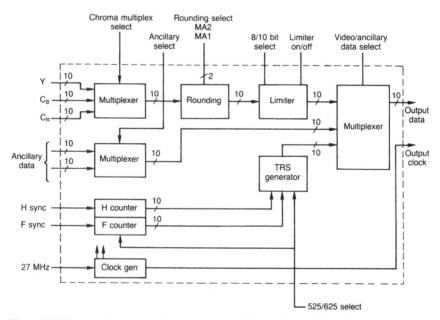

Figure 4.44 The three data streams from component ADCs can be multiplexed into the parallel interface format with the encoder chip shown here.

Figure 4.44 shows a block diagram of the CXD8068G parallel interface encoder. This accepts the parallel input from three component ADCs and multiplexes them to the 27 MHz parallel standard. The rounding process allows 10 bit inputs to be rounded to shorter wordlengths. The limiter prevents out-of-range analog signals from producing all ones or all zeros codes which are reserved for synchronizing. In addition to a 27 MHz clock derived from horizontal sync, the chip requires horizontal and frame drives to operate the timing counters which address the TRS generator. The final multiplexer selects TRS patterns, video data or ancillary data for the 10 bit parallel output.

Figure 4.45(a) shows the SBX1601A serial encoder and Figure 4.45(b) shows the GS9002 serial encoder. Of necessity these chips contain virtually identical processing. Parallel input data are clocked into the input latch by the parallel word clock which is multiplied in frequency by a factor of ten in a phase locked loop to provide a serial bit clock. There is provision for selecting several centre frequencies for composite or component applications. The data latch output is examined by logic which detects input sync patterns and extends 8 bit sync values to ten bits. The parallel data are then serialized in a shift register prior to passing through the scrambler and the transition generator.

Figure 4.46 shows an SDI cable driver chip. The device shown has quadruple outputs and is useful in applications such as distribution amplifiers. Note that each differential amplifier produces a pair of separate SDI outputs. The fact that these are mutually inverted is irrelevant as the SDI signal is not polarity conscious. Note the resistor networks which provide correct cable source termination.

Figure 4.47(a) shows the Gennum GS9005 reclocking receiver. This contains an automatic cable equalizer and a phase locked loop clock recovery circuit which drives a slicer/sampler which recovers the channel waveform to a logic level signal for subsequent descrambling in a separate device. The equalizer operates by estimating the cable length from the input amplitude and driving a voltage-controlled filter from the signal strength. A buffered eye pattern test point is provided. The equalizer output is DC-restored prior to slicing to ensure that the slicing takes place around the waveform centre line. The slicer output will be jittery and so a phase locked loop is used having a loop filter to reject the jitter. The jitter-free clock is used to drive the data latch which samples the slicer output

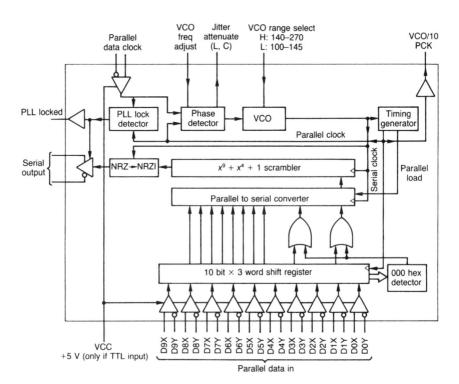

Figure 4.45(a) An SDI encoder chip from Sony; see text for details.

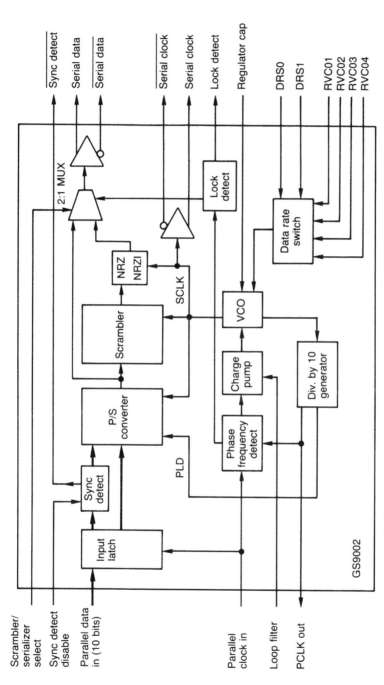

Figure 4.45(b) An SDI encoder chip from Gennum; see text for details.

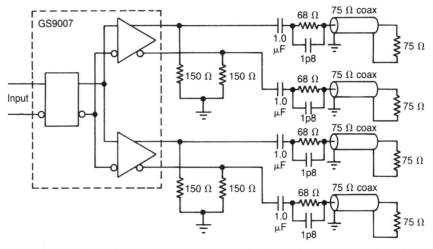

Figure 4.46 SDI cable driver chip provides correct 0.8 V signal level after source termination resistors.

between transitions. The VCO centre frequency can be selected from four values and provision is made for an adjusting potentiometer for each frequency.

Figure 4.47(b) shows the GS9000 serial decoder which complements the GS9005. This contains a descrambler and a serial-to-parallel converter which is synchronized by a sync detector which recognizes TRS in the shift register. The chip also contains an automatic standard detector which can output a two-bit standard code for external indication and to select the centre frequency of the GS9005. The single-ended parallel output can be converted to the differential parallel output standard by a multiple ECL driver such as a VS621.

Figure 4.48 shows the Sony SBX1602A which contains all of the serial receiving functions in one device. Its operation should be self-evident from the description of the Gennum devices above.

Parallel data can be demultiplexed for conversion to analog by the CXD8069G device shown in Figure 4.49 which also extracts ancillary data. The TRS detector identifies sync patterns and uses them to direct the ID word to the Hamming code error correction stage. This outputs corrected timing signals which are decoded to produce analog video timing drives. A FIFO (first in first out) buffer acts as a small timebase corrector to allow the DACs to be driven with a stable clock. Ten-bit video data may be rounded to shorter wordlengths if required, prior to demultiplexing into separate component outputs.

4.22 Embedded audio in SDI

In component SDI, there is provision for ancillary data packets to be sent during blanking. The high clock rate of component means that there is capacity for up to sixteen audio channels sent in four groups. Composite SDI has to convey the digitized analog sync edges and bursts and only sync tip is available for ancillary data. As a result of this and the lower clock rate composite has much less capacity for ancillary data than component although it is still possible to transmit one

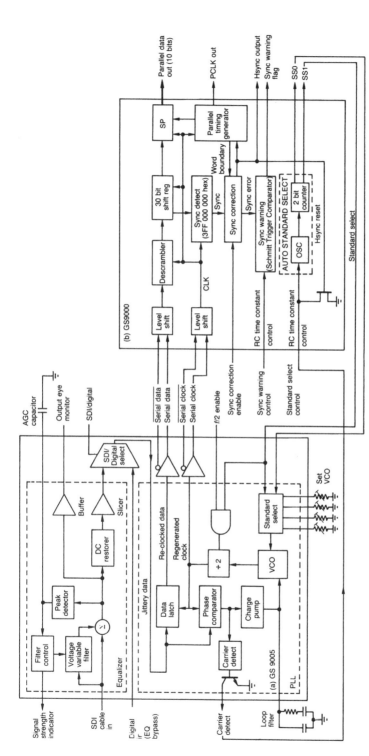

Figure 4.47 (a) Reclocking SDI receiver contains a cable equalizer and is an important building block for SDI routers as well as being the first stage of an SDI decoder. Decoder is shown in (b). Note auto standard sensing outputs which can select VCO frequency in the reclocker.

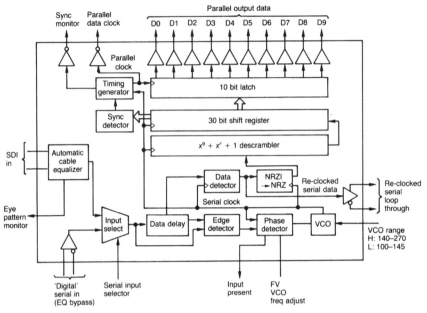

Figure 4.48 Sony SDI receiver chip for comparison with Figure 4.47.

audio data packet carrying four audio channels in one group. Figure 4.50(a) shows where the ancillary data may be located for PAL and Figure 4.50(b) shows the locations for NTSC.

As Figure 4.51 shows, the data content of the AES/EBU digital audio subframe consists of valid (V), user (U) and channel (C) status bits, a 20 bit sample and four auxiliary bits which optionally may be appended to the main sample to produce a 24 bit sample. The AES recommends sampling rates of 48, 44.1 and 32 kHz, but the interface permits variable sampling rates. SDI has various levels of support for the wide range of audio possibilities and these levels are defined in Figure 4.52. The default or minimum level is Level A which operates only with a video-synchronous 48 kHz sampling rate and transmits V, U, C and the main 20 bit sample only. As Level A is a default it need not be signalled to a receiver as the presence of IDs in the ancillary data is enough to ensure correct decoding. However, all other levels require an audio control packet to be transmitted to teach the receiver how to handle the embedded audio data. The audio control packet is transmitted once per field in the second horizontal ancillary space after the video switching point before any associated audio sample data. One audio control packet is required per group of audio channels.

If it is required to send 24 bit samples, the additional four bits of each sample are placed in extended data packets which must directly follow the associated group of audio samples in the same ancillary data space.

There are thus three kinds of packet used in embedded audio: the audio data packet which carries up to four channels of digital audio, the extended data packet and the audio control packet.

In component systems, ancillary data begin with a reversed TRS or sync pattern. Normal video receivers will not detect this pattern and so ancillary data cannot be

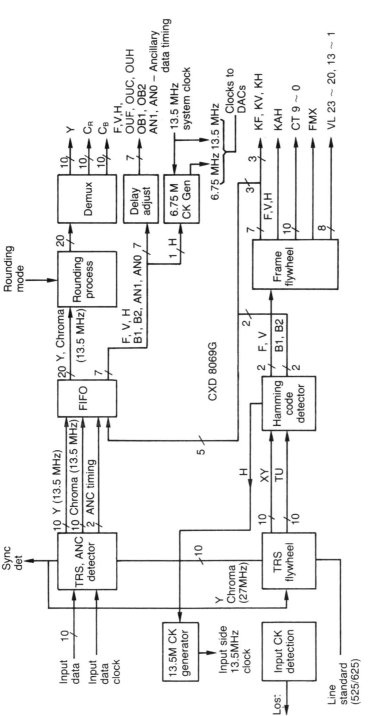

Figure 4.49 This device demultiplexes component data to drive separate DACs for each component as well as stripping out ancillary data.

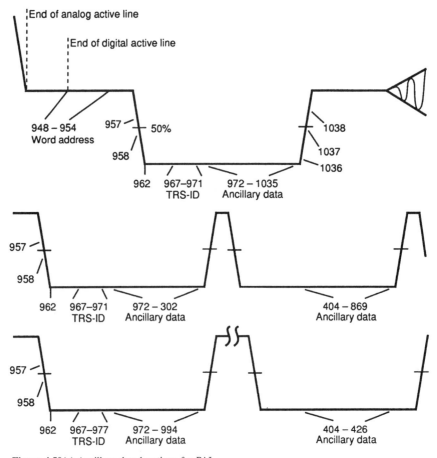

Figure 4.50(a) Ancillary data locations for PAL.

mistaken for video samples. The ancillary data TRS consists of all zeros followed by all ones twice. There is no separate TRS for ancillary data in composite. Immediately following the usual TRS, there will be an ancillary data flag whose value must be $3FC_{16}$. Following the ancillary TRS or data flag is a data ID word which contains one of a number of standardized codes which tell the receiver how to interpret the ancillary packet. Figure 4.53 shows a list of ID codes for various types of packets. Next come the data block number and the data block count parameters. The data block number increments by 1 on each instance of a block with a given ID number. On reaching 255 it overflows and recommences counting. Next, a data count parameter specifies how many symbols of data are being sent in this block. Typical values for the data count are 36_{10} for a small packet and 48_{10} for a large packet. These parameters help an audio extractor to assemble contiguous data relating to a given set of audio channels.

Figure 4.54 shows the structure of the audio data packing. In order to prevent accidental generation of reserved synchronizing patterns, bit 9 is the inverse of bit 8 so the effective system wordlength is 9 bits. Three 9 bit symbols are used

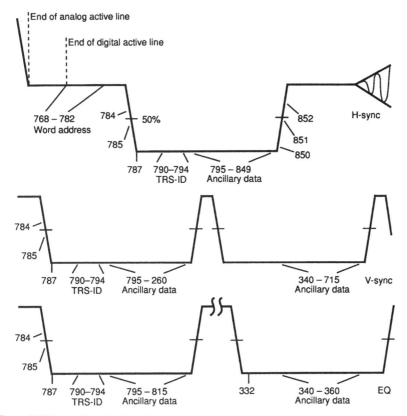

Figure 4.50(b) Ancillary data locations for NTSC.

to convey all of the AES/EBU subframe data except for the four auxiliary bits. Since four audio channels can be conveyed, there are two 'Ch' or channel number bits which specify the audio channel number to which the subframe belongs. A further bit, Z, specifies the beginning of the 192 sample channel status message. V, U and C have the same significance as in the normal AES/EBU standard, but the P bit reflects parity on the three 9 bit symbols rather than the AES/EBU definition. The three-word sets representing an audio sample will then

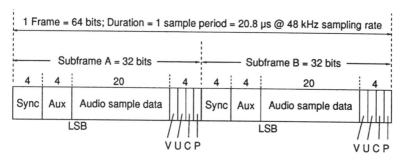

Figure 4.51 Format of the standard two-channel audio interface frame.

	A (Default)	Synchronous 48 kHz, 20 bit audio, 48 sample buffer
	B	Synchronous 48 kHz for composite video. 64 sample buffer to receive
		20 bits from 24 bit data
	C	Synchronous 48 kHz 24 bit with extended packets
	D	Asynchronous audio
	E	44.1 kHz audio
	F	32 kHz audio
	G	32–48 kHz variable sampling rate
	H	Audio frame sequence
	I	Time delay tracking
	J	Non-coincident channel status Z bits in a pair

Needs audio control packet

Figure 4.52 The different levels of implementation of embedded audio. Level A is default.

	Group 1	Group 2	Group 3	Group 4
Audio data	2FF	1FD	1FB	2F9
Audio CTL	1EF	2EE	2ED	1EC
Ext. data	1FE	2FC	2FA	1F8

Figure 4.53 The different packet types have different ID codes as shown here.

Address / Bit	x3	x3 + 1	x3 + 2
B9	$\overline{B8}$	$\overline{B8}$	$\overline{B8}$
B8	A (2^5)	A (2^{14})	P
B7	A (2^4)	A (2^{13})	C
B6	A (2^3)	A (2^{12})	U
B5	A (2^2)	A (2^{11})	V
B4	A (2^1)	A (2^{10})	A MSB (2^{19})
B3	A LSB (2^0)	A (2^9)	A (2^{18})
B2	CH (MSB)	A (2^8)	A (2^{17})
B1	CH (LSB)	A (2^7)	A (2^{16})
B0	Z	A (2^6)	A (2^{15})

Figure 4.54 AES/EBU data for one audio sample is sent as three 9 bit symbols. A = audio sample. Bit Z = AES/EBU channel status block start bit.

be repeated for the remaining three channels in the packet but with different combinations of the Ch bits.

One audio sample in each of the four channels of a group requires twelve video sample periods and so packets will contain multiples of twelve samples. At the end of the packet a checksum is calculated on the entire packet contents.

If 24 bit samples are required, extended data packets must be employed in which the additional four bits of each audio sample in an AES/EBU frame are assembled in pairs according to Figure 4.55. Thus for every twelve symbols conveying the four 20 bit audio samples of one group in an audio data packet two extra symbols will be required in an extended data packet.

The audio control packet structure is shown in Figure 4.56. Following the usual header are symbols representing the audio frame number, the sampling rate,

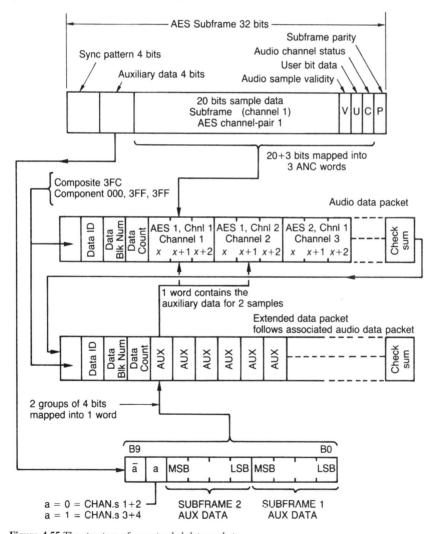

Figure 4.55 The structure of an extended data packet.

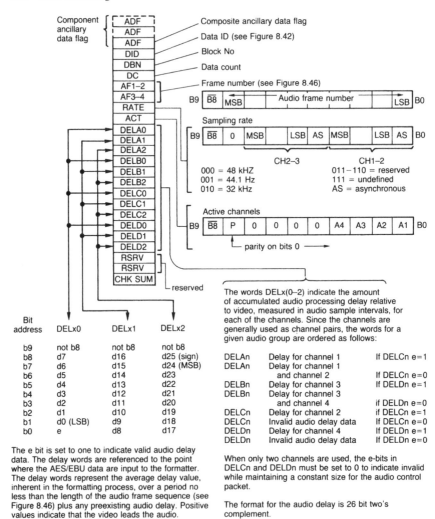

The words DELx(0–2) indicate the amount of accumulated audio processing delay relative to video, measured in audio sample intervals, for each of the channels. Since the channels are generally used as channel pairs, the words for a given audio group are ordered as follows:

DELAn	Delay for channel 1	If DELCn e = 1
DELAn	Delay for channel 1 and channel 2	If DELCn e = 0
DELBn	Delay for channel 3	If DELDn e = 1
DELBn	Delay for channel 3 and channel 4	if DELDn e = 0
DELCn	Delay for channel 2	if DELCn e = 1
DELCn	Invalid audio delay data	If DELCn e = 0
DELDn	Delay for channel 4	If DELDn e = 1
DELDn	Invalid audio delay data	If DELDn e = 0

Bit address	DELx0	DELx1	DELx2
b9	not b8	not b8	not b8
b8	d7	d16	d25 (sign)
b7	d6	d15	d24 (MSB)
b6	d5	d14	d23
b5	d4	d13	d22
b4	d3	d12	d21
b3	d2	d11	d20
b2	d1	d10	d19
b1	d0 (LSB)	d9	d18
b0	e	d8	d17

The e bit is set to one to indicate valid audio delay data. The delay words are referenced to the point where the AES/EBU data are input to the formatter. The delay words represent the average delay value, inherent in the formatting process, over a period no less than the length of the audio frame sequence (see Figure 8.46) plus any preexisting audio delay. Positive values indicate that the video leads the audio.

When only two channels are used, the e-bits in DELCn and DELDn must be set to 0 to indicate invalid while maintaining a constant size for the audio control packet.

The format for the audio delay is 26 bit two's complement.

Figure 4.56 The structure of an audio control packet.

the active channels, the processing delay and some reserved symbols. The sampling rate parameter allows the two AES/EBU channel pairs in a group to have different sampling rates if required. The active channel parameter simply describes which channels in a group carry meaningful audio data. The processing delay parameter denoted the delay the audio has experienced measured in audio sample periods. The parameter is a 26 bit two's complement number requiring three symbols for each channel. Since the four audio channels in a group are generally channel pairs, only two delay parameters are needed. However, if four independent channels are used, one parameter each will be required. The e bit denotes whether four individual channels or two pairs are being transmitted.

The frame number parameter comes about in 525 line systems because the frame rate is 29.97 Hz not 60 Hz. The resultant frame period does not contain a whole number of audio samples. An integer ratio is only obtained over a multiple frame sequence which is shown in Figure 4.57. The frame number conveys the position in the frame sequence. At 48 kHz odd frames hold 1602 samples and even frames hold 1601 samples in a five-frame sequence. At 44.1 and 32 kHz the relationship is not so simple and to obtain the correct number of samples in the sequence certain frames (exceptions) have the number of samples altered. At 44.1 kHz the frame sequence is 100 frames long whereas at 32 kHz it is 15 frames long. As the two channel pairs in a group can have different sampling rates, two frame parameters are required per group. In 50 Hz systems all three sampling rates allow an integer number of samples per frame and so the frame number is irrelevant.

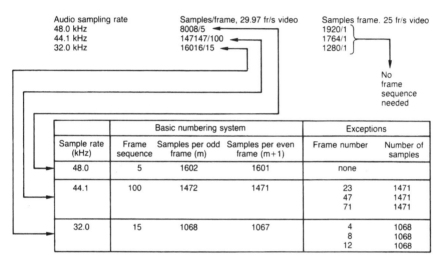

Figure 4.57 The origin of the frame sequences in 525 line systems.

As the ancillary data transfer is in bursts, it is necessary to provide a little RAM buffering at both ends of the link to allow real time audio samples to be time-compressed up to the video bit rate at the input and expanded back again at the receiver. Figure 4.58 shows a typical audio insertion unit in which the FIFO buffers can be seen. In such a system all that matters is that the average audio data rate is correct. Instantaneously there can be timing errors within the range of the buffers. Audio data cannot be embedded at the video switch point or in the areas reserved for EDH packets, but provided that data are evenly spread throughout the frame 20 bit audio can be embedded and retrieved with about 48 audio samples of buffering. If the additional four bits per sample are sent this requirement rises to 64 audio samples. The buffering stages cause the audio to be delayed with respect to the video by a few milliseconds at each insertion. Whilst this is not serious, Level I allows a delay tracking mode which allows the embedding logic to transmit the encoding delay so a subsequent receiver can compute the overall delay. If the range of the buffering is exceeded for any reason, such as a non-synchronous audio sampling rate fed to a Level A encoder, audio samples are periodically skipped or repeated in order to bring the delay under control.

It is permitted for receivers which can only handle 20 bit audio to discard the 4 bit sample extension data. However, the presence of the extension data requires more buffering in the receiver. A device having a buffer of only 48 samples for Level A working could experience an overflow due to the presence of the extension data.

In 48 kHz working, the average number of audio samples per channel is just over three per video line. In order to maintain the correct average audio sampling rate, the number of samples sent per line is variable and not specified in the standard. In practice a transmitter generally switches between packets containing three samples and packets containing four samples per channel per line as required to keep the buffers from overflowing. At lower sampling rates either smaller packets can be sent or packets can be omitted from certain lines.

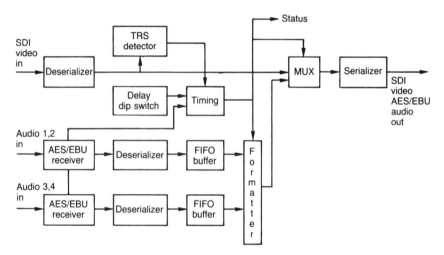

Figure 4.58 A typical audio insertion unit; see text for details.

As a result of the switching, ancillary data packets in component video occur mostly in two sizes. The larger packet is 55 words in length, of which 48 words are data. The smaller packet contains 43 words of which 36 are data. There is space for two large packets or three small packets in the horizontal blanking between *EAV* and *SAV*.

A typical embedded audio extractor is shown in Figure 4.59. The extractor recognizes the ancillary data TRS or flag and then decodes the ID to determine the content of the packet. The group and channel addresses are then used to direct extracted symbols to the appropriate audio channel. A FIFO memory is used to timebase expand the symbols to the correct audio sampling rate.

4.23 Digital video routing

Digital routers have the advantage that they need cause no loss of signal quality as they simply pass on a series of numbers. Analog routers inevitably suffer from crosstalk and noise however well made, and this reduces signal quality on every pass.

Routers are available for serial and parallel formats. The parallel video output signal is cheaper to produce as most equipment has parallel format internally. On

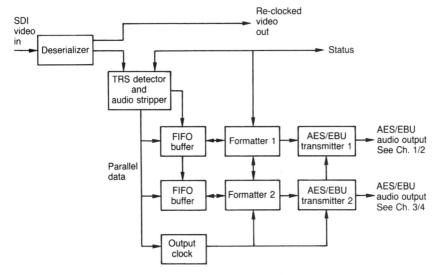

Figure 4.59 A typical audio extractor. Note the FIFOs for timebase expansion of the audio samples.

the other hand a parallel router is complex because of the large number of conductors which need switching for each input. Parallel digital video is also limited to around 50 metres of cable length and so cannot replace the traditional analog router.

A serial router is potentially very inexpensive as it is a single-pole device. It can be easier to build than an analog router because the digital signal is more resistant to crosstalk. Now that SDI chips are available, parallel working is becoming obsolete. Large routers can easily be implemented with SDI and the long cable drive capability means that large broadcast installations can be tackled.

A serial router can be made using wideband analog switches, so that the input waveform is passed from input to output. This is an inferior approach, as the total length of cable which can be used is restricted; the input cable is effectively in series with the output cable and the analog losses in both will add.

The correct approach is for each router input to reclock and slice the waveform back to binary. Figure 4.60 shows a typical reclocking SDI router. Following the input reclocking stage the actual routing takes place on logic level signals prior to a line driver which relaunches a clean signal. The cables to and from the router can be maximum length as the router is effectively a repeater.

It is not necessary to unscramble the serial signal at the router. A phase locked loop is used to regenerate the bit clock. This rejects jitter on the incoming waveform. The waveform is sliced, and the slicer output is sampled by the local clock. The result is a clean binary waveform, identical to the original driver waveform. The Gennum GS9005 is an equalizer/reclocker chip which is suitable for router applications as it does not descramble the data stream.

The router is simply a binary bitstream switch, and is not unduly concerned with the meaning or content of the bitstream. It does not matter whether the bitstream is PAL, NTSC or 4:2:2 or whether or not ancillary data are carried – the information just passes through.

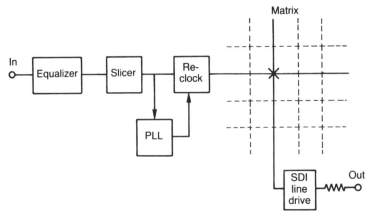

Figure 4.60 A router for SDI signals should be constructed as shown here with a reclocker/slicer at each input to restore the received waveform to clean binary logic levels. The routing matrix proper is then a logic element which is followed by SDI line drivers. If this is not done the output cable is electrically in series with the input cable and the performance margin will be impaired. There is no need to descramble or decode the signal as the router is not interested in its meaning.

The only parameter of any consequence is the bit rate. Component runs at 270 or 360 Mbits/sec, PAL runs at 177 Mbits/sec and NTSC runs at 143 Mbits/sec. Most multistandard routers require a link or DIP switch to be set in each input in order to select the appropriate VCO centre frequency. A separate VCO adjustment will be present for each standard. Otherwise units can be standards independent which allows more flexibility and economy. With a mixed standard router, it is only necessary to constrain the control software so that inputs of a given standard can only be routed to outputs connected to devices of the same standard, and one router can then handle component and composite signals simultaneously.

4.24 Timing in digital installations

The issue of signal timing has always been critical in analog video, but the adoption of digital routing relaxes the requirements considerably. Analog vision mixers need to be fed by equal length cables from the router to prevent propagation delay variation. In the digital domain this is no longer an issue as delay is easily obtained and each input of a digital vision mixer can have its own local timebase corrector. Provided signals are received having timing within the window of the inputs, all inputs are retimed to the same phase within the mixer.

Figure 4.61 shows how a mixing suite can be timed to a large SDI router. Signals to the router are phased so that the router output is aligned to station reference within a microsecond or so. The delay in the router may vary with its configuration, but only by a few microseconds. The mixer reference is set with respect to station reference so that local signals arrive towards the beginning of the input windows and signals from the router (which, having come further, will be the latest) arrive towards the end of the windows. Thus all sources can be retimed within the mixer and any signal can be mixed with any other. Clearly the mixer introduces delay, and the signal feedback to the router experiences further delay. In order to send the mix back to the router a frame synchronizer is needed on the output of the suite. This introduces somewhat less than a frame of delay so that by the time the signal has re-emerged from the router it is aligned to station reference once more, but a frame late. An installation of this kind relies on a genlockable sync pulse generator having multiple outputs with independent phase control.

In an ideal world, every piece of hardware in the station will have component SDI outputs and inputs, and everything is connected by SDI cables. In practice, unless the building is new, this is unlikely. However, there are ways in which SDI can be phased in alongside analog systems. An expensive way of doing this is to fit every composite device with coders and decoders, and every analog device

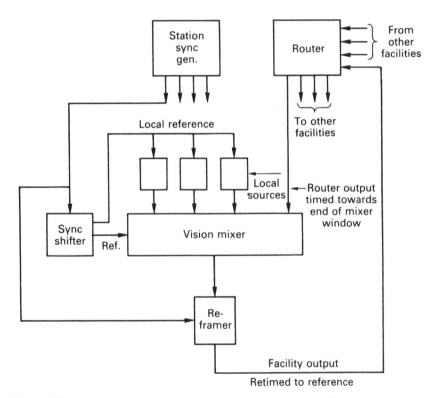

Figure 4.61 In large systems some care is necessary with signal timing as is shown here; see text for details.

with converters so that a component SDI router can be used alone. Figure 4.62 shows an alternative. The SDI router is connected to every piece of digital equipment, using parallel-to-serial adaptors where necessary. Analog VTRs such as Betacam SP or M-II have digital output options which use the data from the TBC directly. One thing to check with digital output SP and M-II machines is that the Y/C timing must be adjusted correctly at the TBC input in the VTR as it cannot be corrected subsequently. These will need DACs to convert SDI signals to analog component inputs. Analog equipment continues to be connected to an analog router, and interconnection paths, called gateways, are created between the two routers. These gateways require converters in each direction, but the number of converters is much less than if every analog device was equipped. The number of gateways will be determined by the number of simultaneous transactions between analog and digital domains.

In many cases the two routers can be made to appear like one large router if appropriate software is available in a common control system. This will only be possible if the SDI router is purchased from the same manufacturer as the existing analog router or if the SDI router manufacturer offers custom software.

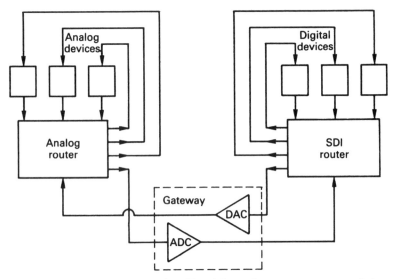

Figure 4.62 Digital routers can operate alongside existing analog routers as an economical means of introducing digital routing.

Whilst modern DVTRs incorporate the audio data in the SDI signal, adapting older devices to do this, and subsequently demultiplexing the audio, could prove expensive. DVTRs tend also to be inflexible in their audio selection. For example it may not be possible to record certain audio channels from embedded SDI data at the same time as other channels from the AES/EBU inputs. Also the embedded audio may not contain timecode even though the standard allows it. As a result, in some installations it may be more appropriate to retain an earlier audio router, or to have a separate AES/EBU digital audio router layer controlled in parallel with the SDI router.

If the analog router handles composite signals, then coders and decoders will be needed in addition to the converters. In this case the use of gateways obviates unnecessary codecs when analog devices are connected together.

4.25 Configuring SDI links

The viability of an SDI link is governed primarily by the data rate and the proposed distance. It is quite easy to establish what grade of cable will be required from the tables in Section 4.19. As can be seen from Figure 4.63, the data integrity deteriorates rapidly beyond a critical cable length. The sudden upswing in bit error rate is known as the 'crash knee' and for reliability only operation to the left of the knee is possible. Do not be tempted to stretch the quoted cable length figures. As SDI is a point-to-point interface all receivers are equipped with an internal terminator. Thus there is no such thing as passive loop-through and use of a coaxial T-piece for monitoring is ruled out. The use of active loop-through means that in the case of a power failure, the loop-through signal will fail. If it is required to drive multiple destinations, a digital distribution amplifier will be needed.

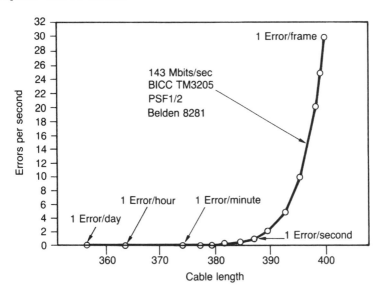

Bit error rates (BER)	NTSC	PAL	270 Mb	360 Mb
1 bit error/field	4.2×10^{-7}	2.8×10^{-7}	1.8×10^{-7}	1.3×10^{-7}
1 bit error/second	7.0×10^{-9}	4.7×10^{-9}	3.1×10^{-9}	2.3×10^{-9}
1 bit error/minute	1.2×10^{-10}	7.8×10^{-11}	5.1×10^{-11}	3.8×10^{-11}
1 bit error/hour	1.9×10^{-12}	1.3×10^{-12}	9.0×10^{-13}	6.4×10^{-13}
1 bit error/day	8.1×10^{-14}	5.4×10^{-14}	3.5×10^{-14}	2.7×10^{-14}
1 bit error/month	2.6×10^{-15}	1.8×10^{-15}	1.2×10^{-15}	8.9×10^{-16}
1 bit error/year	2.2×10^{-16}	1.5×10^{-16}	1.0×10^{-16}	7.4×10^{-17}

Figure 4.63 Because of the multiplicative effect of the large number of factors causing signal degradation the error rate increases steeply after a certain cable length. This sudden onset of errors is referred to as the 'crash knee'.

If the distance required is excessive even for the best grade of cable then a repeater will be required. Unlike an analog repeater, a properly engineered digital repeater causes no generation loss and minimal delay. Figure 4.64 shows a typical reclocking repeater. The repeater is not interested in the meaning of the data and need not descramble or deserialize the data stream. It is only necessary to reclock with a phase locked loop to reject jitter and slice to reject noise. The resultant clean logic level signal can then be used to drive a further SDI waveform generator.

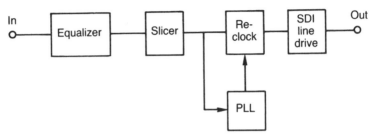

Figure 4.64 In a reclocking repeater the input signal is equalized, sliced and reclocked with a phase-locked loop to recover a clean binary signal which then passes to an SDI line driver.

Such a simple reclocking repeater is of limited use in an EDH system as there is no ability to distinguish errors occurring before or after the repeater. If this is important an EDH supporting repeater will be necessary. By definition such a device must descramble and deserialize the data stream in order to make the error detecting checks on the incoming data. As a result it will cause a greater signal delay than a simple reclocking repeater.

4.26 Testing digital video interfaces

Once video and audio are converted to the digital domain, they become data, or numbers, and if those numbers can be delivered to the other end of a digital interface unchanged then the interface has not caused any loss of quality. This is one of the strengths of digital technology. In the absence of data reduction techniques, the quality is determined in the conversion process and can then be maintained in transmission and recording. In contrast analog signals are subject to generation loss in every recording and to noise and distortion in every transmission. This analog heritage has led to a philosophy where the analog waveform is monitored at every stage so that some adjustment can be made to minimize the quality loss. The waveform monitor and vectorscope tradition is so strong that despite the transition to the radically different digital technology many people think no new monitoring methods are needed.

Unfortunately, traditional analog testing techniques reveal nothing about a digital interface or recorder. Consider the system of Figure 4.65, which could be composite or component. An ADC converts the input waveform to data which is

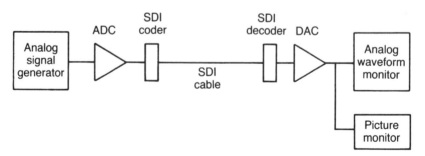

Figure 4.65 Testing waveforms in the analog domain as shown here reveals nothing about the performance margin of the digital interface.

transmitted by the interface. A DAC converts the received data to analog video once more. If a waveform monitor and vectorscope are connected to the DAC, what information is revealed about the interface? If it is assumed that the interface is not suffering bit errors, the monitoring tells us how good the ADC and DAC are, but reveals nothing about the performance of the interface. The interface could be working with 20 dB of noise immunity, or it could be within a whisker of failure. Should the system be marginal such that one bit fails per minute, this will be invisible on an analog monitoring system in the presence of programme material and may just be detectable on colour bars. If the problem is due to a phase locked loop drifting in an SDI receiver or damp penetration in a cable, it is going to get worse and in the absence of a warning the result will be a sudden failure.

Three distinct testing areas are required in digital video systems. Firstly, on installation, it should be possible to verify that the link is working with an adequate safety margin and that the length of the link is not excessive for the cable type selected. Secondly it is necessary to test the data integrity of the link to ensure that the BER (bit error rate) is acceptable and remains acceptable when the system is stressed or *margined* beyond the conditions it will experience in service. Thirdly digital systems can suffer from a problem which has no parallel in the analog domain. This is the protocol error where the data transmission is flawless but the two units concerned cannot understand each other.

Although the SDI signal is digital in that it carries discrete data, it is an analog waveform as far as the cable and receiver equalizer are concerned. Waveform distortions will occur in the cable and noise and jitter will be added. The magnitude of these distortions indicates the likely reliability of the channel. Figure 4.66 shows that a correctly functioning digital receiver is specifically designed to reject the analog waveform distortions by making discrete decisions. By definition, in doing so it denies us knowledge of the signal quality. Thus what is needed is a complementary approach. Instead of rejecting the distortions to obtain discrete data, what is needed is a system which rejects the data in order to measure the magnitude of the distortions.

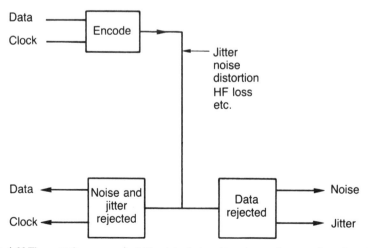

Figure 4.66 The reception process is deliberately designed to reject analog waveform distortions whereas only by measuring these can signal integrity be assessed. Thus the measurement process is diametrically opposed to normal reception and needs special techniques.

One approach is to assess the eye pattern generated by the received waveform. After equalization the eye opening should be clearly visible, and the size of the opening should be consistent with the length and type of cable used. If it is not, the noise and/or jitter margin may be inadequate. However, testing the eye pattern on the SDI requires a fast oscilloscope, or even a sampling scope. The scope probe cannot be just hooked on to the cable as the impedance mismatch this causes will have a damaging effect on the signal. Many SDI receivers have a dedicated, buffered, test point for eye pattern monitoring.

Inspection of the eye pattern is acceptable for establishing that the basic installation is sound and has proper signal levels, termination impedance and equalization, but is not very good at detecting infrequent impulsive noise and requires an expensive oscilloscope which has few other purposes in the studio. Contact noise from electrical power installations such as air conditioners is unlikely to be present for long enough to find with an eye pattern display. The technique of signature analysis is better suited to impulsive noise problems.

4.27 Signature analysis

In a digital routing system reliability is synonymous with data integrity. A data integrity testing system does not care what the video waveform is, or indeed that it is a video waveform at all. A data integrity system considers the digital TV field as a block of binary data and simply checks whether those data were received with bit accuracy or not. The message is to forget the pictures and worry about the data.

Signature analysis is a data integrity testing technique which uses large quantities of data and tests down to extremely low bit error rates. As a digital interface which has no bit errors is transparent, signature analysis is a useful way of verifying the transparency of a channel following installation or maintenance. Signature analysis requires a stationary test signal to be applied at the transmitting end of the interface. Stationary means that in the case of component video every frame contains identical data. In the case of composite video the data repeat every four fields (NTSC) or eight fields (PAL). Digitally generated colour bars are suitable but other patterns work equally well. The received data are then processed to generate a value known as a signature which in typical equipment will be a four-digit hexadecimal number. If the transmitted data are always the same, the received signature should always be the same. Any change in the signature indicates that an error has occurred.

The signature generation process divides the incoming bitstream by a polynomial. The remainder of the division expresses an entire frame in component or an entire colour sequence in composite as a single word which is the signature. A change of a single bit is enough to change the signature. Any number of bit errors up to the number of bits in the word will guarantee to change the signature, whereas larger numbers of errors are detected with a high degree of probability. In the presence of high error rates the occasional misdetection is irrelevant as the goal of the testing is to determine whether or not remedial action is necessary.

Signature analysis is similar in principle to EDH except that the signature is not transmitted with the data. This avoids complexity at the transmitting end and the need to reserve word positions in the data. As the transmitted data are not a codeword, the remainder will not necessarily be non-zero but could have any value. An error is indicated when the received signature changes, not by its absolute value.

Signature analysis can be used in two ways which are shown in Figure 4.67. In absolute analysis, shown in Figure 4.67(a), the test signal comes from a special generator which displays the signature of the data. The data are fed down the channel under test and then into the signature analyser. The signature displayed on the analyser is compared with the signature on the generator. If the two remain identical for an extended period, then no errors are occurring.

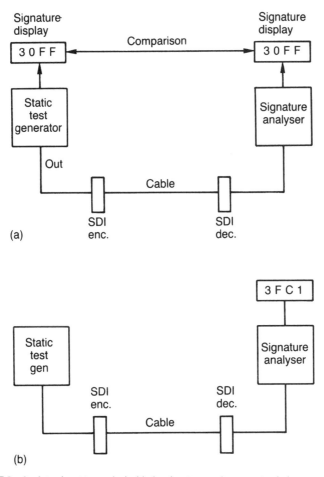

Figure 4.67 In absolute signature analysis (a) the signature at the generator is known and can be compared with the received signature. In relative analysis (b) the signature is unknown but if the generator is known to be static the signature should be constant. Thus changes in the received signature indicate errors.

It is also possible to use a relative detection method, shown in Figure 4.67(b). In relative signature analysis, any stationary generator can be used. The correct signature is not known, but if errors occur, the displayed signature will not be stable but will change. Thus in relative signature analysis the goal is not that the signature is correct but that it should not change for an extended period. Relative signature analysis cannot detect permanent errors, such as a stuck bit in a parallel interface, as the same signature will always be obtained and so its use is restricted to systems which have no hard faults.

In case of doubt, the test pattern signature can easily be obtained by connecting the generator directly to the signature analyser as well as to the path under test.

Signature analysers can be designed to work on specific parts of the transmission only. If the interface is carrying programme material, the signature will vary from frame to frame. However, the ancillary data slots can still be used for signature analysis.

In component systems, the signature analyser may be set to operate on only one selected component. Some machines can be set to operate only on selected bits in the sample, making stuck bits in parallel systems very easy to find.

As signature analysis works in the data domain, it cannot be used to test a channel in which the received data are not necessarily the same as the transmitted data. There are a number of cases in which this could occur. If the digital signal is returned to the analog domain and then converted back to digital, noise in the analog domain will cause data differences. In DVTRs, uncorrectable errors due to dropouts result in concealments which change data values. Thus signature analysis can be used to detect concealment.

Systems which use compression are not transparent and signature analysis is of no use if a compression codec is included in the test channel. In order to test the channel the generator must be connected *after* the compressor and *before* the decoder.

4.28 EDH

The serial digital interface is steadily taking over as the video interface standard for the digital age, but the original standard had no provisions for data integrity checking. EDH is an option for serial digital which goes a long way to rectifying the problem. Figure 4.68 shows an EDH equipped SDI (serial digital interface) transmission system. At the first transmitter, the data from one field are transmitted and simultaneously fed to a cyclic redundancy check (CRC) generator. The CRC calculation is a mathematical division by a polynomial and the result is the remainder. The remainder is transmitted in a special ancillary data packet which is sent early during the vertical interval, before any switching takes place in a router. The first receiver has an identical CRC generator which performs a calculation on the received field. The ancillary data extractor identifies the EDH packet and demultiplexes it from the main data stream. The remainder from the ancillary packet is then compared with the locally calculated remainder. If the transmission is error-free, the two values will be identical. In this case no further action results. However, if as little as one bit is in error in the data, the remainders will not match. The remainder is a 16 bit word and guarantees to detect up to 16 bits in error anywhere in the field. Greater numbers of errors are not guaranteed to be detected, but this is of little consequence as enough fields in error will be detected to indicate that there is a problem.

Should a CRC mismatch indicate an error in this way, two things happen. Firstly an optically isolated output connector on the receiving equipment will present a low impedance for a period of 1 to 2 milliseconds. This will result in a pulse in an externally powered circuit to indicate that a field contained an error. An external error monitoring system wired to this connector can note the occurrence in a log or sound an alarm or whatever it is programmed to do. As the

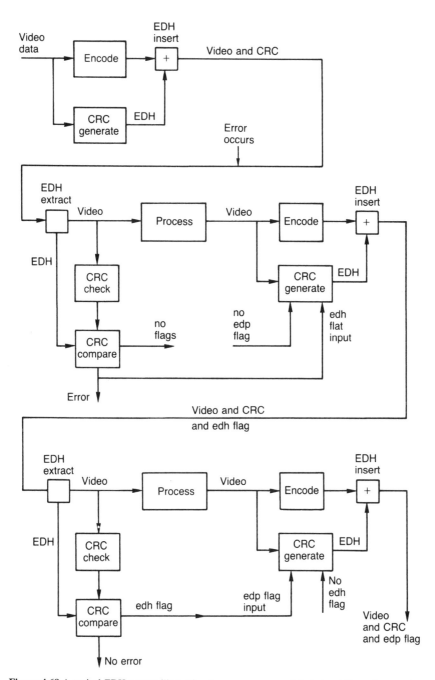

Figure 4.68 A typical EDH system illustrating the way errors are detected and flagged; see text for details.

data are incorrectly received, the fact must also be conveyed to subsequent equipment. It is not permissible to pass on a mismatched remainder. The centre unit in Figure 4.68 must pass on the data as received, complete with errors, but it must calculate a new CRC which matches the erroneous data. When received by the third unit in Figure 4.68, there will then only be a CRC mismatch if the transmission between the second and third devices is in error. This is correct as the job of the CRC is only to locate faulty hardware and clearly if the second link is not faulty the CRC comparison should not fail. However, the third device still needs to know that there is a problem with the data, and this is the job of the error flags which also reside in the EDH packet. One of these flags is called edh (error detected here) and this will be asserted by the centre device in Figure 4.68. The last device in Figure 4.68 will receive edh and transmit eda (error detected already). There are also flags to handle hardware failures (e.g. over temperature or diagnostic failure). The idh (internal error detected here) and ida (internal error detected already) handle this function. Locally detected hardware errors drive the error output socket to a low impedance state constantly to distinguish from the pulsing of a CRC mismatch.

A slight extra complexity is that error checking can be performed in two separate ways. One CRC is calculated for the active picture only, and another is calculated for the full field. Both are included in the EDH packet which is shown in Figure 4.69. The advantage of this arrangement is that whilst regular programme material is being passed in active picture, test patterns can be sent in vertical blanking which can be monitored separately. Thus if active picture is received without error but full field gives an error, the error must be outside the picture. It is then possible to send, for example, pathological test patterns during the vertical interval which stress the transmission system more than regular data to check the performance margin of the system. This can be done alongside the picture information without causing any problems.

In a large system, if every SDI link is equipped with EDH, it is possible for automatic error location to be performed. Each EDH-equipped receiver is connected to a monitoring system which can graphically display on a map of the system the location of any transmission errors. If a suitable logging system is used, it is not necessary for the display to be in the same place as the equipment. In the event of an error condition, the logging system can communicate with the display by dial-up modem or dedicated line over any distance. Logging allows infrequent errors to be counted. Any increase in error rate indicates a potential failure which can be rectified before it becomes serious.

An increasing amount of new equipment is available with EDH circuitry. However, older equipment can still be incorporated into EDH systems by connecting it in series with proprietary EDH insertion and checking modules.

4.29 Margining

It is a characteristic of digital systems that failure is sudden because deteriorations in the signal are initially rejected until they grow serious enough to corrupt data. Put simply, just because a digital system is working today, there is no guarantee that it will work tomorrow unless its performance margin or 'head height' can be measured. Margining is a long established technique used in the computer industry to prove the reliability of a digital process by testing it

Data item	b9 msb	b8	b7	b6	b5	b4	b3	b2	b1	b0 lsb
Ancillary data header, word 1 – component	0	0	0	0	0	0	0	0	0	0
Ancillary data header, word 2 – component	1	1	1	1	1	1	1	1	1	1
Ancillary data header, word 3 – component	1	1	1	1	1	1	1	1	1	1
Auxiliary data flag – composite	1	1	1	1	1	1	1	1	0	0
Data ID (1F4)	0	1	1	1	1	1	0	1	0	0
Block number	1	0	0	0	0	0	0	0	0	0
Data count	0	1	0	0	0	1	0	0	0	0
Active picture data word 0 crc<5:0>	$\bar{P}$	P	C_5	C_4	C_3	C_2	C_1	C_0	0	0
Active picture data word 1 crc<11:6>	$\bar{P}$	P	C_{11}	C_{10}	C_9	C_8	C_7	C_6	0	0
Active picture data word 2 crc<15:12>	$\bar{P}$	P	V	0	C_{15}	C_{14}	C_{13}	C_{12}	0	0
Full-field data word 0 crc<5:0>	$\bar{P}$	P	C_5	C_4	C_3	C_2	C_1	C_0	0	0
Full-field data word 1 crc<11:6>	$\bar{P}$	P	C_{11}	C_{10}	C_9	C_8	C_7	C_6	0	0
Full-field data word 2 crc<15:12>	$\bar{P}$	P	V	0	C_{15}	C_{14}	C_{13}	C_{12}	0	0
Auxiliary data error flags	$\bar{P}$	P	0	ues	ida	idh	eda	edh	0	0
Active picture error flags	$\bar{P}$	P	0	ues	ida	idh	eda	edh	0	0
Full-field error flags	$\bar{P}$	P	0	ues	ida	idh	eda	edh	0	0
Reserved words (7 total)	1	0	0	0	0	0	0	0	0	0
Checksum	$\overline{S8}$	S8	S7	S6	S5	S4	S3	S2	S1	S0

Error flags

All error flags indicate only the status of the previous field; that is, each flag is set or cleared on a field-by-field basis. A logical 1 is the set state and a logical 0 is the unset state. The flags are defined as follows:

edh – error detected here: Signifies that a serial transmission data error was detected. In the case of ancillary data, this means that one or more ANC data blocks did not match its checksum.

eda – error detected already: Signifies that a serial transmission data error has been detected somewhere upstream. If device B receives a signal from device A and device A has set the edh flag, when device B retransmits the data to device C, the eda flag will be set and the edg flag will be unset if there is no further error in the data.

idh – internal error detected here: Signifies that a hardware error unrelated to serial transmission has been detected within a device. This is provided specifically for devices which have internal data error checking facilities, as an error reporting mechanism.

ida – internal error detected already: Signifies that an idh flag was received and there was a hardware device failure somewhere upstream.

ues – unknown error status: Signifies that a serial signal was received from equipment not supporting this error-detection mechanism.

Checkword values

Each checkword value consists of 16 bits of data calculated using the CRC-CCITT polynomial generation method. The equation and a conceptual logic diagram are shown below:

Checkword (16-bit) $= x^{16} + x^{12} + x^5 + 1$

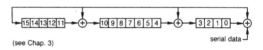

(see Chap. 3)

Figure 4.69 The contents of the EDH packet which is inserted in ancillary data space after the associated field.

under conditions which are more stressful than will be encountered in service. The degree of additional stress which can be applied before failure is a measure of the performance margin. As digital video is only data, margining techniques can be applied to it with great success and if used correctly will give a much-needed confidence factor.

There are two ways in which an SDI system can be stressed. The first of these is to use a special signal generator which produces pathological test patterns. These are bitstreams which mimic the convolution process of the SDI scrambler and result in channel signals which contain less clock content and lower frequencies than usual. Receivers find it harder to decode pathological signals and so they will result in errors unless the system is in good shape.

A simple alternative to the pathological test signal is the use of a cable simulator which has the same effect as increasing the length of the cable between transmitter and receiver. The Faraday 'cable clone' is the best known of these devices. Figure 4.63 showed the non-linear relationship between cable length and error rate and illustrates the 'crash knee' in the characteristic. Testing with a cable simulator depends upon the existence of the crash knee. Figure 4.70(a) shows how the test is made. The cable under test is temporarily broken and the cable clone is inserted. An error monitoring system such as EDH or a signature analyser is connected after the receiver under test.

The configuration shown in Figure 4.70(b) is incorrect as it only tests the cable and the transmitter in conjunction with the receiver in the signature analyser. The important receiver is not tested. The cable clone must be installed in the cable and the signature analyser must be connected after the receiver under test.

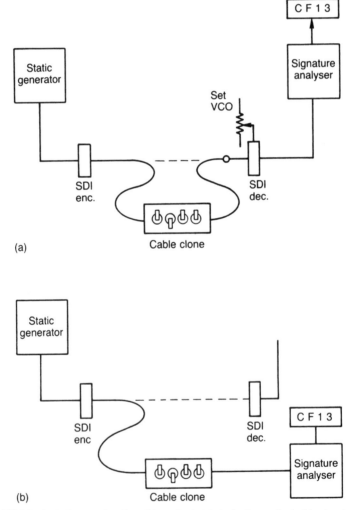

Figure 4.70 Margin testing requires the cable under test to be broken and a 'cable clone' or simulator to be inserted as in (a). The cable length is artificially increased until the crash knee is reached. The configuration in (b) is incorrect as the receiver to be used in service is not being tested. In fact the signature analyser's receiver is being tested: a meaningless exercise.

With the cable clone set to bypass, the system should show no errors. If errors are detected the fault should be rectified. Starting with an error-free system the cable length is gradually increased until a rapid increase in error rate indicates that the crash knee has been reached. The additional length of cable needed to reach the crash knee is a direct measure of the performance margin or head height. It will be seen from Figure 4.63 that the error rate changes from negligible to intolerable with an increase in length of only 20–30 metres. Clearly if less than this figure is achieved in the margining test the system is marginal and should not be put into service.

One potential problem area which is frequently overlooked is to ensure that the VCO in the receiving phase locked loop is correctly centred. If it is not, it will be running with a static phase error and will not sample the received waveform at the centre of the eyes. The sampled bits will be more prone to noise and jitter errors. VCO centring can be checked in a number of ways. If a frequency meter is available, this can be used to display the VCO frequency without input. Another method is to display the control voltage. This should not change significantly when the input is momentarily disconnected. However, the best method is to adjust for minimum error rate in conjunction with a signature analyser (or EDH) and a margining unit or pathological sequence.

Using a cable clone, cable length is added until a slight error rate is caused. The VCO centre frequency is now adjusted one way or the other to see if the error rate can be reduced or even eliminated. If there is a range of error-free adjustment, more cable length should be switched in to make a finer adjustment.

Some SDI receivers run quite hot and the VCO centre frequency changes with temperature. Placing cards on an extender board may change the airflow enough to alter the centre frequency.

4.30 Protocol testing

In digital systems it is possible for problems to occur in which the data transmission is flawless but communication is still not achieved. This can happen where the transmitter and receiver have incompatible protocols. The protocol of a signal includes the nature and positioning of TRS patterns, the location of EDH blocks and embedded audio. A further consideration is that in order correctly to adjust analog-to-digital converters it is necessary to monitor the actual code values coming from a converter and compare them with the original analog voltages.

Such problems can only be addressed by a logic analyser. General purpose logic analysers can be used on parallel interfaces, but for best results a dedicated digital video analyser is to be preferred. Figure 4.71 shows the layout of a video analyser. An SDI receiver and/or a parallel receiver drive a decoder which identifies TRS patterns for synchronizing purposes. Incoming words are written into a page of RAM which can hold the contents of a few lines of video. The analyser thus takes a snapshot of interface activity. The point within the frame at which the snapshot is taken is determined by the trigger criteria which are provided to the RAM write logic.

Once the RAM is written in real time with the digital video snapshot, the data are frozen and can be inspected using the associated PC and its display. Signals can be displayed graphically as they would appear on conventional analog waveform monitors or vectorscopes, but can also be displayed as tabular data so that the exact binary word values and positions can be established. Any

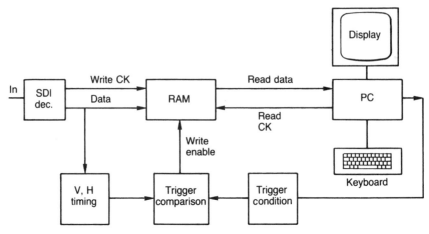

Figure 4.71 A video analyser allows a snapshot of digital video interface activity to be captured in RAM. This data can then be inspected at leisure using a small computer.

departures from correct protocol can be detected by comparing the data with the relevant standards. Figure 4.72 shows a decode table for component TRS which is useful when using an analyser.

4.31 Factors affecting converter quality

In theory the quality of a digital audio system comprising an ideal ADC followed by an ideal DAC is determined at the ADC. The ADC parameters such as the sampling rate, the wordlength and any noise shaping used put limits on the

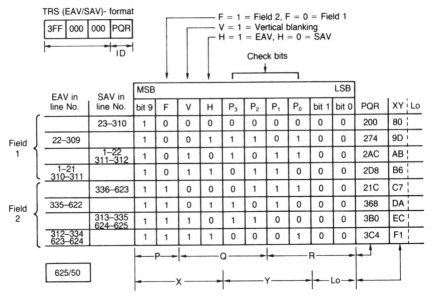

Figure 4.72 Decode table for component TRS.

quality which can be achieved. Conversely the DAC itself may be transparent, because it only converts data whose quality are already determined back to the analog domain. In other words, the ADC determines the system quality and the DAC does not make things any worse.

In practice both ADCs and DACs can fall short of the ideal, but with modern converter components and attention to detail the theoretical limits can be approached very closely and at reasonable cost. Shortcomings may be the result of an inadequacy in an individual component such as a converter chip, or due to incorporating a high quality component in a poorly thought out system. Poor system design can destroy the performance of a converter. Whilst oversampling is a powerful technique for realizing high quality converters, its use depends on digital interpolators and decimators whose quality affects the overall conversion quality.

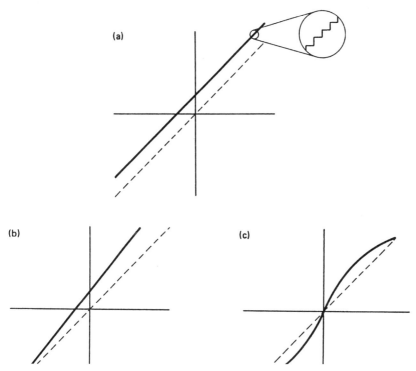

Figure 4.73 Main converter errors (solid line) compared with perfect transfer function (dotted line). These graphs hold for ADCs and DACs, and the axes are interchangeable; if one is chosen to be analog, the other will be digital.

ADCs and DACs have the same transfer function, since they are only distinguished by the direction of operation, and therefore the same terminology can be used to classify the possible shortcomings of both.

Figure 4.73 shows the transfer functions resulting from the main types of converter error:

(a) *Offset error.* A constant appears to have been added to the digital signal. This has a serious effect in video systems because it alters the black level. Offset error is sometimes cancelled by digitally sampling the converter output during blanking and feeding it back to the analog input as a small control voltage.

(b) *Gain error.* The slope of the transfer function is incorrect. Since converters are often referred to one end of the range, gain error causes an offset error. Severe gain error causes clipping.

(c) *Integral linearity.* This is the deviation of the dithered transfer function from a straight line. It has exactly the same significance and consequences as linearity in analog circuits since, if it is inadequate, harmonic distortion will be caused.

(d) *Differential non-linearity* is the amount by which adjacent quantizing intervals differ in size. This is usually expressed as a fraction of a quantizing interval.

(e) *Monotonicity* is a special case of differential non-linearity. Non-monotonicity means that the output does not increase for an increase in input. This can happen in a converter whose current sources are not sufficiently accurate. With a converter input code of 01111111 (127 decimal), the seven low-order current sources of the converter will be on. The next code is 10000000 (128 decimal), where only the eighth current source is operating. If the current it supplies is in error on the low side, the analog output for 128 may be less than that for 127. In an ADC non-monotonicity can result in missing codes. This means that certain binary combinations within the range cannot be generated by any analog voltage. If a device has better than $\frac{1}{2}Q$ linearity it must be monotonic.

(f) *Absolute accuracy.* This is the difference between actual and ideal output for a given input. For video and audio it is rather less important than linearity. For example, if all the current sources in a converter have good thermal tracking, linearity will be maintained, even though the absolute accuracy drifts.

4.32 Setting up converters

Figure 4.74 shows how a video analyser is used to set up a component ADC. Converter set-up is critical as digital systems keep the data the same all down the line so it has to be right from the outset. A precise analog test pattern generator is used to produce colour bars. The signal is looped through an analog waveform

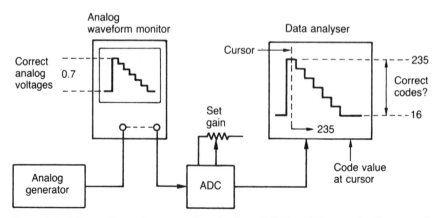

Figure 4.74 Using a video analyser to set the gain of an ADC. The ADC output data is compared with standard values on a known part of the analog waveform.

monitor to the ADC where it should be terminated with the terminator which will be used in practice. This is necessary because terminator tolerance is such that changing a terminator can change the analog level by several digital code values. The generator level is adjusted until the waveform monitor displays exactly the correct amplitude in, say, the white bar.

The analyser then captures the ADC output and the black bar is located in waveform mode with the cursor. The actual data values at the cursor position are displayed, and these can be compared with the ideal so that any offset in the converter can be revealed and adjusted out. By selecting the white bar the luminance converter gain can be adjusted. Some analysers allow timed retriggering so that a new snapshot is taken periodically. This mode is useful when making dynamic gain adjustments. The colour difference signal gains are set up in a similar manner.

The analog Y/C timing should be checked with a suitable signal such as bowtie before returning to colour bars to check the relative timings of the green/magenta transitions in the three digital components. This is not as easy as it sounds as the colour difference sample spacing is twice that of luminance and the sample values need to be interpreted carefully to find the transition.

Chapter 5

Video recording

There are many different applications of video recording and consequently many types of machine will be found. In this chapter the principles of both analog and digital video recorders will be considered. The increasing use of hard disks for video recording warrants an introduction here.

5.1 Introduction

A video recorder is any device designed to record video (and usually audio) waveforms without regard to the medium. A video tape recorder (VTR) uses tape as a medium. Most early VTRs used tape on open reels; later came the video cassette recorder (VCR) where the tape was enclosed. In an attempt to include the essential audio signal in the name, some authorities use the term television tape recorder (TTR), but this is equally lacking as it is difficult to see how the recording process contributes to vision at a distance or how this implies the presence of sound.

The first VCRs did not have very high picture quality and were primarily suited to consumer or industrial uses. Today the term VCR still implies a consumer machine. Even though all digital formats use cassettes, the term used in professional circles is digital video tape recorder (DVTR) or DTTR.

When hard disks are used for video recording, the combination of disk store and control panel is called a workstation. The random access of disks allows the user to jump along the time axis of the recording and the term 'non-linear' is used to describe this. A large disk store found, for example, in a centralized news editing system having several users, is known as a file server or just a server.

Video signals are characterized by a wide bandwidth and this has traditionally led to high tape consumption. Whilst this is acceptable for production purposes where the cost of the tape is a small part of the overall process, high tape consumption is a distinct drawback in the consumer VCR. Consumer recorders, industrial and ENG (electronic news gathering) recorders will cut corners in order to reduce some combination of size, weight or cost. In the analog domain this has led to such techniques as 'colour-under' recording and in the digital domain the result is the use of compression which is also used extensively in disk recording.

A simple recorder needs to do little more than record and play back, but the sophistication of modern production processes requires a great deal more flexibility. A production VTR will need to support most if not all of the following:

- Offtape confidence replay must be available during recording.
- Timecode must be recorded and this must be playable at all tape speeds. Full remote control is required so that edit controllers can synchronize several machines via timecode.
- A high quality video signal is required over a speed range of −1× to +3× normal speed. Audio recovery is required in order to locate edit points from dialogue.
- A picture of some kind is required over the whole shuttle speed range (typically ±50× normal speed).
- Assembly and insert editing must be supported, and it must be possible to edit the audio and video channels independently.
- It must be possible slightly to change the replay speed in order to shorten or lengthen programmes. Full audio and video quality must be available in this mode, known as tape speed override (TSO).
- In digital machines, for editing purposes, there is a requirement to be able to play back the tape with heads fitted in advance of the record head. The playback signal can be processed in some way and re-recorded in a single pass. This is known as pre-read, or read-modify-write operation.

5.2 Magnetic recording

All video recorders, whether analog or digital, disk or tape, rely on the same magnetic physics which will be introduced here.

A magnetic field can be created by passing a current through a coil of wire. When the current ceases, the magnetism disappears. However, many materials, some quite common, display a permanent magnetic field with no apparent power source. Magnetism of this kind results from the spin of electrons within atoms. Atomic theory describes atoms as having nuclei around which electrons orbit, spinning as they go. Different orbits can hold a different number of electrons. The distribution of electrons determines whether the element is diamagnetic (non-magnetic) or paramagnetic (magnetic characteristics are possible). Diamagnetic materials have an even number of electrons in each orbit, and according to the Pauli exclusion principle half of them spin in each direction. The opposed spins cancel any resultant magnetic moment. Fortunately there are certain elements, the transition elements, which have an odd number of electrons in certain orbits. The magnetic moment due to electronic spin is not cancelled out in these paramagnetic materials.

Figure 5.1 shows that paramagnetic materials can be classified as anti-ferromagnetic, ferrimagnetic and ferromagnetic. In some materials alternate atoms are anti-parallel and so the magnetic moments are cancelled. In ferrimagnetic materials there is a certain amount of antiparallel cancellation, but a net magnetic moment remains. In ferromagnetic materials such as iron, cobalt or nickel, all of the electron spins can be aligned and as a result the most powerful magnetic behaviour is obtained.

It is not immediately clear how a material in which electron spins are parallel could ever exist in an unmagnetized state or how it could be partially magnetized by a relatively small external field. The theory of magnetic domains has been developed to explain what is observed in practice. Figure 5.2(a) shows a ferromagnetic bar which is demagnetized. It has no net magnetic moment because it is divided into domains or volumes which have equal and opposite moments. Ferromagnetic material divides into domains in order to reduce its

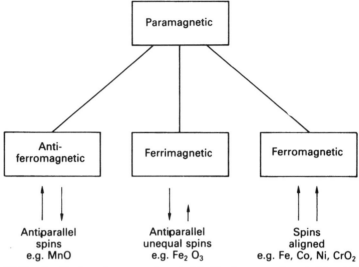

Figure 5.1 The classification of paramagnetic materials. The ferromagnetic materials exhibit the strongest magnetic behaviour.

magnetostatic energy. Figure 5.2(b) shows a domain wall which is around 0.1 micrometres thick. Within the wall the axis of spin gradually rotates from one state to another. An external field of quite small value is capable of disturbing the equilibrium of the domain wall by favouring one axis of spin over the other. The result is that the domain wall moves and one domain becomes larger at the

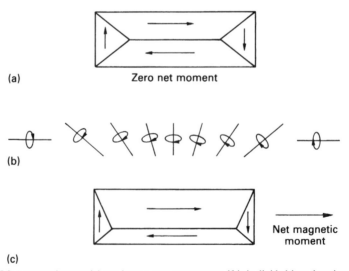

Figure 5.2 A magnetic material can have a zero net moment if it is divided into domains as shown here. Domain walls (b) are areas in which the magnetic spin gradually changes from one domain to another. The stresses which result store energy. When some domains dominate, a net magnetic moment can exist as in (c).

expense of another. In this way the net magnetic moment of the bar is no longer zero, as shown in Figure 5.2(c).

For small distances, the domain wall motion is linear and reversible if the change in the applied field is reversed. However, larger movements are irreversible because heat is dissipated as the wall jumps to reduce its energy. Following such a domain wall jump, the material remains magnetized after the external field is removed and an opposing external field must be applied which must do further work to bring the domain wall back again. This is a process of hysteresis where work must be done to move each way. Were it not for this non-linear mechanism magnetic recording would be impossible. If magnetic materials were linear, tapes would return to the demagnetized state immediately after leaving the field of the head and this chapter would have nothing to describe.

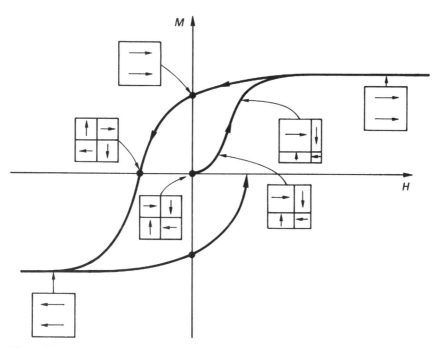

Figure 5.3 A hysteresis loop which comes about because of the non-linear behaviour of magnetic materials. If this characteristic were absent, magnetic recording would not exist.

Figure 5.3 shows a hysteresis loop which is obtained by plotting the magnetization M when the external field H is swept to and fro. On the macroscopic scale, the loop appears to be a smooth curve, whereas on a small scale it is in fact composed of a large number of small jumps. These were first discovered by Barkhausen. Starting from the unmagnetized state at the origin, as an external field is applied, the response is initially linear and the slope is given by the susceptibility. As the applied field is increased a point is reached where the magnetization ceases to increase. This is the saturation magnetization M_s. If the applied field is removed, the magnetization falls, not to zero, but to the remanent magnetization M_r. This remanence is the magnetic memory mechanism which makes recording possible. The ratio of M_r to M_s is called the squareness ratio. In recording media, squareness is beneficial as it increases the remanent magnetization.

If an increasing external field is applied in the opposite direction, the curve continues to the point where the magnetization is zero. The field required to achieve this is called the intrinsic coercive force $_mH_c$. A small increase in the reverse field reaches the point where, if the field were to be removed, the remanent magnetization would become zero. The field required to do this is the remanent coercive force, $_rH_c$.

As the external field H is swept to and fro, the magnetization describes a major hysteresis loop. Domain wall transit causes heat to be dissipated on every cycle around the loop and the dissipation is proportional to the loop area. For a recording medium, a large loop is beneficial because the replay signal is a function of the remanence and high coercivity resists erasure. Heating is not an issue. For a device such as a recording head, a small loop is beneficial. Figure 5.4(a) shows the large loop of a hard magnetic material used for recording media and for permanent magnets. Figure 5.4(b) shows the small loop of a soft magnetic material which is used for recording heads and transformers.

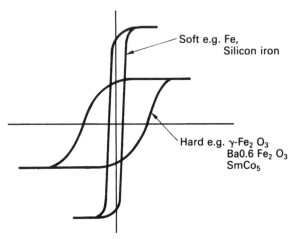

Figure 5.4 The recording medium requires a large loop area (a) whereas the head requires a small loop area (b) to cut losses.

According to the Nyquist noise theorem, anything which dissipates energy when electrical power is supplied must generate a noise voltage when in thermal equilibrium. Thus magnetic recording heads have a noise mechanism which is due to their hysteretic behaviour. The smaller the loop, the less the hysteretic noise. In conventional heads, there are a large number of domains and many small domain wall jumps. In thin film heads there are fewer domains and the jumps must be larger. The noise this causes is known as Barkhausen noise, but as the same mechanism is responsible it is not possible to say at what point hysteresis noise should be called Barkhausen noise.

Figure 5.5 shows the construction of a typical record head, which might be analog or digital. Heads designed for use with tape work in actual contact with the

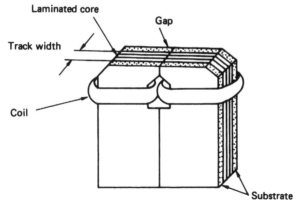

Figure 5.5 A digital record head is similar in principle to an analog head but uses much narrower tracks.

magnetic coating. The tape is tensioned to pull it against the head. There will be a wear mechanism and need for periodic cleaning. A magnetic circuit carries a coil through which the record current passes and generates flux. A non-magnetic gap forces the flux to leave the magnetic circuit of the head and penetrate the medium. The most efficient recording will be obtained when the reluctance of the magnetic circuit is dominated by that of the gap. This means making the ring structure only just large enough to fit the coil to shorten the magnetic circuit as much as possible. The peak current through the head must be set to suit the coercivity of the tape, but is less than the current level which would cause saturation of the medium. In a VTR the amplitude of the current is constant, and recording is performed by reversing the direction of the current with respect to time. As the track passes the head, this is converted to the reversal of the magnetic field left on the tape with respect to distance. The magnetic recording is therefore bipolar. Figure 5.6 shows that the recording is actually made just after the trailing pole of the record head where the

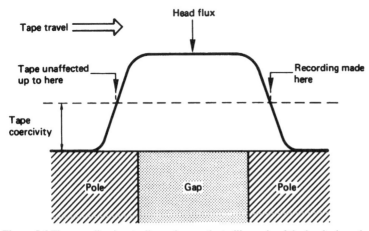

Figure 5.6 The recording is actually made near the trailing pole of the head where the head flux falls below the coercivity of the tape.

flux strength from the gap is falling. The width of the gap is generally made quite large to ensure that the full thickness of the magnetic coating is recorded, although this cannot be done if the same head is intended to replay.

A conventional inductive replay head has a frequency response shown in Figure 5.7. At DC there is no change of flux and no output. As a result inductive heads are at a disadvantage at very low speeds although this is not a problem in rotary-head recorders. The output rises with frequency until the rise is halted by the onset of thickness loss. As the frequency rises, the recorded wavelength falls and flux from the shorter magnetic patterns cannot be picked up so far away. At some point, the wavelength becomes so short that flux from the back of the tape coating cannot reach the head and a decreasing thickness of tape contributes to the replay signal. In VTRs using short wavelengths to cut tape consumption, there is no point in using thick coatings. As wavelength further reduces, the familiar gap loss occurs, where the head gap is too big to resolve detail on the track. The construction of the head results in the same action as that of a two-point transversal filter, as the two poles of the head see the tape with a small delay interposed due to the finite gap. As

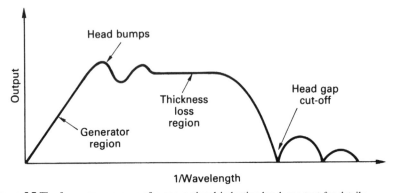

Figure 5.7 The frequency response of a conventional inductive head; see text for details.

expected, the head response is like a comb filter with the well-known nulls where flux cancellation takes place across the gap. Clearly the smaller the gap the shorter the wavelength of the first null. This contradicts the requirement of the record head to have a large gap. In professional analog VTRs, it is the norm to have different record and replay heads for this reason, and the same will be true in digital machines which have separate record and playback heads. Clearly in consumer and industrial recorders, where the same pair of heads are used for record and play, the head gap size will be determined by the playback requirement.

As can be seen, the frequency response is far from ideal, and steps must be taken to ensure that recorded waveforms do not contain frequencies which suffer excessive losses.

5.3 Noise and track width

In a recorder with high quality electronics, the signal-to-noise ratio (SNR) of the replay signal is determined by the tape. In an analog recorder, the tape quality directly affects the signal quality and tape noise will be superimposed on the replay video signal.

When an analog tape is copied, noise from the replay of the first tape is added to the noise of the second tape, and so inevitably the noise level of the copy must rise. If multigeneration work is a requirement, as will be the case for a production recorder, then the signal-to-noise ratio of a single generation recording must be much higher than necessary so that noise can build up over several generations of copying without impairing the signal quality excessively.

The SNR is a function of the track width. If a track of a given width has a certain SNR, consider what would happen if the same waveform were to be recorded in another track alongside the first. If, on replay, the signal from the two tracks were to be linearly added, the signal would be coherent and would double in voltage; i.e. it would increase by 6 dB. However, the noise in the two tracks would be incoherent and so the noise power would double. This would increase the noise voltage by only 3 dB. Thus every doubling of track width results in a 3 dB improvement in SNR.

As a consequence, analog production recorders requiring multigeneration performance will use wider tracks than consumer recorders which only require single-generation performance. This reflects in the tape consumption: the professional C-format recorder uses twenty times as much tape area as the consumer VHS format for the same recording time.

In digital recording it is only necessary to distinguish a one and a zero and this can be done with a relatively low SNR in comparison to analog recording. In addition there is no generation loss when copying digital recordings. However, expressing an analog voltage as a binary number having eight or ten bits requires a higher frequency response than in an analog recorder. As a result analog recorders tend to have short, wide tracks, whereas digital recorders tend to have long, narrow tracks such that a segmented recording is needed. In both analog and digital recording, the bandwidth required is in excess of the capabilities of a stationary head with a reasonable linear tape speed.

5.4 Rotary heads

The attractions of the rotary-head recorder are that the head-to-tape speed and hence bandwidth are high, whereas the linear tape speed is not. The space between tracks is determined by the linear tape speed, not by multitrack head technology. Rotary-head machines make better use of the tape area, particularly if azimuth recording is used. The high head speed raises the frequency of offtape signals, and since output is proportional to frequency, playback signals are raised above head noise even with very narrow tracks.

With stationary heads, the offtape frequency is proportional to the linear tape speed and this makes recovery of data at other than the correct speed extremely difficult as demodulators tend to work well only over a narrow speed range. In contrast, with rotary heads the scanning speed dominates head-to-tape speed and variations in the linear speed of the tape have a smaller effect, especially if the rotational speed is modulated by the linear speed. Thus picture-in-shuttle and slow motion are readily accommodated in a rotary-head machine.

D.L.I.A.D.T. Library

5.5 Helical geometry

Figure 5.8 shows the general arrangement of the two major categories of rotary-head recorder. In transverse-scan recorders, relatively short tracks are recorded

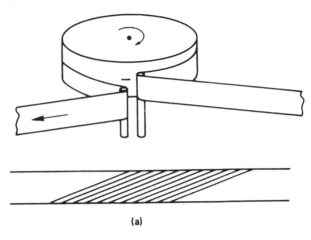

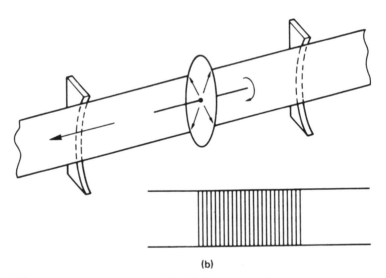

(a)

(b)

Figure 5.8 Types of rotary-head recorder. (a) Helical scan records long diagonal tracks. (b) Transverse scan records short tracks across the tape.

almost at right angles to the direction of tape motion by a rotating headwheel containing four or six heads. The transverse scan approach allows for a compact construction and the signals replayed from the short tracks suffer relatively little timebase error. In helical-scan recorders, the tape is wrapped around the drum in such a way that it enters and leaves in two different positions along the drum axis. This causes the rotating heads to record long slanting tracks, with the penalty that the mechanism is rather larger. Timebase error is increased because of the longer tracks. In both approaches, the pitch of the tracks (defined as the spacing between the same feature on successive tracks) is determined by the linear tape speed rather than by head design. The space between tracks can easily be made much smaller than in stationary-head recorders; in fact it can be zero or even negative.

As video signals consist of discrete lines and frames, it is possible to conceal the interruptions in the tracks of a rotary-head machine by making them coincident with the time when the CRT is blanked during flyback. The first video recorders developed by Ampex used the transverse-scan approach, with four evenly spaced heads on the rotor: hence the name quadruplex which was given to this system. The tracks were a little shorter than the two-inch width of the tape, and several sweeps were necessary to build up a video frame. The geometry of the scanning was arranged so that one head would reach the end of a track just as the next head reached the beginning of the next track. The change-overs between the heads were made during the horizontal synchronizing pulses.

Variable-speed operation in rotary-head machines is obtained by deflecting the playback heads along the drum axis to follow the tape tracks. Periodically the heads will need to jump in order to omit or repeat a field. In transverse scan the number of tracks needed to accommodate one field is high, and the head deflection required to jump fields was virtually impossible to achieve.

In helical scanning, the tracks become longer, so fewer of them are needed to accommodate a field. Figure 5.9 shows that the head displacement needed for field jumping is then reduced.

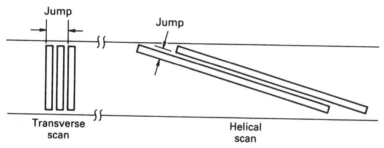

Figure 5.9 Helical scan results in longer tracks so a shorter distance needs to be jumped to miss out or repeat a field.

For professional use, the quadruplex format gave way to one-inch analog C-format, which used helical scan and an almost total wrap to fit an entire field into a slant track about 15 in (380 mm) long. The change-over between tracks was then made in the vertical interval. Field jumps could then be made with a head displacement of single track.

In digital recorders the analog-to-digital conversion process represents the video signal in a form which requires a much smaller signal-to-noise ratio but with a much higher bandwidth. As a result, tracks on the tape are required to be narrower but longer. A single track containing an entire digital field would be impractically long and in practice fields are inevitably segmented into between six (NTSC D-2, Digital Betacam) and sixteen (D-5) tracks, but as the tracks are so much narrower in digital recorders the head displacement required is of the same order as on analog machines.

Figure 5.10 shows the two fundamental approaches to drum design. In the rotating upper drum system, one or more heads are mounted on the periphery of a revolving drum (also known as the scanner). The fixed base of the drum carries a helical ramp in the form of a step or, for greater wear resistance, a hardened band

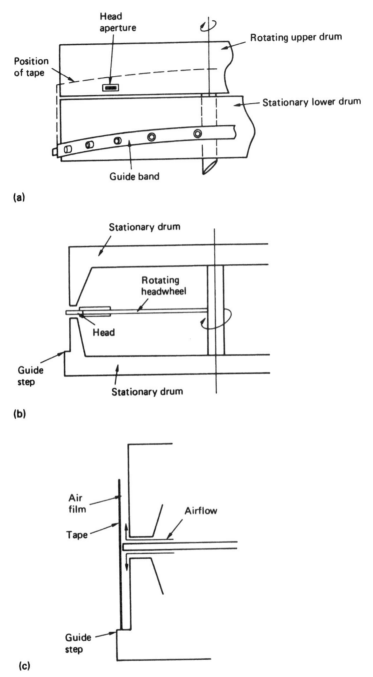

Figure 5.10 (a) Rotating-top-type scanner. The upper drum is slightly smaller than the lower drum due to the air film it develops. Helical band guides lower edge of tape. (b) Stationary-top scanner, where headwheel rotates in a slot between upper and lower drums. (c) Airflow in stationary-top scanner. Headwheel acts as a centrifugal pump, producing air film between tape and drums.

which is suitably attached. Alternatively, both top and bottom of the drum are fixed, and the headwheel turns in a slot between them. Both approaches have advantages and disadvantages. The rotating upper drum approach is simpler to manufacture than the fixed upper drum, because the latter requires to be rigidly and accurately cantilevered out over the headwheel. The rotating part of the drum will produce an air film which raises its effective diameter. The rotor will thus need to be made a slightly different diameter to the lower drum, so that the tape sees a constant diameter as it rises up the drum. There will be plenty of space inside the rotor to install individually replaceable heads.

The fixed upper drum approach requires less power, since there is less air resistance. The headwheel acts as a centrifugal pump, and supplies air to the periphery of the slot where it lubricates both upper and lower drums, which are of the same diameter. It is claimed that this approach gives head contact which is more consistent over the length of the track, but it makes the provision of replaceable heads more difficult, and it is generally necessary to replace the entire headwheel as an assembly.

The presence of the air film means that the tape surface is not normally in contact with the cylindrical surface of the drum. Many drums have a matt etched finish, which does not become polished in service because there is no contact. The thickness of the air film is that where the pumping effect of the rotating drum reaches equilibrium with the tape tension. Figure 5.11 shows that the heads project out of the drum by a distance which must exceed the air film thickness in order to deform the tape slightly. In the absence of such a deformation there would be no contact pressure. It will be clear that the tape tension must be maintained accurately if the desired head contact pressure is to be obtained.

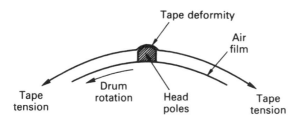

Figure 5.11 The tape is supported on an air film and the heads must project by a greater distance to achieve contact pressure.

The creation and collapse of the deformities in the tape result in appreciable acoustic output, in the form of an irritating buzz. The production of a deformity in the tape due to head impact results in the propagation of a wave motion down the tape. This has a finite velocity and the velocity of the head must always be slower or it will produce a shock wave resulting in tremendous contact forces and rapid wear.

The presence of the air film means that the tape is only located around the drum by one edge. It must be arranged to follow the helical step without drifting away from it. Two sets of fixed guides, known as the entry and exit guides, lead the tape to and from the ramp. Figure 5.12 shows the tape path around the drum as if it had been unrolled into a plane. It will be seen that the step on the drum acts as a single flanged guide. The two fixed guides are arranged to contact only

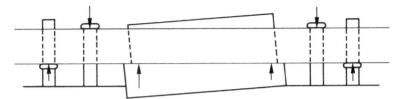

Figure 5.12 The head drum is shown here as if it had been unrolled to make the tape straight. It can then be seen that the drum step acts as a single flanged guide. The entry and exit guides work in conjunction with the drum step to locate the tape accurately.

one edge of the tape each. The height and angle of the tape are set by the drum step and the lower flange of the outer guide. The tape is prevented from leaving that path by the upper flange of the inner guide. The reference flanges are fixed, and will be made of some wear-resistant material such as ceramic. The other flanges may be spring loaded to accommodate slight variations in tape width.

The tape may wrap around the drum by various amounts. Some early analog machines used a complete circuit around the drum which led the tape to cross itself in the so-called alpha wrap. The C-format used almost a complete circuit of the drum where the tape turns sharply around the entrance and exit guides in the shape of an omega. These techniques were necessary to allow the use of a single head, which avoided banding in analog recording, but the result is a machine which is difficult to lace and cannot use a cassette. In DVTRs the tape passes between half-way and three-quarters of the way around the drum. The total angle of drum rotation for which the heads touch the tape is called the *mechanical wrap angle* or the *head contact angle*. The angle over which a useful recorded track is laid down is always somewhat shorter than the mechanical wrap angle. This is not only to allow the head/tape contact to settle after the initial impact, but also to allow the entire track to be read when the track following heads are deflected. Figure 5.13 shows that successive tracks start at a different distance along the tape. Deflecting a head to follow a different track results in that track being read earlier or later than normal, and an extended wrap is necessary to guarantee head contact with a deflected head.

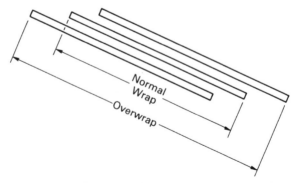

Figure 5.13 In helical scan recordings, successive tracks start at a different distance along the tape. These appear displaced around the drum and so an overwrap is needed to allow the whole track to be read by a deflected head.

It will be evident that as the tape is caused to travel along the drum axis by the ramp, it actually takes on the path of a helix. The head rotates in a circular path, and so will record diagonal tracks across the width of the tape. So it is not really the scanning which is helical, it is the tape path.

In practical machines the tape may, in normal forward motion, travel up the ramp (e.g. C-format) or down the ramp (e.g. D-3). This reverses the slant angle of the tracks as will be seen in Figure 5.14. In addition, the drum can rotate either with (e.g. U-matic) or against (e.g. C-format) the direction of linear tape motion.

If the tape is stationary, as in Figure 5.14(a) the head will constantly retrace the same track, and the angle of the track can be calculated by measuring the rise of the tape along the drum axis, and the circumferential distance over which this rise takes place. The latter can be obtained from the diameter of the drum and the wrap angle. The tangent of the *helix angle* is given by the rise over the distance. It can also be obtained by measuring the distance along the ramp corresponding to the wrap angle. In conjunction with the rise, this dimension will give the sine of the helix angle.

However, when the tape moves, the angle between the tracks and the edge of the tape will not be the helix angle. Figure 5.14(b) shows an example in which tape climbs up the drum which rotates against the direction of tape travel (e.g. D-2). When the head contact commences, the tape will be at a given location, but when the head contact ceases, the tape will have moved a certain linear distance and the resultant track will be longer.

Figure 5.14(c) shows what happens when the tape moves down the drum in the same direction as head rotation. In this case the track is shorter. In order to obtain the *track angle* it is necessary to take into account the tape motion. The length of the track resulting from scanning a stationary tape, which will be at the helix angle, can be resolved into two distances at right angles as shown in Figure 5.15. One of these is across the tape width, the other is along the length of the tape. The tangent of the helix angle will be the ratio of these lengths. If the length along the tape is corrected by adding or subtracting the distance the tape moves during one scan, depending upon whether tape motion aids or opposes drum rotation, the new ratio of the lengths will be the tangent of the track angle. In practice this process will often be reversed, because it is the track angle which is standardized in a given format, and the transport designer has to find a helix angle which will produce it.

It can also be seen from Figure 5.14 that when a normally recorded tape is stopped, the head must be deflected by a triangular waveform or ramp in order to follow the track. A further consequence of the track angle being different to the helix angle is that when azimuth recording is used, the azimuth angles at which the heads are mounted in the drum are not the same as the angles between the transitions and the edge of the track. One of the angles is slightly increased and one is slightly reduced. In D-3, for example, the difference is 0.017 degrees.

The relative direction of drum and tape motion is unimportant, as both configurations work equally well. Often the direction is left undefined until many other parameters have been settled. If the segmentation and coding scheme proposed result in the wavelengths on tape being on the short side, opposite rotation will be chosen, as this lengthens the tracks and with it the wavelength. Sometimes the direction of rotation is a given; in Digital Betacam, playback of analog tapes was a requirement, so the rotation direction had to be the same as in analog Betacam.

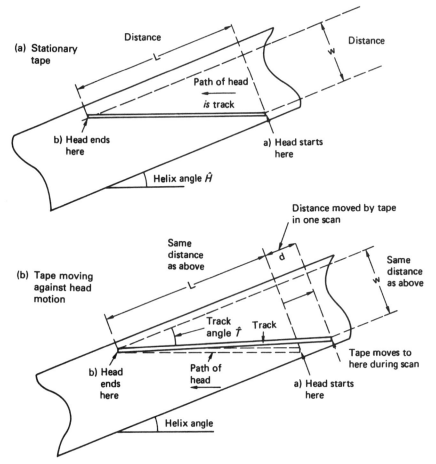

Figure 5.14 When the tape is moving the track laid down will be at an angle which is different from the helix angle, because the tape is in a different place at the end of the scan than at the beginning. Track length can be considered as two components L and w for stationary case, and $L \pm d$ and w for moving case.

Provided that the tape linear speed and drum speed remain the same, the theoretical track angle will remain the same. In practice this will only be the case if the tape tension is constant. Figure 5.16 shows that if the back tension changes, the effective length of the tape will also change, and with it the track angle. It will be evident that the result is a tracking error which increases towards the ends of the track. In addition the changed track length will alter the signal timing, advancing it at one end of the track whilst delaying it at the other, a phenomenon known as *skew*. As shown above, tension errors also affect the air film thickness and head contact pressure. All digital rotary-head recorders need some form of tape tension servo to maintain the tape tension around the drum constant irrespective of the size of the pack on the supply hub. In practice tension servos can only control the tension of the tape entering the drum. Since there will be

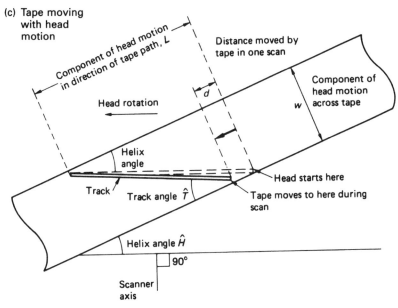

(c) Tape moving with head motion

Figure 5.14 (c).

friction between the edge of tape and the drum step, the tape tension will gradually increase between the entrance and exit guides, and so the tape will be extended more towards the exit guide. When the tape subsequently relaxes, it will be found that the track is actually curved. The ramp can be made to deviate from a theoretical helix to counteract this effect, or all drums can be built to the same design, so that effectively the track curvature becomes part of the format. Another possibility is to use some form of embedded track following system, or a system like azimuth recording which tolerates residual tracking errors.

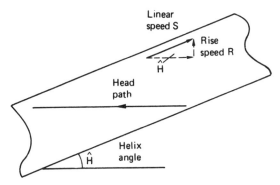

Figure 5.15 The linear speed of the tape S can be resolved into the speed of the tape along the scanner axis which is the rise speed R. $R = S \sin \hat{H}$. Dividing the rise speed by the head passing frequency gives the track pitch. Head passing frequency is simply the number of heads multiplied by the scanner rotational frequency. Thus track pitch is proportional to tape speed.

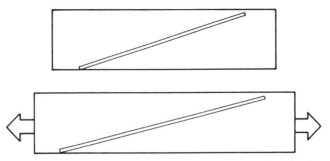

Figure 5.16 Tape is flexible, so change of tension will result in change of length. This causes a change in track angle known as skew, shown exaggerated here.

When the tape direction reverses, the sense of the friction in the drum will also reverse, so the back tension has to increase to keep the mid-span tension the same as when going forward.

When verifying the track angle produced by a new design, it is usual to develop a tape which it has recorded with magnetic fluid, and take measurements under a travelling microscope. With the very small track widths of digital recorders, it is usually necessary to compensate for skew by applying standard tension to the tape when it is being measured, or by computing a correction factor for the track angle from the modulus of elasticity of the tape.

5.6 Track and head geometry

The *track pitch* is the distance, measured at right angles to the tracks, from a given place on one track to the same place on the next. The track pitch is a function of the linear tape speed, the head passing frequency and the helix angle. It can be seen in Figure 5.15 that the linear speed and the helix angle determine the rise rate (or fall rate) with respect to the drum axis, and the knowledge of the rotational period of the drum will allow the travel in one revolution to be calculated. If the travel is divided by the number of active heads on the drum, the result will be the track pitch. If everything else remains equal, the track pitch is proportional to the linear tape speed. Note that the track angle will also change with tape speed.

Figure 5.17(a) shows that in guard band recording, the track pitch is equal to the width of the track plus the width of the guard band. The track width is determined by the width of the head poles, and the linear tape speed will be high enough so that the desired guard band is obtained. In guard band recording, the erase head is wider than the record head, which in turn is wider than the replay head, as shown in Figure 5.18(a). This ensures that despite inevitable misalignments, the entire area to be recorded is erased and the playback head is entirely over a recorded track.

In azimuth recording the situation is different, depending upon whether it is proposed to use flying erase heads. In Figure 5.17(b) the head width is greater than the track pitch, so that the tape does not rise far enough for one track to clear the previous one. Part of the previous track will be overwritten, so that the track width and the track pitch become identical. As Figure 5.18(b) shows, this approach guarantees that, when re-recording, previous tracks are fully over-

(a)

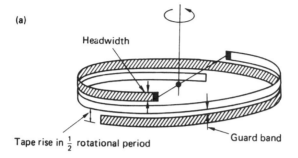

Headwidth

Tape rise in $\frac{1}{2}$ rotational period

Guard band

(b)

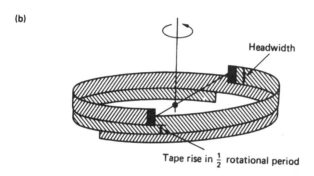

Headwidth

Tape rise in $\frac{1}{2}$ rotational period

(c)

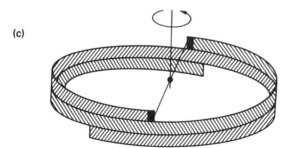

Figure 5.17 In the absence of azimuth recording, guard bands (a) must be left between the tracks. With azimuth recording, the record head may be wider than (b) or of the same width as (c) the track.

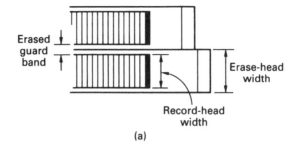

Erased guard band

Erase-head width

Record-head width

(a)

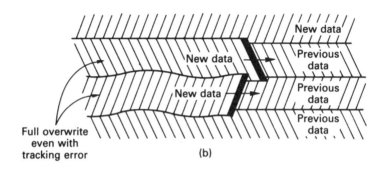

New data

New data

New data

New data

Previous data

Previous data

Previous data

Full overwrite even with tracking error

(b)

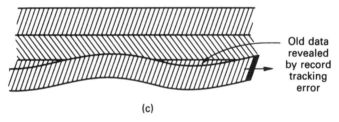

Old data revealed by record tracking error

(c)

Figure 5.18 (a) The erase head is wider than the record head in guard-band recording. In (b) If the azimuth record head is wider than the track, full overwrite is obtained even with misalignment. In (c) if the azimuth record head is the same width as the track, misalignment results in failure to overwrite and an erase head becomes necessary.

written as the overlapping heads cover the entire tape area at least once, and in places twice. For some purposes, flying erase heads are not then necessary.

The alternative shown in Figure 5.17(c) is for the track width to be exactly the same as the track pitch so there is no overlapping. In this case misalignment during re-recording can allow a thin strip of a previous track to survive unless a flying erase head is used. This is shown in Figure 5.18(c).

5.7 Timebase correction

One of the characteristics of tape recording is that the time axis is not particularly stable owing to the flexibility of the tape. In consumer VCRs the problem is handled by allowing the scanning process of the display to follow the

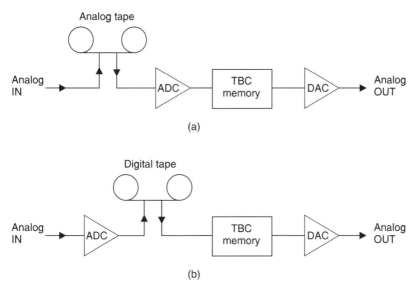

Figure 5.19 (a) Analog VTR digitizes on replay to facilitate timebase correction. (b) Digital VTR digitizes before recording.

instabilities. In most monitors and TV sets the scanning oscillators are heavily damped and the frequency cannot change rapidly. This makes the picture more stable on a broadcast signal when interference interrupts the sync pulses. However, when a VCR input is selected, the display must reduce the damping in the timebase oscillators so that they can track the offtape instability.

In professional VTRs, the solution is to insert a variable delay in the replay signal which opposes the timebase error. Delay is most readily achieved in the digital domain using random access memory. Consequently, even analog VTRs use digital timebase correction. Figure 5.19(a) shows that in an analog VTR,

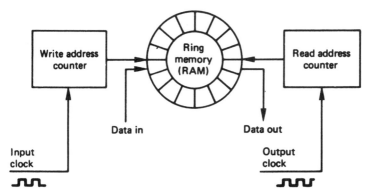

Figure 5.20 If the memory address is arranged to come from a counter which overflows, the memory can be made to appear circular. The write address then rotates endlessly, overwriting previous data once per revolution. The read address can follow the write address by a variable distance (not exceeding one revolution) and so a variable delay takes place between reading and writing.

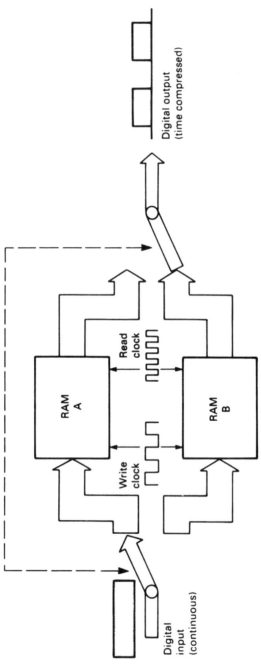

Figure 5.21 In time compression, the unbroken real-time stream of samples from an ADC is broken up into discrete blocks. This is accomplished by the configuration shown here. Samples are written into one RAM at the sampling rate by the write clock. When the first RAM is full, the switches change over, and writing continues into the second RAM whilst the first is read using a higher-frequency clock. The RAM is read faster than it was written and so all of the data will be output before the other RAM is full. This opens spaces in the data flow which are used as described in the text.

there is an ADC following the replay stage. This converts the replay signal into the digital form so that the delay can operate on it. The digital signal is subsequently converted back to analog. In a digital recorder, shown in Figure 5.19(b), the ADC precedes the recorder which now records data. The replay data can be timebase corrected directly. In a sense the difference between the analog and digital recorder is the position of the transport with respect to the ADC.

Figure 5.20 shows that the relationship between the read and write addresses makes the RAM into a variable delay. The addresses are generated by counters which overflow to zero after they have reached a maximum count. As a result the memory space appears to be circular. The read and write addresses chase one another around the circle. If the read address follows close behind the write address, the delay is short. If it just stays ahead of the write address, the maximum delay is reached. If the input and output have an identical data rate, the address relationship will be constant. When a VTR is playing back there will be variations in the instantaneous data rate from the tape. The timebase corrector absorbs these variations by varying its delay in the opposite sense. The write address changes at the varying rate from the tape, but the read address changes at a stable rate.

5.8 Time compression

Time compression is a technique which allows the instantaneous time axis of the recording to be different from that of the input signal. It is used in all digital and some analog recorders. The process is related to timebase correction, but is a deliberate technique used on recording. An equal and opposite process is needed on replay.

Figure 5.21 shows an ADC feeding a pair of RAMs. When one is being written by the ADC, the other can be read, and vice versa. As soon as the first RAM is full, the ADC output switches to the input of the other RAM so that there is no loss of samples. The first RAM can then be read at a higher clock rate than the sampling rate. As a result the RAM is read in less time than it took to write it, and the output from the system then pauses until the second RAM is full. The information is now time compressed into blocks with convenient pauses in

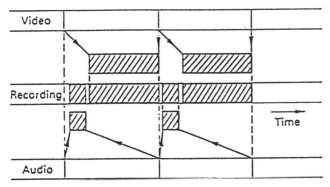

Figure 5.22 Time compression is used to shorten the length of track needed by the video. Heavily time-compressed audio samples can then be recorded on the same track using common circuitry.

between them. In a digital system the time compressed data are recorded directly. In an analog system the data must be passed through a DAC first.

In digital VTRs, the video data are time compressed so that part of the track is left for audio data. Figure 5.22 shows that heavy time compression of the audio data raises the instantaneous audio data rate up to that of the video data so that the same tracks, heads and much common circuitry can be used to record both.

In the Betacam and M-II analog component recorders, the two colour difference signals are recorded in a single track using time compression. Figure 5.23 shows that lines of colour difference are time compressed by a factor of 2 so that both will fit in the standard line period. This allows three components to be recorded in only two tracks. As the colour difference signals have half the bandwidth of luminance, time compression gives the two tracks the same bandwidth.

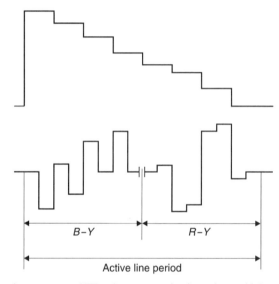

Figure 5.23 In analog component VTRs, time compression is used to multiplex two colour difference signals into one tape track.

Subsequently, any time compression can be reversed by time expansion. Samples are written into a RAM at the incoming clock rate, but read out at the standard sampling rate. Unless there is a design fault, time compression is undetectable. In a practical VTR, the time expansion stage can be combined with the timebase correction stage so that speed variations in the medium can be eliminated at the same time. The use of time compression is universal in digital recording but less common in analog. In general the *instantaneous* data rate at the medium is not the same as the rate at the converters, although clearly the *average* rate must be the same.

5.9 The basic rotary-head transport

Figure 5.24 shows the important components of a rotary-head helical scan tape transport. There are four servo systems which must correctly interact to obtain all modes of operation: two reel servos, the drum servo and the capstan servo. The capstan and reel servos together move and tension the tape, and the drum servo moves the heads. For variable speed operation a further servo system will be necessary to deflect the heads.

There are two approaches to capstan drive: those which use a pinch roller and those which do not. In a pinch roller drive, the tape is held against the capstan by pressure from a resilient roller which is normally pulled toward the capstan by a solenoid. The capstan only drives the tape over a narrow speed range, generally the range in which broadcastable pictures are required. Outside this range, the pinch roller retracts, the tape will be driven by reel motors alone, and the reel motors will need to change their operating mode; one becomes a velocity servo whilst the other remains a tension servo.

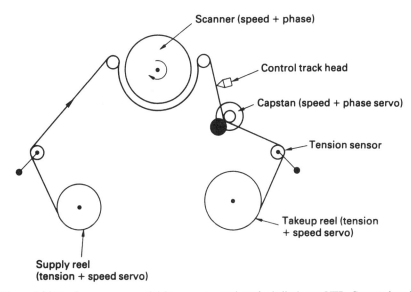

Figure 5.24 The four servos essential for proper operation of a helical scan VTR. Cassette-based units will also require loading and threading servos, and for variable speed a track-following servo will be necessary.

In a pinch-roller-less transport, the tape is wrapped some way around a relatively large capstan, to give a good area of contact. A drilled capstan connected to a suction pump can also be used to obtain extra adhesion. The tape is always in contact with the capstan, irrespective of operating mode, and so the reel servos never need to change mode. A large capstan has to be used to give sufficient contact area, and to permit high shuttle speed without excessive motor rpm. This means that at play speed it will be turning slowly, and must be accurately controlled and free from cogging. A multipole ironless rotor pancake type brush motor is often used, or a sinusoidal drive brushless motor.

The simplest operating mode to consider is the first recording on a blank tape. In this mode, the capstan will rotate at constant speed, and drive the tape at the linear speed specified for the format. The drum must rotate at a precisely determined speed, so that the correct number of tracks per unit distance will be laid down on the tape. Since in a segmented recording each track will be a constant fraction of a television field, the drum speed must ultimately be determined by the incoming video signal to be recorded. To take the example of a PAL D-2 or D-3 recorder having two record head pairs, eight tracks or four segments will be necessary to record one field, and so the drum must make exactly two complete revolutions in one field period, requiring it to run at 100 Hz. In the case of NTSC D-2 or D-3, there are six tracks or three segments per field, and so the drum must turn at one and a half times field rate, or a little under 90 Hz. The phase of the drum rotation with respect to input video timing depends upon the time delay necessary to shuffle and interleave the video samples. This time will vary from a minimum of about one segment to more than a field, depending on the format.

5.10 Controlling motor speed

In various modes of operation, the capstan and/or the drum will need to have accurate control of their rotational speed. During crash record (a mode in which no attempt is made to lock to a previous recording on the tape), the capstan must run at an exact and constant speed. When the drum is first started, it must be brought to the correct speed before phase lock can be attempted. The principle of speed control commonly used will be examined here. Figure 5.25(a) shows that the motor whose speed is to be controlled is fitted with a toothed wheel or slotted disk. For convenience, the number of slots will usually be some power of two. A sensor, magnetic or optical, will produce one pulse per slot, and these will be counted by a binary divider. A similar counter is driven by a reference frequency. This may often be derived by multiplying the input video field rate in a phase locked loop.

The outputs of the two counters are taken to a full adder, whose output drives a DAC which in turn drives the motor. The bias of the motor amplifier is arranged so that a DAC code of one-half of the quantizing range results in zero drive to the motor, and smaller or larger codes will result in forward or reverse drive.

If the count in the tacho divider lags the count in the reference divider, the motor will receive increased power, whereas if the count in the tacho divider leads the count in the reference divider, the motor will experience reverse drive, which slows it down. The result is that the speed of the motor is exactly proportional to the reference frequency. In principle the system is a phase locked loop, where the voltage controlled oscillator has been replaced by a motor and a frequency-generating (FG) wheel.

5.11 Phase locked servos

In a VTR the rotational phase of the drum and capstan must be accurately controlled. In the case of the drum, the phase must be controlled so that the heads reach the beginning of a track at a time which is appropriate to the station reference video fed to the machine.

A slightly more complex version of the speed control system of Figure 5.25(a) is required, as will be seen in Figure 5.25(b). In addition to a toothed wheel or slotted disk, the motor carries a reference slot which produces a rotational phase reference commonly called *once-round tach*. This reference pre-sets the tach divider, so that the tach count becomes an accurate binary representation of the actual angle of rotation.

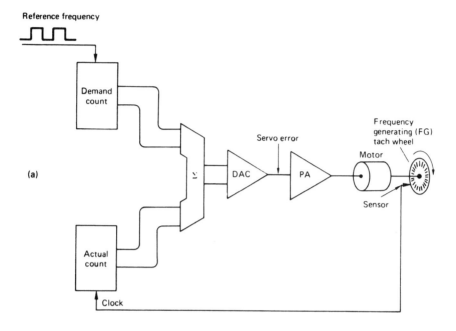

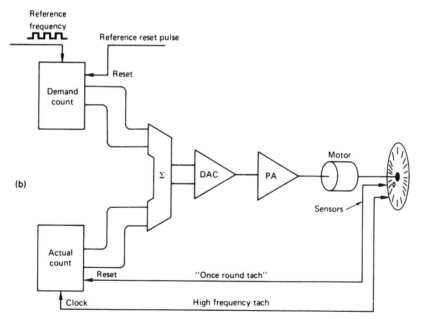

Figure 5.25 (a) Motor speed control using frequency generator on motor shaft. Pulses from FG are compared with pulses from reference to derive servo error. (b) An additional sensor resets the actual count once per revolution, so it counts motor phase angle. Demand count is reset by reference timing. Thus motor phase is locked to reference.

A similar divider is fed by a reference clock as before, and pre-set at appropriate intervals. The reference clock has the same frequency as the tooth passing frequency of the tacho at normal speed. In a segmented machine which needs two drum rotations per field, the counter will need to be pre-set twice per field, or, more elegantly, the counter will have an additional high order bit which does not go to the adder, and then it can be pre-set once per field, since neglect of the upper bit will cause two repeated counts of half a field duration each, with an overflow between.

The adder output will increase or decrease the motor drive until the once-round tach occurs exactly opposite the reference pre-set pulse, because in this condition the sum of the two inputs to the adder is always zero.

The binary count of the tach counter can be used to address a rotation phase PROM. This will be programmed to generate signals which enable the different sectors of the recorded format to be put in the correct place on the track. For example, if it is desired to edit one audio channel without changing any other part of a recording, the record head must be enabled for a short period at precisely the correct drum angle. The drum phase PROM will provide the timing information needed.

When the tape is playing, the phase of the control track must be locked to reference segment phase in order to achieve accurate tracking.

Figure 5.26 shows that a similar configuration to the drum servo is used, but there is no once-round tach on the capstan wheel. Instead, the tach counter is reset by the segment pulses obtained by replaying the control track. Since the

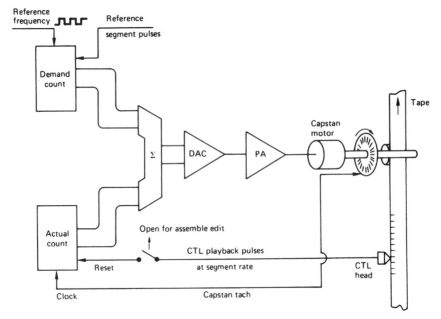

Figure 5.26 If the encoded counter is reset by CTL pulses, it will count linear tape phase, i.e. distance between CTL pulses. Controlling demand counter from reference segment pulses phase-locks tape CTL track to segment rate resulting in correct tracking. At an assemble edit the reset is disabled and the capstan servo makes a smooth transition to the velocity control mode of Figure 5.25(a).

speed of the control track is proportional to the capstan speed, resetting the tach count in this way results in a count of control track phase. The reference counter is reset by segment rate pulses, which can be obtained from the drum, and so the capstan motor will be driven in such a way that the phase error between control track pulses and reference pulses is minimized. In this way the rotary heads will accurately track the diagonal tracks.

During an assemble edit, the capstan will phase lock to control track during the pre-roll, but must revert to constant speed mode at the in-point, since the control track will be recorded from that point. This transition can be obtained by simply disabling the capstan tach counter reset, which causes the system to revert to the speed control servo of Figure 5.25.

5.12 Tension servos

It has been shown that tape tension control is critical in helical scan machines, primarily to ensure interchange and the correct head contact. Tension control will also be necessary for shuttle to ensure correct tape packing.

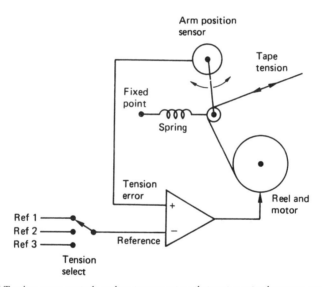

Figure 5.27 Tension servo controls reel motor current so that motor extends sprung arm. Sensor determines extension of spring and thus tape tension.

Figure 5.27 shows a typical back tension control system. A swinging guide called a tension arm is mounted on a position sensor which can be optical or magnetic. A spring applies a force to the tension arm in a direction which would make the tape path longer. The position sensor output is connected to the supply reel motor amplifier which is biased in such a way that when the sensor is in the centre of its travel the motor will receive no drive. The polarity of the system is arranged so that the reel motor will be driven in reverse when the spring contracts. The result is that the reel motor will apply a reverse torque which will extend the spring as it attempts to return the tension arm to the neutral position.

If the system is given adequate loop gain, a minute deflection of the arm will result in full motor torque, so the arm will be kept in an essentially constant position. This means that the spring will have a constant length, and so the tape tension will be constant. Different tensions can be obtained by switching offsets into the feedback loop, which result in the system null being at a different extension of the spring.

The error in the servo will only be small if the reel can accelerate fast enough to follow tape motion. In a machine with permanent capstan engagement, the capstan can accelerate much faster than the reels can. If not controlled, this would lead to the tension arm moving to one or other end of its travel, resulting in tape stretch, or a slack loop which will subsequently snatch tight with the same results. A fixed acceleration limit on the capstan servo would prevent the problem, but it would have to be set to allow a full reel on a large size cassette to keep up. The motion of a small cassette with vastly reduced inertia would be made artificially ponderous. The solution is to feed back the displacement of the tension sensors to the capstan servo. If the magnitude of the tension error from either tension arm is excessive, the capstan acceleration is cut back. In this way the reels are accelerated as fast as possible without the tension becoming incorrect.

In a cassette-based recorder, the tension arms usually need to be motorized so that they can fit into the mouth of the cassette for loading, and pull tape out into the threaded position. It is possible to replace the spring which provides tape tension with a steady current through the arm motor. By controlling this current, the tape tension can be programmed.

5.13 Tape remaining sensing

It is most important in a cassette to prevent the tape running out at speed. The tape is spliced to a heavy leader at each end, and this leader is firmly attached to the reel hub. In an audio cassette, there is sufficient length of this leader to reach to the other reel, and so the impact of a run-off can be withstood. This approach cannot be used with a video cassette, because the heavy leader cannot be allowed to enter the drum, as it would damage the rotating heads.

The transport must compute the tape remaining in order to prevent running off at speed. This may be done by measuring the linear speed of the tape and comparing it with the rotational speed of the reel. The linear speed will be the capstan speed in a permanent capstan drive transport; a timer roller will be necessary in a pinch roller type transport. Alternatively, tape remaining may be computed by comparing the speed of the two reels. The rotational speed of the reels will be obtained from a frequency generator on the reel motors. Figure 5.28 shows a simple method of computing the tape remaining. Pulses from the capstan FG cause a counter to increment. When a reel FG pulse occurs, the count will be transferred to a latch, and the counter will be reset. When the reel is full, there will be many capstan FG pulses between reel FG pulses, but as the radius of the tape pack falls, the count transferred to the latch will also fall. It will be possible to determine the limit count from a knowledge of the capstan and reel hub diameters, and the number of teeth on their generators. The latch count is not quite the pack radius, because if the tension arm is moving due to an acceleration, the linear speed of the tape at the capstan will not be the same as the linear speed at the reel. To prevent false shutdowns when accelerating near the end of the, tape, the tension arm signal may be

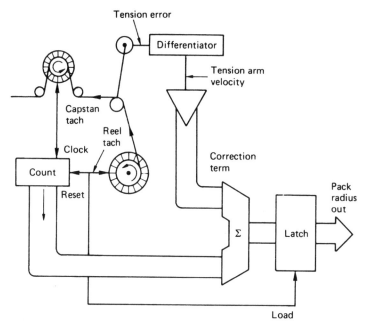

Figure 5.28 Tape remaining is calculated by comparing capstan tach with reel tach. If tension arm is moving, tape speed at reel and capstan will be different, so correction term from tension arm sensor is added. Pinch-roller-type transports disengage the capstan in shuttle, and so the timer roller tacho would be used instead.

differentiated, to give an arm velocity signal, and this can be digitized and used to produce a correction factor for the radius parameter.

To prevent run-offs, the reel pack radius of the reel which is unwinding profiles the allowable shuttle speed, so that as the pack radius falls, the tape speed falls with it. Thus when the tape finally runs out, it will be travelling at very low speed, and the photo-electric sensor which detects the leader will be able to halt the transport without damage.

5.14 Video cassettes

The first video recording format, Quadruplex, used two-inch tape on open reels. The B- and C-formats used one-inch tape, again on open reels. All subsequent analog and digital formats use cassettes. The main advantages of a cassette are that the medium is better protected from contamination whilst out of the transport, and that an unskilled operator or a mechanical elevator can load the tape.

Unfortunately a cassette takes up more space than a tape reel, because it must contain two such reels, only one of which will be full at any one time. In some cases it is possible to reduce the space needed by using flangeless hubs and guiding liner sheets as is done in the Compact Cassette and RDAT, or pairs of hubs with flanges on opposite sides, as in U-matic. Whilst such approaches are acceptable for consumer and industrial products, they are inappropriate for the professional cassettes, because these will be expected to wind at high speeds in automation and editing systems. Accordingly the professional cassette contains two fully flanged reels side by side. The centre of each hub is fitted with a thrust pad and when the cassette is not in the drive a spring acts on this pad and presses the lower flange of each reel firmly against the body of the cassette to exclude dust. When the cassette is in the machine the relative heights of the reel turntables and the cassette supports are such that the reels seat on the turntables before the cassette comes to rest. This opens a clearance space between the reel flanges and the cassette body by compressing the springs. This should be borne in mind if a machine is being tested without the cassette elevator as a suitable weight must be placed on the cassette in order to compress the springs.

The use of a cassette means that it is not as easy to provide a range of sizes as it is with open reels. Simply putting smaller reels in a cassette with the same hub spacing does not produce a significantly smaller cassette. The only solution is to specify different hub spacings for different sizes of cassette. This gives the best volumetric efficiency for storage, but it does mean that the transport must be able to reposition the reel drive motors if it is to play more than one size of cassette.

Some formats, such as VHS and Video-8 allow only one cassette size. Some, such as Betacam and U-matic, offer two cassette sizes, whereas almost all other formats offer three. If the small, medium and large cassettes are placed in a stack with their throats and tape guides in a vertical line, the centres of the hubs will be seen to fall on a pair of diagonal lines going outwards and backwards. This arrangement was chosen to allow the reel motors to travel along a linear track in machines which accept more than one size.

5.15 Threading the tape

It is inherent in helical scan recorders that the tape enters and leaves the head drum at different heights. In open reel recorders, the reels were simply mounted at different heights, but in a cassette this is not practicable. The tape must be geometrically manipulated in some way. There are several approaches to the geometrical problem; two examples are given here.

In the Sony D-2 transports, the first approach is taken to the tape guidance. Figure 5.29(a) shows tape wrapping a drum, with the usual elevation difference between entrance and exit. In Figure 5.29(b) the drum has been tilted so that entrance and exit guides are at the same height. The tape now approaches in the wrong plane. It will be found that if the wrap angle on the entry and exit guides is reduced, an angle can be found where the edge of the tape enters and leaves in the plane of the cassette, as shown in Figure 5.29(c). At this stage the tape edge is in the cassette plane, but its surface is not at right angles to that plane: it is leaning over. The entry and exit guides are now tilted in the plane of the tape tangential to the drum until the tape feeding them is at right angles to the cassette plane, as in Figure 5.29(d). In this way, the tape is not subjected to any twisting as it always remains planar. This approach allows a very shallow transport construction which is highly suitable for portable operation.

Figure 5.30 shows the second approach used in the Sony D-1 transport. This uses an extended wrap angle in order to reduce the frequencies at the heads. The previous approach is difficult to use with an extended wrap. The drum axis is

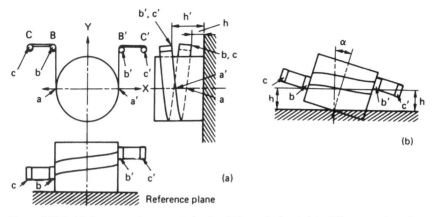

Figure 5.29 In (a) the scanner has a vertical axis which results in a height difference and a twist between the entrance plane *BC* and the exit plane *B'C'*.

In (b) the scanner has been tilted through an angle α such that points *b* and *b'* are both at height *h*.

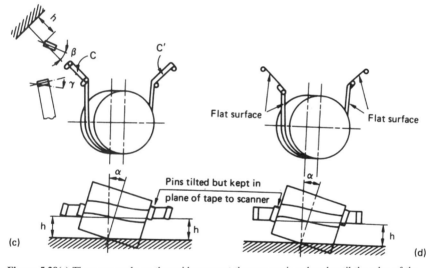

Figure 5.29(c) The wrap angle on the guides nearest the scanner is reduced until the edge of the tape lies in the reference plane. The tape in planes *C* and *C'* remains flat. The pins now incline at angle β to the reference surface.

In (d) the outer pins can be made vertical if the plane of *C* and *C'* is brought perpendicular to the reference surface. This is done by tilting the inner pins but keeping them in the plane of the tape from inner pin to scanner. Tape entry and exit are now coplanar. (Based on drawings courtesy of Sony Broadcast.)

vertical and tape is led down from the supply reel to the drum entrance. Tape then climbs up the drum ramp, and is led down once more to the cassette plane.

Various methods exist to achieve the helical displacement of the tape. Some VTR transports have used conical posts, but these have the disadvantages that there is a considerable lateral force against the edge of the tape, and that they cannot be allowed to revolve or the tape would climb off them. Angled pins do

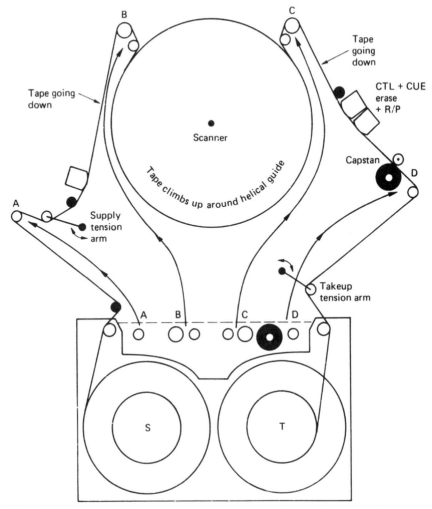

Figure 5.30 In the Sony D-1 transport an extended wrap is used, and guides move on both sides of the scanner to create the wrap. Tape begins the helix below the cassette plane and ends the scan above it. This contrasts with the Ampex approach where the tape begins the helix far below the cassette plane and ends in the cassette plane.

not suffer side force, but again cannot be allowed to revolve. The friction caused by non-rotating pins can be reduced by air lubrication from a compressor, as used in Ampex transports, or by vibrating them ultrasonically with a piezo-electric actuator, as is done in certain Sony transports.

In the Ampex D-2 and DCT transports, the tape in the plane of the cassette is slightly twisted on a long run, and then passes around a conventional guide which causes it to leave the cassette plane at an angle. The twist is too small to approach the elastic limit of the tape, which is quite unharmed. A second guide set at the same angle as the drum axis passes the tape to the drum. Figure 5.31 contrasts the tape twist and angled guide methods.

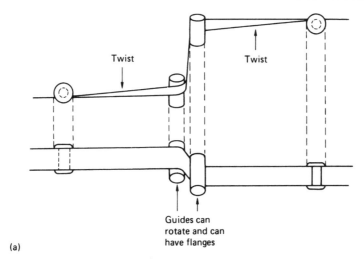

Twist

Twist

Guides can
rotate and can
have flanges

(a)

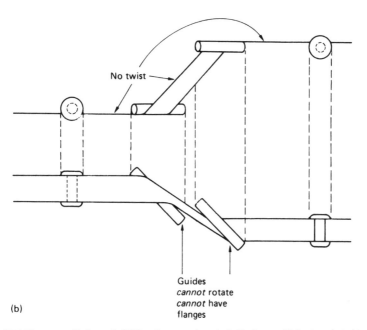

No twist

Guides
cannot rotate
cannot have
flanges

(b)

Figure 5.31 The contradictions of shifting the tape plane in helical scan. If the tape is twisted, the guides can rotate. If it is not, they cannot. Long gentle twist is good, but not compact enough for portable use.

The threading process will be considered using the Panasonic D-3/D-5 transport as an example. As with any VCR, the guides start inside the cassette, and move to various positions as threading proceeds. The sequence can be followed in Figure 5.32. The entry side threading is performed by guide P2 which swings anticlockwise on an arm to wrap the tape onto fixed guide P1 and the full

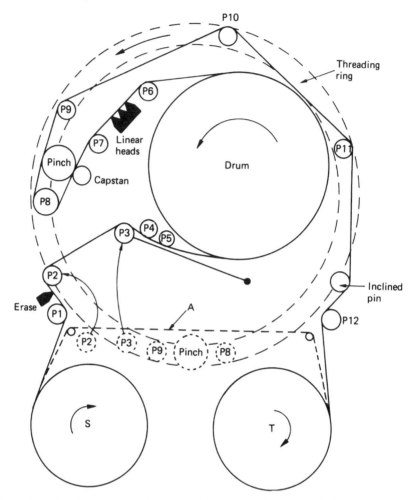

Figure 5.32 Threading sequence of Panasonic D-3 transport. When cassette is first loaded, tape runs straight between the cassette pins (dashed line shown at A) in front of the moving guide pins P2, P3, P9, P8 and the pinch roller. Guides P2 and P3 wrap the entry side by swinging on arms. P3 is in fact the tension arm. The pinch roller and its guides travel anticlockwise on the large threading ring. As the ring rotates P10 and P11 guide the return loop. The inclined pin hinges over the edge of the tape and does not need to be in the cassette mouth at threading start.

width erase head and by the tension arm guide P3 which swings clockwise to bring the tape across the drum entry guides P4 and P5. The drum wrapping and exit side threading is performed by guides which move in a circular path on a threading ring, which rotates around the drum and capstan. When the cassette is initially lowered, guide P8, the pinch roller and guide P9 are inside the front run of tape. As the threading ring turns anticlockwise, these guides take a loop of tape from the cassette and begin to wrap it around the drum. As the threading ring proceeds further, guide P10 and then guide P11 come into contact with the return loop, and the leading guide completes the wrap of the drum and wraps fixed exit guide P6, the fixed heads, fixed capstan guide P7 and the capstan. The pinch roller completes its travel by locating in a cage which is operated by the pinch solenoid. It is no longer supported by the threading ring.

5.16 The signal path

The tape, heads and mechanism of a VTR do not understand the meaning of the waveforms they record. Consequently there is no fundamental difference between analog and digital recorders at this level. The difference is purely in the way that replayed signals are interpreted. In an analog machine, the varying replay signal directly represents the varying video waveform. In a digital machine the replay signal still varies, but it is interpreted as discrete levels representing binary data. These data then represent the video signal. Consequently the transports of analog and digital machines have a lot in common, whereas the signal systems are totally different.

In professional work it is important to be quite certain that a recording is being made, and the only way of guaranteeing that this is so is actually to play the tape as it is being recorded. Extra heads are fitted to the revolving drum in such a way that they pass along the slant tracks directly behind the record heads. The drum must carry additional rotary transformers so that signals can simultaneously enter and leave the rotating head assembly. As can be seen in Figure 5.33 the input

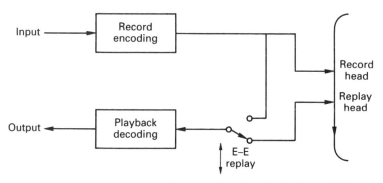

Figure 5.33 A professional DVTR uses confidence replay, where the signal recorded is immediately played back. If the tape is not running, the heads are bypassed in E–E mode so that all of the circuitry can be checked.

signal will be made available at the machine output if all is well. In analog machines the quality of the recording can only be assessed by watching a picture monitor connected to the confidence replay output during recording. With a digital machine this is not necessary, and instead the rate at which the replay channel performs error corrections should be monitored. In some machines the error rate is made available at an output socket so that remote or centralized data reliability logging can be used.

It will be seen from Figure 5.33 that when the machine is not running, a connection is made which bypasses the record and playback heads. The output signal in this mode has passed through every process in the machine except the actual tape/head system. This is known as E–E (electronics to electronics) mode, and it is used in both analog and digital machines as a good indication that the circuitry is functioning.

5.17 Analog video recording

In a rotary-head recorder the head revolves at high speed and the tape contact is intermittent. When the head first makes contact with the tape the resultant impact combines with the flexibility of the tape to cause a damped mechanical resonance whereby the pressure between the head and the tape varies. Under these conditions direct recording, as used for example with analog audio, is of no use as the contact variations affect the amplitude and frequency response. In order to overcome the amplitude instability of rotary-head recorders, frequency modulation was adopted from the earliest formats and has since become universal in analog machines.

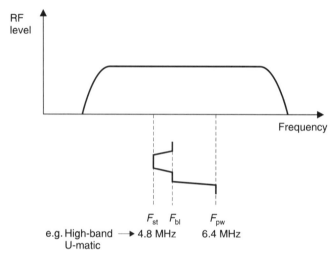

Figure 5.34 In FM recording the video signal voltage determines the frequency of an oscillator. For each format, frequencies for sync tip, blanking and peak white are defined.

Figure 5.34 shows the principle of frequency modulation (FM). A voltage-controlled oscillator (VCO) is supplied with the video signal and the result is a frequency proportional to the video voltage. The frequencies for sync tip, blanking and peak white are defined for a given format. On replay, the signal is amplified by a very large gain factor and then clipped, so that amplitude variations are largely eliminated. The FM radio transmission system uses a similar principle to reduce the effect of interference. A further advantage of FM recording is that the effects of magnetic non-linearity are eliminated and no bias is required. The penalty of frequency modulation is that the bandwidth required at the tape is increased. Figure 5.35(a) shows that when a carrier is frequency modulated, the result is a series of sidebands which are spaced above and below the carrier by integer multiples of the modulation frequency. The relative amplitudes of the various sidebands can be calculated using Bessel functions; however, these are beyond the scope of this book. In practice only the first order sidebands are used as the energy in the second and higher sidebands is small and, in the case of the upper sidebands, an excessively high frequency response is required.

In order to reduce the bandwidth required on tape, the carrier frequency is chosen to be as low as possible. When the ratio of the modulating frequency to the carrier frequency is high, a large *modulation index* is said to be in use. This results in the second and higher order lower sidebands having negative frequencies which fold back around into the first order passband as shown in Figure 5.35(b). If the amplitude of such folded sidebands is excessive, the result is *beat* or difference frequencies which interfere with the baseband signal on demodulation. The resultant patterns on the picture are called moiré after the interference effect observed in finely woven cloth.

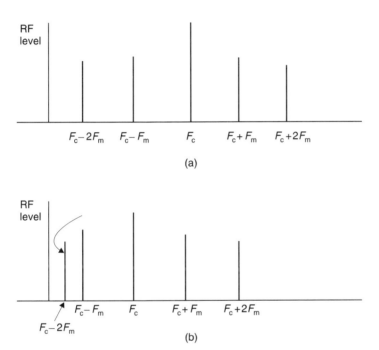

Figure 5.35 (a) Frequency modulation gives rise to a series of sidebands. (b) When a large modulation index is used, the lower sidebands fold about zero Hz to become positive frequencies.

A frequency-to-voltage converter, otherwise known as a demodulator or discriminator, is used to return to a baseband video signal. Although the *absolute* amplitude of a frequency modulated signal is relatively unimportant, the relative amplitude of the carrier and the first order sidebands must be maintained otherwise the baseband video signal will be distorted. As Section 5.2 showed, the frequency response of a magnetic tape channel is far from flat and suffers a loss at high frequencies owing to the head gap effect. A practical VTR will require a replay equalizer which opposes the gap loss in order to balance the amplitudes of the sidebands. As the heads wear the equalizer will need to be adjusted.

It is a characteristic of FM systems that the noise in the channel is proportional to frequency. Stated differently, the signal-to-noise ratio is triangular and so the upper sideband contributes more noise than the lower sideband. Figure 5.36 shows why this should be so. An ideal demodulator removes amplitude disturbances by clipping the offtape signal. The demodulator works by analysing the position of zero crossings in the FM signal with respect to the time axis. Noise added to a sloping signal can change the position of a zero crossing, and cause the estimated frequency to be in error, resulting in noise in the demodulated baseband signal. Figure 5.36 shows that as frequency rises, the period of a signal becomes smaller. As a result, a given disturbance on the time axis assumes a greater proportion of the signal period at high frequencies than it does at low frequencies. As a result, the noise is proportional to frequency. Stated in technical terms, the SNR deteriorates at 6 dB per octave.

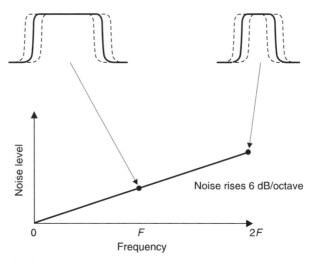

Figure 5.36 Noise disturbs the position of zero crossings. In an FM signal the effect forms a greater proportion of the cycle as frequency rises, hence the triangular noise spectrum.

Fortunately it was discovered that if the gain of the lower side band is increased whilst the gain of the upper sideband is reduced *by the same amount*, no distortion occurs. Thus if the replay signal, after equalization, is subject to a filter with a frequency response falling at 6 dB per octave, the demodulated signal is undistorted and a useful improvement in signal-to-noise ratio is obtained because the higher noise level in the upper sideband has less effect on the demodulated signal. A further improvement may be obtained if the video signal is subject to *pre-emphasis* on recording and a matching *de-emphasis* on replay. Pre-emphasis causes high frequencies to be boosted with respect to low frequencies.

5.18 The FM channel

Figure 5.37 shows a typical FM record/playback channel. In order to meet the format specification, it is important that the correct frequencies are produced by the appropriate video signal levels. The first step is to use a black-level clamp on the input signal. In consumer equipment, it is assumed that camera aperture control may be less than perfect such that the amplitude of the video signal to be

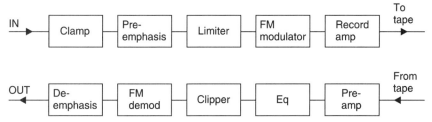

Figure 5.37 The essential stages in an FM record/playback channel; see text for details.

recorded may be less than the signal gamut allows. In this case an automatic gain control (AGC) system will be used to boost low amplitude video until it exercises the entire gamut.

In industrial or low-end professional recorders the AGC is used to make the black-to-sync level constant.

Professional recorders assume that the user has the signal levels under better control and use a system which ensures that the frequency of the FM carrier is correct during blanking. This is done using a local demodulator and a crystal oscillator which runs at the blanking frequency specified by the standard. Figure 5.38 shows how the system works. During blanking, the video waveform must have the correct voltage due to the action of the black-level clamp. Thus if the output frequency of the frequency modulator is incorrect it must be due to drift in the modulator. The local demodulator in the record channel is switched between the modulator output during blanking and the crystal oscillator at other times. If the modulator is correctly calibrated, the demodulator output will not change. However, if there is a frequency drift in the modulator, locally demodulated blanking will not produce the same voltage as demodulated crystal reference. The voltage error can be fed back to the DC component of the modulator in such a sense as to cancel the error.

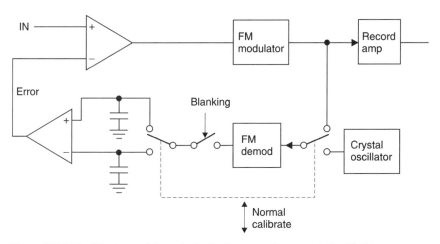

Figure 5.38 Self-calibrating modulator checks for the correct frequency during blanking.

5.19 Wideband composite recording

In composite video there is a single waveform to be recorded which carries the chroma information as a superimposed carrier. In a wideband recorder such as B- and C-format, this waveform is fed directly to a single modulator. The presence of the colour subcarrier causes a large component at high frequencies. Figure 5.39 shows that the first order sidebands will spread over a large range, with a centre frequency which depends upon the luminance level.

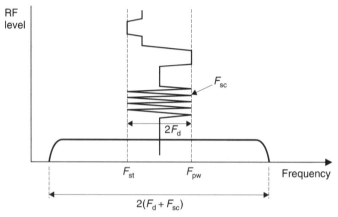

Figure 5.39 When using FM with composite video, the chroma produces strong sidebands around the frequency determined by the luminance level.

As the dominant high frequency energy in a composite FM recording is due to the chroma, which is at a known frequency, it is possible to predict where the folded sidebands will appear for a given carrier frequency. The signal-to-noise ratio is not a simple function of the carrier frequency, but has a series of steps, or shelves, which result from the interaction of the real and reflected sidebands. As a result it is possible to select a carrier frequency at which the moiré is minimized by making the folded sidebands appear at a frequency which is less significant. This technique is known as *shelf working*.

As the subcarrier frequencies of PAL and NTSC are different, it follows that different carrier frequencies will be needed in composite FM VTRs, and this is indeed the case.

Noise in the replay signal has the effect of moving zero crossings in the chroma burst. Thus the burst SNR determines the accuracy of subsequent chroma decoding. An effective improvement in burst SNR of 6 dB can be obtained by recording it at double amplitude and switching in a gain reduction on playback. This technique is used in, for example, the C-format.

In direct composite recoding, the effect of incorrect equalization is that the relative amplitudes of high and low video frequencies change. The lowest video frequency is due to sync pulses, whose amplitude is easy to measure. The composite burst is a high frequency of standard amplitude and this can also be measured on replay. If the equalizer is correctly set, the relative amplitudes of sync to blanking and burst should be correct. If the equalizer is set wrongly, the relative levels will be incorrect. This is the principle of the *auto-chroma* system used on certain production VTRs. The relative levels of sync and burst are used to programme the equalizer so that the correct equalization is automatically arrived at. In a simple auto-chroma system, filtering is used so that the equalizer response stays essentially the same for an entire field. More advanced systems use *line-by-line auto-chroma* in which the machine builds up a map of the equalization required in each picture line and changes the equalization dynamically throughout the frame. This overcomes the dynamic changes in frequency response caused by the tape elasticity interacting with head impacts.

5.20 Colour-under recording

In production applications the direct recording of composite video at full bandwidth is essential. However, for many purposes a lower resolution picture with a luminance bandwidth of around 3 MHz is acceptable, particularly in consumer and industrial use. Unfortunately composite video concentrates the colour information in a high frequency subcarrier and simple bandwidth reduction removes the colour.

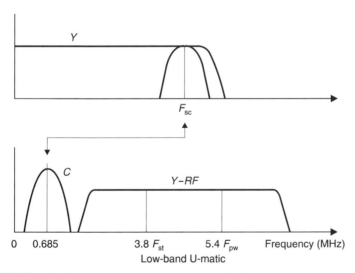

Figure 5.40 The principle of colour-under recording where the chroma is downconverted.

Colour-under recording was developed to allow composite video to be recorded without full-bandwidth luminance. Figure 5.40 shows the principle. The incoming composite signal is split by a low-pass filter which removes chroma to give a luminance signal and a bandpass filter which outputs chroma (and high frequency luminance). The chroma signal is then *heterodyned* or multiplied by the signal from an oscillator. This results in sum and difference frequencies. The sum frequency is rejected, but a new *down-converted* chroma signal is produced at the difference frequency.

The luminance signal is supplied to a frequency modulator as normal, and the downconverted chroma is linearly added to the FM luminance for recording. Thus luminance is recorded using FM, whereas chroma is directly recorded using the FM video as linearizing bias. Figure 5.41(a) shows the resultant spectrum for low-band U-matic in which it can be seen that the chroma is recorded at frequencies below those needed by the luminance. Figure 5.41(b) shows the spectrum of high-band U-matic.

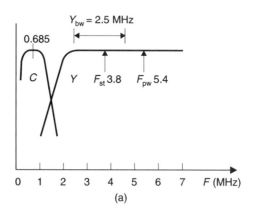

(a)

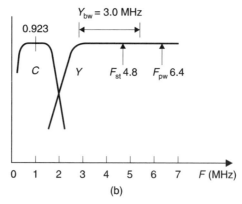

(b)

Figure 5.41 (a) Spectrum on tape for low-band U-matic. (b) In high-band U-matic the tape frequencies are raised to improve performance.

On replay the offtape signal is band split. The chroma signal is heterodyned once more by a suitable local oscillator to produce chroma at the correct frequency again.

Whilst colour-under recording works well, one consequence of its use is that there are very few cycles of burst in the downconverted signal. This increases the chances of chroma phase errors. In U-matic the problem is overcome by recording additional bursts during blanking. These can be used on replay to determine subcarrier phase more accurately, but are removed from the composite output.

The colour-under process has been very successful and is used in U-matic, Betamax, VHS and Video-8. In U-matic, guard bands are provided between the tracks, whereas in later formats guard-band-less azimuth recording is used. As has been explained earlier, the azimuth effect fails at low frequencies and this affects the downconverted chroma signal. The solution is to reject chroma crosstalk in a different way. The heterodyne frequency is chosen so that the new downconverted subcarrier changes phase by one quadrant per field. When the replay head picks up crosstalk from the two adjacent tracks, that from one track will lead by 90 degrees whereas that from the other track will lag by 90 degrees. As a result the two crosstalk signals will be antiphase and will effectively cancel one another out.

5.21 *Y/C* recording

One of the most difficult processes in composite video is the separation of luminance and chroma. In the S-VHS format the colour-under system is used, but the chroma and luminance are kept separate as much as possible. Figure 5.42 shows

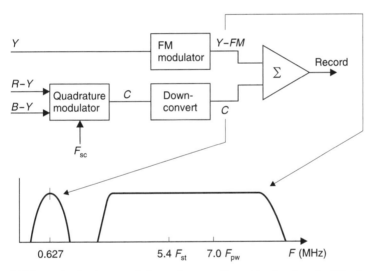

Figure 5.42 Separating luminance and chroma in composite working is extremely difficult. S-VHS solves the problem by keeping them separate.

how S-VHS works. Using the component output of a camera, an S-VHS recorder will produce a quadrature-modulated chroma signal, but this will not be added to luminance to make a conventional composite signal. Instead the chroma is directly recorded and the luminance is frequency modulated. On replay the downconverted chroma is heterodyned to standard subcarrier frequency, but separate *Y* and *C* outputs are provided. With a suitable decoder, the *Y/C* separation stage can be bypassed and the chroma is directly demodulated to colour difference signals. Thus although S-VHS is subcarrier-based, it is strictly speaking not a composite format because *Y* and *C* are kept separate. It is not, however, a pure component system because the colour difference signals are quadrature modulated.

5.22 Analog component recording

The first analog component recorders, such as Betacam and M-I, were designed for ENG purposes where full broadcast bandwidth was sacrificed for portability. Prior to these formats, the only alternative had been the use of colour-under recording of a composite signal. Component signals have the advantage that there is no subcarrier. If the bandwidth of a component video system is reduced, the picture simply becomes progressively softer, whereas in composite the colour will be lost. Whilst not as good as broadcast formats, the early analog component machines were a definite improvement over colour-under. Subsequent tape and head developments allowed the bandwidth of analog component formats to be increased to meet broadcast standards. Betacam SP and M-II both used metal particle tape and raised carrier frequencies.

In analog components, there are three signals to be recorded: full bandwidth luminance and two reduced bandwidth colour difference signals. Analog component recorders are therefore multichannel devices. Recording signals of different bandwidths is inefficient and an elegant solution was devised. As Section 5.8 showed, time compression is used to multiplex the colour difference signals into one channel having the same bandwidth as that of the luminance channel. With this technique, only two simultaneous channels are required. The drum on the tape transport carries pairs of heads which work in parallel. These heads have opposite azimuth and can record tracks which are adjacent on the tape.

5.23 Introduction to the digital VTR

Whilst the DVTR is a complex device, it is not necessarily difficult to understand. The machine can be broken down into major areas and then the processes performed there can be further broken down into smaller steps, each of which is relatively easy to follow. The main difficulty with study is to appreciate where the small steps fit in the overall picture. Some of the major steps, such as helical transports and time compression, have already been considered. Further components are considered here to introduce the block diagram of a digital machine.

5.24 Error correction and concealment

As anyone familiar with analog recording will know, magnetic tape is an imperfect medium. It suffers from noise and dropouts, which in analog recording are visible. Upon reproduction of binary data, a bit is either correct or wrong, with no intermediate stage. Small amounts of noise are rejected, but inevitably, infrequent noise impulses cause some individual bits to be in error. Dropouts cause a larger number of bits in one place to be in error. An error of this kind is called a burst error. Whatever the medium and whatever the nature of the mechanism responsible, data are either recovered correctly, or suffer some combination of bit errors and burst errors.

The visibility of a bit error depends upon which bit of the sample is involved. If the LSB of one sample was in error in a detailed, contrasty picture, the effect would be totally masked and no-one could detect it. Conversely, if the MSB of one sample was in error in a flat field, no-one could fail to notice the resulting spot. Clearly a means is needed to render errors from the medium inaudible. This is the purpose of error correction.

In binary, a bit has only two states. If it is wrong, it is only necessary to reverse the state and it must be right. Thus the correction process is trivial and perfect. The main difficulty is in identifying the bits which are in error. This is done by coding the data by adding redundant bits. Adding redundancy is not confined to digital technology – airliners have several engines and cars have twin braking systems. Clearly the more failures which have to be handled, the more redundancy is needed. If a four-engined airliner is designed to fly normally with one engine failed, three of the engines have enough power to reach cruise speed, and the fourth one is redundant. The amount of redundancy is equal to the amount of failure which can be handled. In the case of the failure of two engines, the plane can still fly, but it must slow down; this is graceful degradation. Clearly the chances of a two-engine failure on the same flight are remote.

In digital recording, the amount of error which can be corrected is proportional to the amount of redundancy. Within this limit, the samples are returned to exactly their original value. Consequently *corrected* samples are undetectable. If the amount of error exceeds the amount of redundancy, correction is not possible, and, in order to allow graceful degradation, concealment will be used. Concealment is a process where the value of a missing sample is estimated from those nearby. The estimated sample value is not necessarily exactly the same as the original, and so under some circumstances concealment can be audible, especially if it is frequent. However, in a well designed system, concealments occur with negligible frequency unless there is an actual fault or problem.

Concealment is made possible by rearranging the sample sequence prior to recording. This is shown in Figure 5.43 where odd-numbered samples are separated from even-numbered samples prior to recording. The odd and even sets of samples may be distributed over two tape tracks, so that an uncorrectable burst

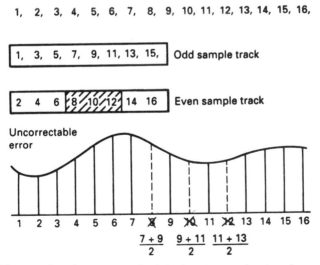

Figure 5.43 In cases where the error correction is inadequate, concealment can be used provided that the samples have been ordered appropriately in the recording. Odd and even samples are recorded in different places as shown here. As a result an uncorrectable error causes incorrect samples to occur singly, between correct samples. In the example shown, sample 8 is incorrect, but samples 7 and 9 are unaffected and an approximation to the value of sample 8 can be had by taking the average value of the two. This interpolated value is substituted for the incorrect value.

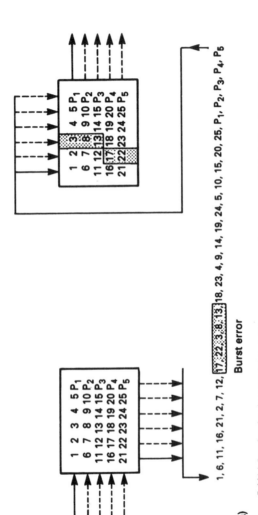

(a)

1, 6, 11, 16, 21, 2, 7, 12, `17, 22, 3, 8, 13,` 18, 23, 4, 9, 14, 19, 24, 5, 10, 15, 20, 25, P_1, P_2, P_3, P_4, P_5

Burst error

Figure 5.44(a) Interleaving is essential to make error correction schemes more efficient. Samples written sequentially in rows into a memory have redundancy P added to each row. The memory is then read in columns and the data sent to the recording medium. On replay the non-sequential samples from the medium are de-interleaved to return them to their normal sequence. This breaks up the burst error (shaded) into one error symbol per row in the memory, which can be corrected by the redundancy P.

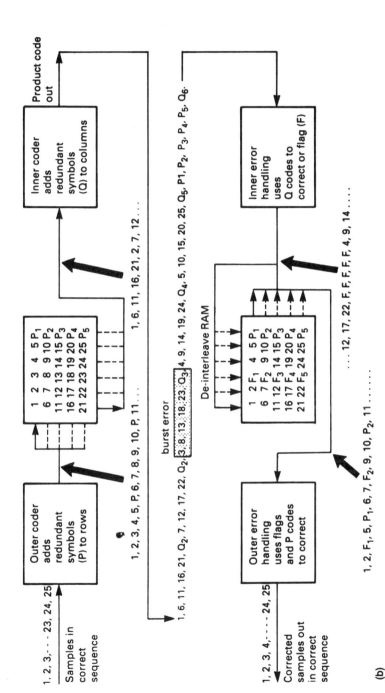

Figure 5.44(b) In addition to the redundancy P on rows, inner redundancy Q is also generated on columns. On replay, the Q code checker will pass on flags F if it finds an error too large to handle itself. The flags pass through the de-interleave process and are used by the outer error correction to identify which symbol in the row needs correcting with P redundancy. The concept of crossing two codes in this way is called a product code.

(b)

error only affects one set. On replay, the samples are recombined into their natural sequence, and the error is now split up so that it results in every other sample being lost in a two-dimensional structure. The picture is now described half as often, but can still be reproduced with some loss of accuracy. This is better than not being reproduced at all, even if it is not perfect. Almost all digital recorders use such an odd/even distribution for concealment. Clearly if errors are fully correctable, the distribution pattern is of no consequence; it is only needed if correction is not possible.

The presence of an error-correction system means that the video (and audio) quality is independent of the tape/head quality, within limits. There is no point in trying to assess the health of a machine by watching a monitor or listening to the audio, as this will not reveal whether the error rate is normal or within a whisker of failure. The only useful procedure is to monitor the frequency with which errors are being corrected, and to compare it with normal figures. Professional DVTRs have an error rate display for this purpose and in addition most allow the error correction system to be disabled for testing.

5.25 Product codes

The higher the recording density, the more data are lost in a given sized dropout. Adding redundancy equal to the size of a dropout to every code is inefficient. Figure 5.44(a) shows that the efficiency of the system can be raised using interleaving. Following distribution, sequential samples from the ADC are assembled into codes, but these are not recorded in their natural sequence. A number of sequential codes are assembled along rows in a memory. When the memory is full, it is copied to the medium by reading down columns. On replay, the samples need to be de-interleaved to return them to their natural sequence. This is done by writing samples from tape into a memory in columns, and when it is full, the memory is read in rows. Samples read from the memory are now in their original sequence so there is no effect on the recording. However, if a burst error occurs on the medium, as is shown shaded on the diagram, it will damage sequential samples in a vertical direction in the de-interleave memory. When the memory is read, a single large error is broken down into a number of small errors whose size is exactly equal to the correcting power of the codes and the correction is performed with maximum efficiency.

An extension of the process of interleave is where the memory array has not only rows made into codewords, but also columns made into codewords by the addition of vertical redundancy. This is known as a product code. Figure 5.44(b) shows that in a product code the redundancy calculated first and checked last is called the outer code, and the redundancy calculated second and checked first is called the inner code. The inner code is formed along tracks on the medium. Random errors due to noise are corrected by the inner code and do not impair the burst-correcting power of the outer code. Burst errors are declared uncorrectable by the inner code which flags the bad samples on the way into the de-interleave memory. The outer code reads the error flags in order to locate the erroneous data. As it does not have to compute the error locations, the outer code can correct more errors.

The interleave, de-interleave, time-compression and timebase-correction processes cause delay and this is evident in the timing of the confidence replay output of DVTRs.

5.26 Shuffling

When a product-code-based recording suffers an uncorrectable error the result is a rectangular block of failed sample values which require concealment. Such a regular structure would be visible even after concealment, and an additional process is necessary to reduce the visibility. Figure 5.45 shows that a shuffle process is performed prior to product coding in which the pixels are moved around the picture in a pseudo-random fashion. The reverse process is used on

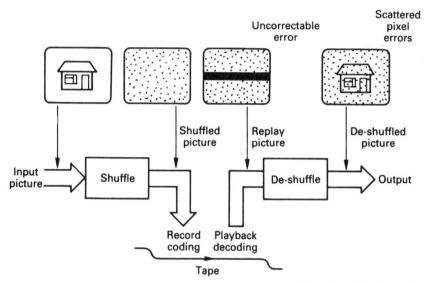

Figure 5.45 The shuffle before recording and the corresponding de-shuffle after playback cancel out as far as the picture is concerned. However, a block of errors due to dropout only experiences the de-shuffle, which spreads the error randomly over the screen. The pixel errors are then easier to conceal.

replay, and the overall effect is nullified. However, if an uncorrectable error occurs, this will only pass through the de-shuffle and so the regular structure of the failed data blocks will be randomized. The errors are spread across the picture as individual failed pixels in an irregular structure.

5.27 Channel coding

In most recorders used for storing digital information, the medium carries a track which reproduces a single waveform. Clearly, data words representing audio samples contain many bits and so they have to be recorded serially, a bit at a time. DVTRs usually have two or four tracks which are read or written simultaneously. At high recording densities, physical tolerances cause phase shifts, or timing errors, between tracks and so it is not possible to read them in parallel. Each track must still be self-contained until the replayed signal has been timebase corrected.

As was seen in Chapter 4, serial transmission requires a coding step to pass a signal down a single channel. Figure 5.46 shows that a DVTR is just a tape recorder which can handle the serial waveform. Clearly, serialized raw data

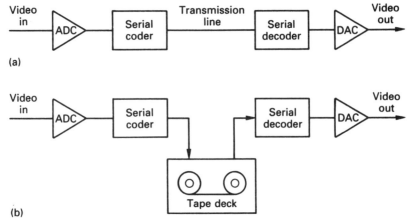

Figure 5.46 A minimal digital video system (a) converts analog video to data which are then serialized for cable transmission. A recorder might in principle be one shown in (b) which simply records the serial waveform of (a). A practical recorder will be much more complex.

cannot be recorded directly: it has to be modulated into a waveform which contains an embedded clock irrespective of the values of the bits in the samples. On replay a circuit called a data separator can lock to the embedded clock and use it to separate strings of identical bits.

The process of modulating serial data to make it self-clocking is called channel coding. Channel coding also shapes the spectrum of the serialized waveform to make it more efficient. With a good channel code, more data can be stored on a given medium.

5.28 Video compression

Digital video operates with an extremely high data rate, particularly in high definition, and one approach to the problem is to reduce that rate without affecting the subjective quality of the picture. The human eye is not equally sensitive to all spatial frequencies, so some coding gain can be obtained by quantizing more coarsely the frequencies which are less visible. Video images typically contain a great deal of redundancy where flat areas contain similar pixel values repeated many times. Furthermore, in many cases there is little difference between one field and the next, and interfield data reduction can be achieved by sending only the differences. Whilst this may achieve considerable reduction, the result is difficult to edit because individual fields can no longer be identified in the data stream. Thus for production purposes, data reduction is restricted to exploiting the redundancy within each field individually. Production DVTRs such as Sony's Digital Betacam and the Ampex DCT use only very mild compression of about 2:1. This allows simple algorithms to be used and also permits multiple generations without artifacts being visible.

Clearly a consumer DVTR needs only single-generation operation and has simple editing requirements. A much greater degree of compression can then be used, which might also take advantage of redundancy between fields.

Data reduction requires an encoder prior to the recording medium and a decoder after it. Unless the matching decoder is available, the recording cannot be played. Data reduction and the corresponding decoding are complex processes and take time, adding to existing delays in signal paths. Concealment of uncorrectable errors is also more difficult on reduced data.

5.29 DVTR block diagram

Figure 5.47(a) shows a representative block diagram of a full bit rate DVTR. Following the converters will be the distribution of odd and even samples and a shuffle process for concealment purposes. An interleaved product code will be formed prior to the channel coding stage which produces the recorded waveform. On replay the data separator decodes the channel code and the inner and outer codes perform correction as in Section 5.25. Following the de-shuffle the data channels are recombined and any necessary concealment will take place. Figure 5.47(b) shows the block diagram of a DVTR using compression. Data from the converters is rearranged from the normal raster scan to sets of pixel blocks upon which the data reduction unit works. A common size is eight pixels horizontally by four vertically. The blocks are then shuffled for concealment purposes. The shuffled blocks are passed through the data reduction unit. The output of this is distributed and then assembled into product codes and channel coded as for a conventional recorder. On replay, data separation and error correction take place as before, but there is now a matching data expansion unit which outputs pixel blocks. These are then de-shuffled prior to the error concealment stage. As concealment is more difficult with pixel blocks, data from another field may be employed for concealment as well as data within the field.

5.30 Operating modes of a digital recorder

The digital video recorder is expected to do much more than record and replay in a modern installation. The main operating modes will be examined here, followed by the more obscure modes.

In *crash record* the tape is either blank or is considered to be blank, and no reference will be made to any previous information on the tape. As with analog video recorders, if a crash recording is made in the middle of an existing recording, the playback will lose lock at the transition. In this mode the full width erase head will be active, and the entire tape format will be laid down, including audio blocks and control track. There are a fixed number of segments in a field, and so the drum speed will be locked to incoming video. The drum phase will be determined by the delay needed to shuffle and encode the data in a segment. Owing to the encoding delay, the recording heads on the drum will begin tracing a segment some time after the beginning of the input field. The capstan will simply rotate at constant speed, driving the tape at the speed specified in the format. As the rotating heads begin a diagonal track, a segment pulse will be recorded in the control track. Once per field, the segment pulse will be accompanied by a field pulse. There will also be a colour frame pulse recorded at appropriate intervals.

5.31 Colour framed playback

Ordinary framing in component recorders only requires that the segmentation on tape is properly undone, so that the all of the segments (if more than one) in one

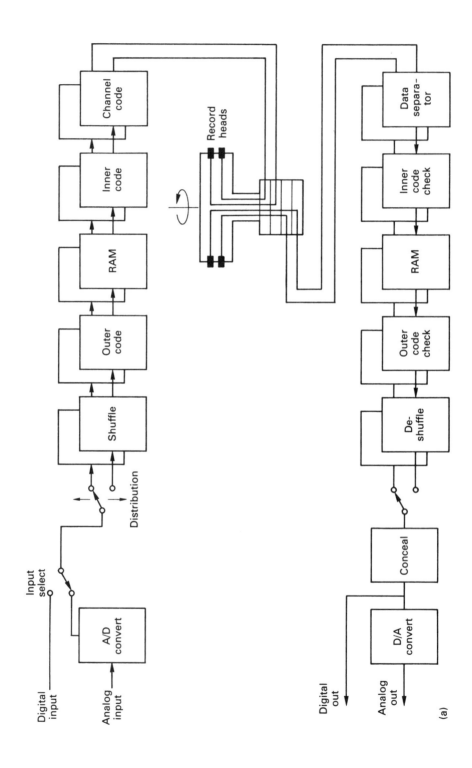

Digital input

Analog input

A/D convert

Input select

Distribution

Shuffle

Outer code

RAM

Inner code

Channel code

Record heads

Data separator

Inner code check

RAM

Outer code check

De-shuffle

Conceal

D/A convert

Digital out

Analog out

(a)

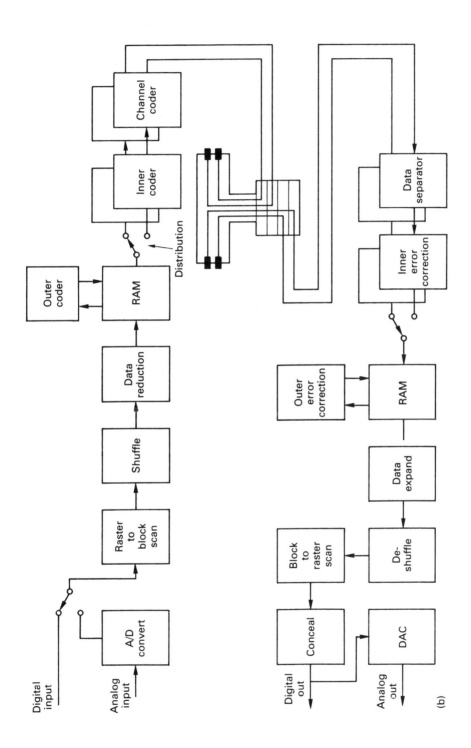

Digital input

Analog input

A/D convert

Raster to block scan

Shuffle

Data reduction

Outer coder

RAM

Distribution

Inner coder

Channel coder

Data separator

Inner error correction

Outer error correction

RAM

Data expand

De-shuffle

Block to raster scan

Conceal

DAC

Digital out

Analog out

(b)

field are assembled together, and that the interlace sequence is synchronous with reference, so that an odd field comes from tape when there is an odd field in the station reference. Composite recorders require colour framing, shown in Figure 5.48(a). On replay, the off-tape field must also be the same type of field in the four- or eight-field sequence as exists in the reference. Many component formats support colour framing which is useful in case they need to record decoded composite signals which may later be re-encoded. If the component replay is colour framed, artifacts due to residual chroma in luminance can be minimized.

The error correction and de-interleaving processes of digital machines and the timebase correction in all machines require a finite time in which to operate, and so the transport must play back segments ahead of real time. The drum speed will be synchronous with reference, and the drum phase will be determined by the decoding delay.

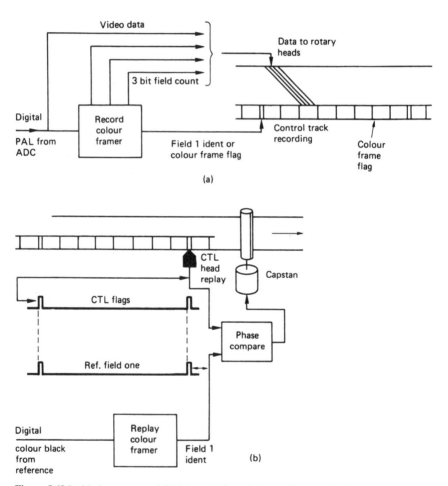

Figure 5.48 In (a) the presence of field 1 on the input is denoted by a colour frame flag on the control track. The field sequence is also written in the rotary tracks.

In (b), on replay the capstan speed will be changed until offtape colour frame flags coincide with reference field 1 identification. Replay video will then be colour framed to reference.

The capstan system will be responsible for tracking and framing, and will need to vary the speed of the tape until framing is achieved. It will then vary the phase of the tape to optimize tracking.

Figure 5.48(b) shows that the capstan and tape form part of a phase locked loop where the phase of the control track pulses is compared with reference pulses. In order to achieve colour framing, the phase comparison must be between reference colour frame pulses and offtape colour frame pulses. In this way the linear motion of the tape is phased such that reference and offtape framing are the same. The capstan speed must vary during this part of the lock-up sequence, and the picture may be temporarily degraded unless the machine has provision for operating at non-normal speed.

Once framing or colour framing is achieved, the capstan will switch to a different mode in order to obtain accurate tracking. The phase comparison will now be made more often using all of the control track pulses. If the phase error is used to modify the capstan drive, the error can be eliminated, since the capstan drives the tape which produces the control track segment pulses. Eliminating this timing error results in the rotating heads following the tape tracks properly. Artificially delaying or advancing the reference pulses from the drum will result in a tracking adjustment.

5.32 Assembly editing

In an assemble edit, new material is appended to an existing recording in such a way that the video timing structure continues unbroken over the edit point. In a component recording only the syncs need to be unbroken, whereas in a composite recording the subcarrier phase will also need to be continuous.

The recording will begin at a vertical interval, and it will be necessary to have a pre-roll in order to synchronize tape and drum motion to the signal to be recorded. The procedure during the pre-roll is similar to that of framed playback, except that the input video timing is used. The goal of the pre-roll process is to ensure that the record head is at the beginning of the first segment in a field exactly one encode delay after the beginning of the desired field in the input video signal. At this point the record head will be turned on. After the assemble point, there will not necessarily be a control track, and the capstan must smoothly enter constant speed mode without a disturbance to tape motion. The control track will begin to record in a continuation of the phase of the existing control track. This process will then continue indefinitely until halted.

5.33 Insert editing

An insert differs from an assemble in that a short part of a recording is replaced by new material somewhere in the centre. An insert can only be made on a tape which has a continuous control track and timecode to allow edit control, because the in- and out-point edits must both be synchronous. The pre-roll will be exactly as for an assemble edit, and the video record process will be exactly the same, but the capstan control will be achieved by playing back the control track at all times, so that the new video tracks are laid down in exactly the same place as the previous recording. At the out-point, the record heads will be turned off at the end of the last segment in a field. The flying erase heads will also be used for a short period at the beginning of an assemble edit until the tape erased by the full-width stationary erase head has reached the scanner.

5.34 Edit optimize

When an edit is made, it is important that the new slant tracks are laid down in exactly the correct place along the tape so that a change of track phase does not occur at the edit point. On a perfectly adjusted machine editing a tape which it has itself recorded this will not happen, but when the tape being edited was recorded elsewhere, there may be a discrepancy between the locations of the control track heads on the two machines concerned.

Edit optimize is an operating mode in which the edit is not made by recording tracks in the *correct* place, but by recording tracks having the *same tracking error* as those already on the tape. As a result the edited tape will require the same tracking adjustment everywhere. This is particularly useful when it is required to edit only the audio blocks in a digital recording as a tracking error during an audio edit results in sectors having an offset as shown in Figure 5.49. Such a track cannot be played properly at any setting of the tracking control.

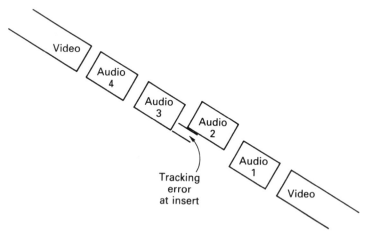

Figure 5.49 If an insert edit of one audio channel is made on a tape containing a tracking error the resultant track has no optimum tracking position. Edit optimize matches the tracking error so that the same tracking can be used for all sectors.

In edit optimize, prior to an edit, the machine plays the tape with the record heads and varies the capstan phase in order to locate the tracking setting where the maximum signal level, or the minimum error rate, is obtained. This tracking will then be employed during the edit so that new tracks have the same or nearly the same alignment as the old tracks.

Whilst edit optimize is a useful feature, it should not be used to excess or when it is not essential. A series of assembly edits, in which each one is optimized to the end of the last recording, may result in tolerance buildup where the tracking slowly changes at each edit as a result of residual error in the optimize system.

5.35 Timecode

Timecode is simply a label attached to each frame on the tape which contains the time at which it was recorded measured in hours, minutes, seconds and frames. It is used for editing, in order to repeatedly return to a selected frame, and for synchronization between audio and video recorders.

There are two ways in which timecode data can be recorded. The first is to use a dedicated linear track, usually alongside the control track, in which there is one timecode entry for every tape frame. Such a linear track can easily be played back over a wide speed range by a stationary head. Timecode of this kind is known as LTC (linear timecode).

LTC clearly cannot be replayed when the tape is stopped or moving very slowly. In DVTRs with track-following heads, particularly those which support pre-read, head deflection may result in a frame being played which is not the one corresponding to the timecode from the stationary head. The player software needs to modify the LTC value as a function of the head deflection.

An alternative timecode is where the information is recorded in the video field itself, so that the above mismatch cannot occur. This is known as vertical interval timecode (VITC) because it is recorded in a line which is in the vertical blanking period. VITC is used in both analog and digital recorders because it has the advantage that it can be recovered with the tape stopped. However, it cannot be recovered in shuttle because the rotary heads do not play entire tracks in this mode. Consequently a machine must be able to switch source according to its operating mode. Most VTRs do not record the whole of the vertical blanking period, and if VITC is to be used, it must be inserted in a line which is within the recorded data area of the format concerned.

5.36 Fast striping

Many machines have a mode in which the control track and timecode tracks can be written or *striped* at high speed. The tape is driven at typically three times normal speed and artificially higher frequency signals are generated and supplied to the stationary heads which record these linear tracks. In some machines this fast striping can be done in coplanar mode, where the tape does not contact the drum and rotary head wear is avoided. In others the drum is still wrapped and must rotate in order to develop an air film, but clearly no slant tracks can be recorded at such a linear speed.

Fast striping records only the control and timecode tracks, which is sufficient reference to allow insert editing to be used. However, when the inserts are made, it is important that the entire slant track is recorded by recording video *and* all of the audio channels. If this is not done, the tape format is violated by recording, say, the video but no audio. On replay the machine will find blank lengths of track where it is expecting ID codes and an error condition may occur.

5.37 Tape speed override

One of the most useful features of a production recorder is the ability to operate at variable speed. The variable speed modes variously available are TSO (tape speed override), slow motion/jog and shuttle.

In TSO, the speed is only changed by a maximum of about 15 per cent from normal in order to trim a programme to fit a broadcast time slot. Clearly the audio must be fully recovered, and so in a digital machine no replay head jumping is permissible. The speed of the entire transport is changed by changing the transport timing reference with respect to station reference. The drum and the capstan change speed in proportion so that the heads still follow all of the slant tracks properly. All of the audio blocks are recovered, and full quality digital audio is output. Owing to the speed change, the audio sampling rate will not be exactly 48 KHz, and a digital pitch changer or sampling rate converter can be used if necessary. Clearly the offtape field rate will no longer match reference, and the difference is accommodated by a framestore/timebase corrector, which is written at offtape speed and read at reference speed. Fields will occasionally be skipped or repeated as TBC addresses lap one another.

5.38 Variable speed replay

The variable speed range first achieved by the C-format analog machines has essentially become the yardstick by which later formats are measured. It is important for the success of a VTR that at least an equal speed range is available. It was seen in Section 5.5 that the movement of the tape results in the tracks having an angle different from the helix angle. The rotary head will only be able to follow the track properly if the tape travels at the correct speed. At all other speeds, the head will move at an angle to the tracks. If the head is able to move along the drum axis as it turns, it will be possible to follow whole tracks at certain tape speeds by moving the head as a function of the rotational angle of the drum. The necessary function can be appreciated by considering the situation when the tape is stopped. The tape track will, of course, be at the track angle, but the head will rotate at the helix angle. The head can be made to follow a stationary track by deflecting it at constant rate by one segment pitch per sweep. In other words, a ramp or triangle waveform is necessary to deflect the head. The slope of the ramp is proportional to the speed *difference*, since at normal speed the difference is zero and no deflection is needed. Clearly the deflection cannot continue to grow forever, because the head will run out of travel, and it must then jump to miss out some tracks and reduce the deflection.

There are a number of issues to be addressed in providing a track-following system. The use of segmented formats means that head jumps necessary to omit or repeat one or more fields must jump over several tracks. This requires a mechanical head positioning system which has the necessary travel and will work reliably despite the enormous acceleration experienced at the perimeter of the drum. In many formats the wrap is 180 degrees and two heads traverse the tape alternately. For variable speed, two movable heads are needed, and they must be independently controlled since they are mounted in opposition on the drum. In segmented formats a control system is required which will ensure that jumps only take place at the end of a field to prevent a picture from two different fields being displayed. The degree of accuracy required is much higher in digital formats because the tracks are much narrower.

When the tape speed is close to three times normal, most of the time a two-field jump will be necessary at the end of every field. Figure 5.50 shows what happens in a segmented format having four tracks per field (PAL D-3). Since the control track phase is random, an offset of up to $\pm\frac{1}{2}$ a field will be superimposed

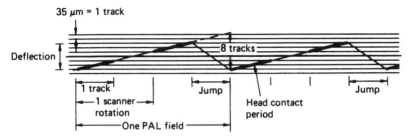

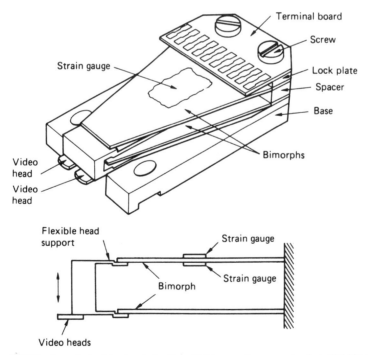

Figure 5.50 Head deflection waveform for PAL D-3 at +3× normal speed. This requires a jump of two fields between every field played, and this corresponds to eight tracks. Since head pairs trace the tape alternately, the head has half a revolution in which to jump, so the actual jump is only six tracks. However, the vertical position of the above waveform is subject to an uncertainty of plus or minus two tracks because capstan phase is random during variable speed.

on the deflection, so that if a two-field jump must always be possible, a total deflection of three fields must be available. This, along with the segmentation employed, determines the mechanical travel that the heads must be capable of.

5.39 The head actuator

In most machines, the actuator used for head deflection is based on piezo-electric elements. Figure 5.51 shows the construction of the Sony dynamic tracking head.

Figure 5.51 The dynamic tracking head of a Sony D-2 transport uses a pair of parallel bimorphs to maintain head zenith angle. Note use of strain gauges for feedback. (Courtesy Sony Broadcast)

A pair of parallel piezo-electric bimorphs is used, to ensure that head zenith is affected as little as possible by deflection. The basic principle of the actuator is that an applied voltage causes the barium titanate crystal to shrink. If two thin plates are bonded together to create a bimorph, the shrinkage of one of them will result in bending. A stale sandwich displays the same effect. Application of voltage to one or other of the elements allows deflection in either direction, although care must be taken to prevent reverse voltage being applied to an element since this will destroy the inherent electric field. In view of the high-g environment, which attempts to restore the actuator to the neutral position, high deflection voltages are necessary. The deflection amplifiers are usually static, and feed the drum via slip rings which are often fitted on the top of the drum. When worn, these can spark and cause interference. This is visible on the picture in analog machines, whereas in digital machines it serves to increase the error rate. Piezo-electric actuators display hysteresis, and some form of position feedback is necessary to allow a linear system. This is obtained by strain gauges which are attached to one of the bimorphs, and can be seen in the figure. When power is first applied to the transport, the actuator is supplied with a gradually decaying sinusoidal drive signal, which removes any unwanted set from the bimorph.

In some machines a moving coil actuator is used. Using rare earth magnets which offer high field strength with low mass, the moving coil actuator works like a miniature loudspeaker and has the advantage that high voltages are not required.

5.40 Non-linear video editing

Non-linear video editing has no parallel in analog equipment and takes advantage of the freedom to store digitized image data in any suitable medium and the signal processing techniques developed in computation. The images may have originated on film or video. Recently images which have been synthesized by computer have been added. Although aesthetically film and video have traditionally had little in common, from a purely technological standpoint many of the necessary processes are similar.

In all types of editing the goal is the appropriate sequence of material at the appropriate time. In an ideal world the difficulty and cost involved in creating the perfect edited work are discounted. In practice there is economic pressure to speed up the editing process and to use cheaper media. Editors will not accept new technologies if they form an obstacle to the creative process, but if a new approach to editing takes nothing away, it will be considered. If something is added, such as freedom or flexibility, so much the better. When there was only film or video tape editing, it did not need a qualifying name. Now that images are stored as data, alternative storage media have become available which allow editors to reach the same goal but using different techniques. Whilst digital VTR formats copy their analog predecessors and support field accurate editing on the tape itself, in all other digital editing samples from various sources are brought from the storage media to various pages of RAM. The edit is viewed by selectively processing two (or more) sample streams retrieved from RAM. Thus the nature of the storage medium does not affect the form of the edit in any way except the amount of time needed to execute it.

Tapes only allow serial access to data, whereas disks and RAM allow random access and so can be much faster. Editing using random access storage devices is very powerful as the shuttling of tape reels is avoided. The technique is sometimes called non-linear editing. This is not a very helpful name, as in these systems the editing itself is performed in RAM in the same way as before. In fact it is only the time axis of the storage medium which is non-linear.

5.41 The structure of a workstation

Figure 5.52 shows the general arrangement of a hard-disk-based workstation. The VDU in such devices has a screen which is a montage of many different signals, each of which appear in windows. In addition to the video windows there

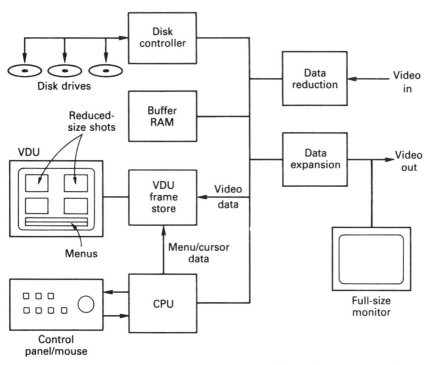

Figure 5.52 A hard-disk-based workstation. Note the screen which can display numerous clips at the same time.

will be a number of alphanumeric and graphic display areas required by the control system. There will also be a cursor which can be positioned by a trackball or mouse. The screen is refreshed by a framestore which is read at the screen refresh rate. The framestore can be simultaneously written by various processes to produce a windowed image. In addition to the VDU, there may be a second screen which reproduces full size images for preview purposes.

A master timing generator provides reference signals to synchronize the internal processes. This also produces an external reference to which source devices such as VTRs can lock. The timing generator may free-run in a standalone system, or genlock to station reference to allow playout to air.

Digital inputs and outputs are provided, along with optional converters to allow working in an analog environment. In many workstations, data reduction is employed, and the appropriate coding and decoding logic will be required adjacent to the inputs and outputs. With mild compression, the video output of the machine may be used directly for some purposes. This is known as online editing. Alternatively a high compression factor may be used, and the editor is then used only to create an edit decision list (EDL). This is known as offline editing. The EDL is then used to control automatic editing of the full bandwidth source material, probably on tape.

Disk-based workstations fall into two categories depending on the relative emphasis of the vertical or horizontal aspects of the process. High end post-production emphasizes the vertical aspect of the editing as a large number of layers may be used to create the output image. The length of such productions is generally quite short and so disk capacity is not an issue and data reduction will not be employed. In contrast a general purpose editor used for television programme or film production will emphasize the horizontal aspect of the task. Extended recording ability will be needed, and data reduction is more likely.

The machine will be based around a high data rate bus, connecting the I/O, RAM, disk subsystem and the processor. If magnetic disks are used, these will be Winchester types, because they offer the largest capacity. Exchangeable magneto-optic disks may also be supported.

Before any editing can be performed, it is necessary to have source material on line. If the source material exists on MO disks with the appropriate file structure, these may be used directly. Otherwise it will be necessary to input the material in real time and record it on magnetic disks via the data reduction system. In addition to recording the data reduced source video, reduced size versions of each field may also be recorded which are suitable for the screen windows.

Inputting the image data from film rushes requires telecine to disk transfer. Inputting from video tape requires dubbing. Both are time-consuming processes. Time can be saved by involving the disk system at an early stage. In video systems, the disk system can record camera video and timecode alongside the VTRs. Editing can then begin as soon as shooting finishes. In film work, it is possible to use video assisted cameras where a video camera runs from the film camera viewfinder. During filming, the video is recorded on disk and both record the same timecode. Once more, editing can begin as soon as shooting is finished.

5.42 Locating the edit point

Digital editors must simulate the 'rock and roll' process of edit-point location in VTRs or flatbeds where the tape or film is moved to and fro by the action of a shuttle knob, jog wheel or joystick. Whilst DVTRs with track-following systems can work in this way, disks cannot. Disk drives transfer data intermittently and not necessarily in real time. The solution is to transfer the recording in the area of the edit point to RAM in the editor. RAM access can take place at any speed or direction and the precise edit point can then be conveniently found by monitoring signals from the RAM. In a window-based display, a source recording is attributed to a particular window, and will be reproduced within that window, with timecode displayed adjacently.

Figure 5.53 shows how the area of the edit point is transferred to the memory. The source device is commanded to play, and the operator watches the replay in the

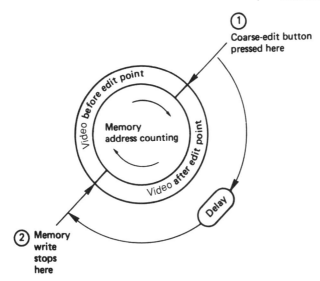

Figure 5.53 The use of a ring memory which overwrites allows storage of samples before and after the coarse edit point.

selected window. The same samples are continuously written into a memory within the editor. This memory is addressed by a counter which repeatedly overflows to give the memory a ring-like structure rather like that of a timebase corrector, but somewhat larger. When the operator sees the rough area in which the edit is required, he or she will press a button. This action stops the memory writing, not immediately, but one-half of the memory contents later. The effect is then that the memory contains an equal number of samples before and after the rough edit point. Once the recording is in the memory, it can be accessed at leisure, and the constraints of the source device play no further part in the edit-point location.

There are a number of ways in which the memory can be read. If the field address in memory is supplied by a counter which is clocked at the appropriate rate, the edit area can be replayed at normal speed, or at some fraction of normal speed repeatedly. In order to simulate the analog method of finding an edit point, the operator is provided with a jog wheel or rotor, and the memory field address will change at a rate proportional to the speed with which the rotor is turned, and in the same direction. Thus the recording can be seen forward or backward at any speed, and the effect is exactly that of turning the wheel on a flatbed or VTR.

If the position of the jog address pointer through the memory is compared with the addresses of the ends of the memory, it will be possible to anticipate that the pointer is about to reach the end of the memory. A disk transfer can be performed to fetch new data further up the time axis, so that it is possible to jog an indefinite distance along the source recording in a manner which is transparent to the user.

The act of pressing the coarse edit-point button stores the timecode of the source at that point, which is frame-accurate. As the rotor is turned, the memory address is monitored, and used to update the timecode.

Before the edit can be performed, two edit points must be determined: the out-point at the end of the previously recorded signal, and the in-point at the beginning of the new signal. The second edit point can be determined by moving the cursor to a different screen window in which video from a different source is displayed. The jog wheel will now roll this material to locate the second edit point while the first source video remains frozen in the deselected window. The editor's microprocessor stores these in an edit decision list (EDL) in order to control the automatic assemble process.

It is also possible to locate a rough edit point by typing in a previously noted timecode, and the image in the window will automatically jump to that time. In some systems, in addition to recording video and audio, there may also be text files locked to timecode which contain the dialog. Using these systems one can allocate a textual dialog display to a further window and scroll down the dialog or search for a key phrase as in a word processor. Unlike a word processor, the timecode pointer from the text access is used to jog the video window. As a result an edit point can be located in the video if the actor's lines at the desired point are known.

5.43 Editing with disk drives

Using one or other of the above methods, an edit list can be made which contains an in-point, an out-point and a filename for each of the segments of video which need to be assembled to make the final work, along with a timecode-referenced transition command and period for the vision mixer. This edit list will also be stored on the disk. When a preview of the edited work is required, the edit list is used to determine what files will be necessary and when, and this information drives the disk controller.

Figure 5.54 shows the events during an edit between two files. The edit list causes the relevant blocks from the first file to be transferred from disk to memory, and these will be read by the signal processor to produce the preview output. As the edit point approaches, the disk controller will also place blocks from the incoming file into the memory. In different areas of the memory there will be simultaneously the end of the outgoing recording and the beginning of the incoming recording. Before the edit point, only pixels from the outgoing recording are accessed, but as the transition begins, pixels from the incoming recording are also accessed, and for a time both data streams will be input to the vision mixer according to the transition period required. The output of the signal processor becomes the edited preview material, which can be checked for the required subjective effect. If necessary the in- or out-points can be trimmed, or the crossfade period changed, simply by modifying the edit-list file. The preview can be repeated as often as needed, until the desired effect is obtained. At this stage the edited work does not exist as a file, but is re-created each time by a further execution of the EDL. Thus a lengthy editing session need not fill up the disks.

It is important to realize that at no time during the edit process were the original files modified in any way. The editing was done solely by reading the files. The power of this approach is that if an edit list is created wrongly, the original recording is not damaged, and the problem can be put right simply by correcting the edit list. The advantage of a disk-based system for such work is that location of edit points, previews and reviews are all performed almost instantaneously, because of the random access of the disk. This can reduce the time taken to edit a programme to a fraction of that needed with a tape machine.

During an edit, the disk controller has to provide data from two different files simultaneously, and so it has to work much harder than for a simple playback. If there are many close-spaced edits, the controller and drives may be hard-pressed

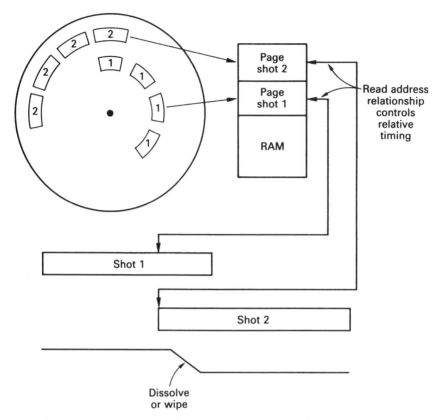

Figure 5.54 Sequence of events for a hard-disk edit; see text for details.

to keep ahead of real time, especially if there are long transitions, because during a transition a vertical edit is taking place between two video signals and the source data rate is twice as great as during replay. A large buffer memory helps this situation because the drive can fill the memory with files before the edit actually begins, and thus the instantaneous sample rate can be met by allowing the memory to empty during disk-intensive periods.

Some drives rotate the sector addressing from one cylinder to the next so that the drive does not lose a revolution when it moves to the next cylinder. Disk-editor performance is usually specified in terms of peak editing activity which can be achieved, but with a recovery period between edits. If an unusually severe editing task is necessary where the drive just cannot access files fast enough, it will be necessary to rearrange the files on the disk surface so that files which will be needed at the same time are on nearby cylinders. An alternative is to spread the material between two or more drives so that overlapped seeks are possible.

Once the editing is finished, it will generally be necessary to transfer the edited material to form a contiguous recording so that the source files can make way for new work. In offline editing, the source files already exist on tape or film and all that is needed is the EDL. This will be used to conform the original material to the edit points decided using the non-linear workstation. The disk files can simply be erased. In online editing the disks hold original recordings and will need to be backed up to tape if they will be required again. In large broadcast systems, the edited work can be broadcast directly from the disk file server. In smaller systems it will be necessary to output to some removable medium, since the Winchester drives in the editor have fixed media.

5.44 Disk drives

Disk drives came into being as random-access file-storage devices for digital computers. The explosion in personal computers has fuelled demand for low cost high-density disk drives and the rapid access offered is increasingly finding applications in digital video. After lengthy development, optical disks are also emerging in digital video applications.

In a disk drive, the data are recorded on a circular track. In hard-disk drives, the disk rotates at several thousand rev/min so that the head-to-disk speed is of the order of 100 miles per hour. At this speed no contact can be tolerated, and the head flies on a boundary layer of air turning with the disk at a height measured in microinches. The longest time it is necessary to wait to access a given data block is a few milliseconds. To increase the storage capacity of the drive without a proportional increase in cost, many concentric tracks are recorded on the disk surface, and the head is mounted on a positioner which can rapidly bring the head to any desired track. Such a machine is termed a moving-head disk drive. An increase in capacity could be obtained by assembling many disks on a common spindle to make a disk pack. The small size of magnetic heads allows the disks to be placed close together. If the positioner is designed so that it can remove the heads away from the disk completely, it can be exchanged. The exchangeable-pack moving-head disk drive became the standard for mainframe and minicomputers for a long time.

Later came the so-called Winchester technology disks, where the disk and positioner formed a compact sealed unit which allowed increased storage capacity but precluded exchange of the disk pack alone.

Disk drive development has been phenomenally rapid. The first flying head disks were about three feet across. Subsequently disk sizes of 14, 8, $5\frac{1}{4}$, $3\frac{1}{2}$ and $1\frac{7}{8}$ inches were developed. Despite the reduction in size, the storage capacity is not compromised because the recording density has increased and continues to increase. In fact there is an advantage in making a drive smaller because the moving parts are then lighter and travel a shorter distance, improving access time.

There are numerous types of optical disk, which have different characteristics. There are, however, three broad groups which can be usefully compared.

1. The Compact Disc and LaserVision are examples of a read-only laser disk, which is designed for mass duplication by stamping. They cannot be recorded.
2. Some laser disks can be recorded, but once a recording has been made, it cannot be changed or erased. These are usually referred to as write-once-read-many (WORM) disks. The general principle is that the disk contains a thin layer of metal; on recording, a powerful laser melts holes in the layer. Clearly once a pattern of holes has been made, it is permanent.

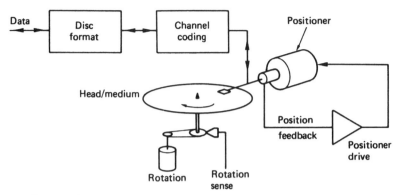

Figure 5.55 The main subsystems of a typical disk drive.

3. Erasable optical disks have essentially the same characteristic as magnetic disks, in that new and different recordings can be made in the same track indefinitely, but there is usually a separate erase cycle needed before a new recording can be made since overwrite is not always possible.

Figure 5.55 introduces the essential subsystems of a disk drive which will be discussed here. Magnetic drives and optical drives are similar in that both have a spindle drive mechanism to revolve the disk, and a positioner to give radial access across the disk surface. In the optical drive, the positioner has to carry a collection of lasers, lenses, prisms, gratings and so on, and will be rather larger than a magnetic head. The heavier pickup cannot be accelerated as fast as a magnetic-drive positioner, and access time is slower. A large number of pickups on one positioner makes matters worse. For this reason, and because of the larger spacing needed between the disks, multiplatter optical disks are uncommon. Instead, 'juke box' mechanisms have been developed to allow a large library of optical disks to be mechanically accessed by one or more drives. Access time is sometimes reduced by having more than one positioner per disk, a technique adopted rarely in magnetic drives. A penalty of the very small track pitch possible in laser disks, which gives the enormous storage capacity, is that very accurate track following is needed, and it takes some time to lock on to a track. For this reason tracks on laser disks are usually made as a continuous spiral, rather than the concentric rings of magnetic disks. In this way, a continuous data transfer involves no more than track-following once the beginning of the file is located.

Glossary

3:2 Pulldown Process used in telecine to produce 60 Hz video from 24 fps film.

AES/EBU Also known as AES-3. Professional digital audio interface.

Active line Part of television line on which the visible part of the image is portrayed. Distinguishes the line blanking area which is not visible.

Aliasing Generation of incorrect samples due to input frequencies exceeding one-half the sampling rate.

Anti-aliasing filter Filter which restricts the frequency range of an analog signal to less than one-half the sampling rate.

Aperture effect A loss of resolution caused by the image being scanned or sampled by a non-ideal system in which the scanning beam has finite area.

Artifact Undesirable erroneous effect visible on screen.

Aspect ratio Ratio of picture width to height, e.g. 4:3.

Azimuth recording Twisting alternate magnetic heads left and right to record adjacent tracks which can be read without crosstalk. Also called guard-band-less recording.

B video signal representing blue component of image.

BER Bit error rate. Rate at which incorrect bits are received.

Back porch Blanked area between sync pulse and beginning of video.

Bit Binary digit.

Blanking Voltage corresponding to black on screen. Below blanking = invisible.

Bottles Colour ident signals inserted in vertical blanking to synchronize D_r, D_b sequence in SECAM. No longer mandatory but still in use.

Bowtie Test signal used to check relative timing of analog component video signals.

Breezeway Space between end of burst and active line.

Burst Signal used to synchronize local subcarrier oscillator in composite decoder.

Buzzword A specialist term which performs two functions: (a) to those who understand its meaning it makes technical conversations briefer; (b) to those who do not understand its meaning it is a way of preventing communication.

Byte Set of bits, generally eight.

CCIR International Radio Consultative Committee, now known as ITU-RB (Radio branch of International Telecommunications Union).

CCTV   Closed circuit television: cameras connected to monitors by private cabling (as opposed to broadcast). Often used for security.

CIE   Commission Internationale d'Eclairage. Standards body for colorimetry. Branch of ISO (q.v.)

CRC   Cyclic redundancy check. Error detection technique.

Clamp   Circuit which forces video signal to correct level during blanking.

Colour framing   A process which synchronizes the subcarrier and sync timing in composite VTRs to a reference. This allows edits without jumps or breakup on replay.

Colour-under   Recording technique which downconverts chroma signal to lower frequency to save tape.

Composite video   (a) (Old usage) video signal carrying sync pulses as well as picture. (b) (Modern usage) video signal carrying subcarrier-based chroma.

Compression   Also called bit-rate reduction or data reduction. Process which allows pictures to be represented with less data. Picture quality may suffer if used to excess.

Concealment   Process used when error correction is not possible. Interpolates or estimates missing pixel values from those nearby.

Contribution quality   Describes a signal which is going to be further post-produced and so must have high quality.

Convergence   Causing all three electron beams in a shadow mask tube to fall in the same place.

Crushing   Some of contrast range is lost, typically because of wrongly adjusted brightness control.

Cutting list   Data sheet containing edit frame numbers. Used by film laboratory to conform negative. Equivalent of EDL.

Cylinder address   Code sent to disk drive positioner to control radial head movement.

D_b Colour difference signal used in SECAM. $D_b = 1.505(B - Y)$.

D_r Colour difference signal used in SECAM. $D_r = -1.902(R - Y)$.

DCT   Discrete cosine transform. Mathematical technique which analyses blocks of an image to determine which spatial frequencies are present. Used in compression.

DSB   Direct satellite broadcasting. System where a consumer antenna can receive broadcast.

Data integrity   General term for any action or strategy which minimizes the proportion of data bits in a system which are corrupted.

Decimator   Digital filter which reduces sampling rate.

Dielectric   Insulating material used between the conductors in transmission lines.

Digitizing   In non-linear editors the process of transferring input images and audio onto the system disks. May include a compression step.

Distribution   (a) In DVTRs, sharing data between two or more heads in a DVTR allows concealment if one head clogs. (b) In statistics the shape of the probability curve.

Dither   Random signal added to analog input to linearize subsequent quantizing step.

EDH   Error detection and handling. Optional data integrity package for SDI (q.v.)

EDL   Edit decision list. Set of instructions determining what sections of material are to be edited together to produce a finished work.

E–E   Electronics to electronics. A mode in a VTR where the tape and heads are bypassed but the signal passes through everything else.

EBU   European Broadcasting Union.

EMC   Electromagnetic compatibility. General term for set of regulations and procedures to ensure that electronic equipment neither suffers from nor generates interference.

ENG   Electronic news gathering. Recording news images using video rather than film.

ESP   Extended studio PAL. BBC-developed wide bandwidth composite signal compatible with composite digital VTRs.

Edit gap   In a DVTR, a space left on the recorded track allowing data on one side of the space to be edited without corrupting data on the other side.

Entropy   The unpredictable part of a signal which has to be transmitted by a compression system if quality is not to be lost.

Equalizer   Circuit needed to compensate for a reduction of certain frequencies in recording or transmission.

Eye-pattern   Characteristic appearance of serial digital signal on oscilloscope.

FM   Frequency modulation. Used in analog VTRs.

F_{sc} Frequency of subcarrier.

Film-for-video   System in which material intended for television broadcast or videocassette release is shot on film.

Flatbed   A traditional film editing machine having a viewer and means to drive the film to and fro.

Flyback   Retrace prior to a further scan.

Flywheel sync   System used in TV sets to resist sync loss due to interference. Effectively a phase locked loop.

Four-field sequence   A repetition rate which occurs in NTSC due to the subcarrier frequency having a half-line offset. The subcarrier can only return to a given phase after an even number of lines and this requires two frames or four fields.

Front porch   Blanked area after video but before H sync pulse.

Fukinuki hole   Space theoretically clear in ideal 3-D PAL spectrum.

G   Video signal representing green component of image.

Gs   Video signal representing green component of image with synchronizing pulses added.

Gamma   Non-linear relationship between video signal voltage and screen brightness.

Gamut   Allowable range of signal voltage.

Gigabyte   Measure of data storage. Equal to 1024 megabytes.

Guard band   In older VTRs a space left between the tracks to reduce crosstalk.

H   Horizontal.

H-coherent   Having a frequency which is an integer multiple of H.

Helix angle   In VTRs the mechanical inclination of the tape path.

Helper   Additional signal which when optionally decoded in more complex receiver enhances picture.

Horizontal editing   Edit process which primarily involves the time axis, e.g. cuts. Contrasts with vertical editing.

Hue   The dominant wavelength in a colour (*see* Saturation).

I   Signal used in NTSC chroma. $I = -0.27(B - Y) + 0.74(R - Y)$

IEC   International Electrotechnical Commission. Branch of ISO (q.v.)

IRE (unit)   Institute of Radio Engineers unit which is 1 per cent of black to white voltage swing.

ISO   International Standards Organisation.

Illuminant   Light source having standardized position on chromaticity diagram.

Insertion loss   reduction in signal level due to incorporating a device in a series circuit.

Inter-coding   Compression scheme in which redundancy between successive images is eliminated.

Interlaced scan   The frame is scanned by two or more fields where not all lines are included in each scan.

Interleave   Regular re-ordering of data to assist in error correction.

Interpolator   Digital filter which increases sampling rate.

Intra-coding   Compression scheme in which only redundancy within the individual image is eliminated.

JPEG (Joint Photographic Experts Group)   A compression standard for still images or individual frames.

Jitter   Statistical distribution of events on time axis which ideally are equally spaced.

Judder   Artifact occurring when motion is incorrectly portrayed.

K-factor   Figure of merit for linear distortions in a transmission system. Tested with pulse and bar signal.

Kell factor   Degree by which a display approaches ideal resolution set by line spacing.

Keycode   Signal recorded on the edge of film which allows individual frames to be located according to the time at which they were shot (*see* Timecode).

Keying   Electronic equivalent of matte in which part of one image is replaced with part of another.

Kilobyte   Measure of data storage equal to 1024 bytes.

Latency   Access delay in disk drive due to mechanical motion.

Lightning   Screen display of all three colour difference signals allowing rapid assessment of correct adjustment.

Loop-through   Connecting the same signal to several destinations in a daisy chain.

MAC   Multiplexed analog components. An alternative to composite video for colour broadcast from satellites.

MPEG (Moving Picture Experts Group)   A compression technique using intercoding for moving pictures.

MTF   Modulation transfer function. The ratio of output to input contrast index in an optical system.

Margining   Checking performance of a system by measuring the amount of deliberate degradation needed to cause a failure.

Masking   In human hearing the reduced sensitivity to one sound in the presence of another.

Matrix   (a) Circuit for converting between component and colour difference signals. (b) Switching element of a router.

Megabyte   Measure of data storage equal to 1024 kilobytes.

Moiré   Artifact in composite analog VTRs caused by high order sidebands folding into baseband.

Motion vector   Parameter in a compression system or standards converter which tells the decoder how to shift pixels from a previous picture so it more nearly resembles the current picture.

Non-linear   An editing system in which random access storage is used so that the time axis of access to the material can be non-linear.

NTSC   Never Twice the Same Colour. A television system in which the colours are a function of where the hue control was left by an unskilled viewer.

OIRT   East European equivalent of EBU, merged with EBU in 1992.

Offline   System where low quality images are used for decision-making purposes. Low quality is not seen by end viewer.

Online   System where the quality seen by the operator is the same as that seen by the end viewer.

Optic flow axis   Axis passing through space–time relative to which part of a moving image appears stationary.

Orthogonal   Signals or processes which are on independent axes. e.g. U and V in PAL chroma.

Oversampling   Temporary use of a higher than necessary sampling rate in converters in order to simplify analog filters.

PAL   Phase alternating line. Composite video colour system.

PALPlus   16:9 version of PAL.

P_b Standard colour difference signal. $P_b = 0.56433(B - Y)$.

PCM   Pulse code modulation. Sending analog signal by discrete representation.

P_r Standard colour difference signal. $P_r = 0.71327(R - Y)$.

Patch   Tube face area illuminated by the flying spot in telecine.

Pedestal   In NTSC black level may be raised to 7.5 IRE units instead of zero to guarantee retrace is invisible.

Pel   *See* Pixel.

Phase locked loop   An electronic circuit which extracts the average phase from a jittery signal in a manner analogous to a flywheel (*see* Reclocker).

Phosphor   Substance which emits light when struck by electron beam.

Pixel   Short for picture cell. A point sample of a picture. Also called a pel (*see also* Square pixel).

PLUGE   Picture line-up generator; a test signal for adjusting monitors.

Power factor   In electrical supplies, power factor measures the efficiency of transmission. If current is out of phase with voltage, the power factor is poor and transmission losses increase.

Product code   Error correction strategy where pixels are formed into a rectangular array with check words calculated on both rows and columns.

Progressive scan   Scanning proceeds from top to bottom of frame taking in every line in sequence.

Purity   Degree to which colour monitor can produce a primary colour.

Q Signal used in NTSC chroma. $Q = 0.41(B - Y) + 0.48(R - Y)$.

Quadrature   When two signals have 90 degree relative phase.

Quantizer   A device which breaks an analog signal's voltage range into even intervals and outputs the number of the interval in which the analog input lies.

Quincunx   Sampling grid where pixels on alternate rows are shifted to create a pattern resembling the five of dice.

R Video signal representing red component of image.

RFI Radio frequency interference. Interference which is radiated rather than conducted.

Random access Storage device like a disk where contents can be output in any order. Contrasts with serial access.

Randomizing *See* Scrambling.

Reclocker A combination of a slicer and a phase locked loop which can remove noise and jitter from a digital signal.

Reconstruction Filtering process which converts a series of samples back to a continuous waveform.

Redundancy (a) In error correction, extra check bits appended to the wanted data. (b) In compression, that part of a signal which can be predicted and so need not be sent.

Reed–Solomon code Powerful error-correcting code named after its inventors.

Router Equivalent of a telephone exchange for video, audio and control signals.

Rushes Film developed urgently after a day's shooting for confirmation purposes.

SDI Serial digital interface for composite and component video.

SECAM French colour system, essentially contrary to the American method.

SMPTE Society of Motion Picture and Television Engineers (USA).

Sampling A process in which some continuous variable is measured at discrete (usually uniform) intervals.

Saturation Lack of dilution of a colour by white; e.g. red is saturated, pink is desaturated.

ScH Subcarrier to horizontal sync phase.

Scrambling Process in digital transmission which spreads signal spectrum and increases clock content.

Segmentation In VTRs the use of several parallel tracks to record one field.

Seek Process of moving disk drive heads from one track to another.

Serial access Storage system such as tape where data comes out in a fixed sequence. Contrasts with random access.

Set-up *See* Pedestal.

Shuffling Random pixel reordering process used in DVTRs which spreads uncorrected pixels over a large area to aid concealment.

Skew In analog VTRs a timing error caused by incorrect tape tension.

Slicer Electronic circuit which judges an input to be above or below a threshold. Used to clean up binary signals (*see* Reclocker).

Split edit Edit in which the image and soundtrack transition at different times.

Square pixel An image sampling process in which the vertical and horizontal sampling spacing is the same.

Stripview Graphical representation of the time axis through an edit sequence.

TRS Timing reference signal. Equivalent of sync pulses in digital interfaces.

TSO Tape speed override. Means of changing speed of VTR to stretch or squeeze duration of a programme.

Tally Signal which retraces signal routing path to operate on-air light.

Telecine Machine which drives film past an optical scanning system in order to output a video signal.

Television   Literally seeing at a distance. This implies some long cable or radio transmission between camera and display. If there is no such distance, television becomes video.

Terminator   Device fitted at the ends of a transmission line to match its characteristic impedance and prevent signal reflections.

Timecode   A signal recorded down the side of a video tape allowing individual frames to be located according to the time at which they were shot (*see* Keycode).

Time compression   Process used to squeeze the time taken to send a given quantity of data by raising the data rate.

Track angle   In VTRs the angle between track and edge of tape.

Transmission line   Cable which is long compared with wavelength of signals carried.

Triad   Set of three primary phosphor dots in CRT.

Twitter   Artifact due to interlace where horizontal picture transitions flicker.

U Scaled component signal used in PAL. $U = 0.493(B - Y)$.

V Scaled component signal used in PAL. $V = 0.877(R - Y)$.

VCR   Video cassette recorder, generally implying a consumer device.

VSB   Vestigial sideband. System used for terrestrial TV transmission in which lower sideband is heavily curtailed.

VTR   Video tape recorder.

V-switch   Vertical axis switch reversing phase of $R - Y$ component on alternate lines in PAL.

Vector   Multidimensional quantity. In TV generally a 2D representation of a pair of colour difference signals.

Vertical editing   Editing where manipulations take place within the picture, e.g. layering, chroma key. Contrasts with horizontal editing.

Video   Literally 'I see'. An electrical signal which represents a picture.

Wavelet transform   Technique for analysing spatial frequencies of an image which does not use blocks. Used in compression.

Weighting   Modifying measurements to give better correspondence to human perception.

Winchester disk   Disk drive having heads and disks sealed in one unit allowing higher speed and capacity.

Working positive   A viewable print made from a master negative, used for making edit decisions. Damage to the working positive is irrelevant as it is only used to create a cutting list (q.v.).

Wrap angle   Number of degrees of circumference of VTR drum over which the tape is in contact.

Y Luminance signal.

Y/C Recording system used in S-VHS where chroma and luma are kept separate to avoid decoding stage.

Ys Luminance signal with sync pulses added.

Zenith angle   Angular error which takes a head out of the plane of the tape, resulting in poor contact.

Index

791.450232/ WAT